South of Forgiveness

Scribe Publications
2 John St, Clerkenwell, London, WC1N 2ES, United Kingdom
18–20 Edward St, Brunswick, Victoria 3065, Australia

First published by Scribe 2017
This edition published 2018

Typeset in Fournier MT by the publishers
Printed and bound in the UK by CPI Group (UK) Ltd, Croydon
CR0 4YY

Scribe Publications is committed to the sustainable use of natural
resources and the use of paper products made responsibly from those
resources.

9781911617136 (UK edition)
9781925321951 (Australian edition)
9781925307979 (e-book)

CIP records for this title are available from the British Library
and the National Library of Australia.

scribepublications.co.uk
scribepublications.com.au

South of Forgiveness

Placing responsibility where it belongs

Thordis Elva
Tom Stranger

SCRIBE

Melbourne • London

Preface to this paperback edition

Some people remember where they were when the Berlin Wall came down. Other people can recall exactly what they were doing when the Twin Towers collapsed. I will never forget the day when #metoo spread over the internet like wildfire. I instantly knew that this was big. This was revolutionary. This was going to change the way we see the world.

A few months earlier, in February 2017, I told the world about my experience of being raped at the age of sixteen in a TED talk that went viral. I did so while standing next to the man who raped me. Tom and I were teenage sweethearts until a dark, December night when he made a decision that changed both of our lives forever. It took eight years of careful analysis and a week-long meeting in person, sixteen years later, to get a full understanding of the consequences. It was the time needed for me to shed the responsibility I'd wrongfully shouldered, and for the ownership to be fully taken by Tom.

To our knowledge, a survivor and perpetrator of rape had never before joined forces and publicly shared their story. The aim was simple: we wanted to contribute our experience to an ever growing global debate about sexual violence within relationships, to challenge victim-blaming, and to raise awareness about the perpetrator's responsibility, as well as the importance of always seeking consent in intimate situations.

Needless to say, our collaboration was controversial. I'd expected nothing less, and neither had the people who supported me and Tom along the way. In all fairness, the majority of reactions were positive and supportive, but those who questioned our collaboration made their opinions very clear. The most outraged critics claimed that a perpetrator of sexual violence should not be seen and heard in public. I couldn't help but wonder if they lived on the same planet as me? In the world where I live, we see and hear perpetrators all the time. They direct the films we watch, they compete in our biggest sporting events, they shape our world view every day – all the while denying their actions and minimizing their consequences with the effect of normalizing violence. One of them has even been rewarded with the presidency of the United States, despite bragging about sexually assaulting women. They continue to cause hurt to their victims by refusing to take responsibility for what they did, much like Harvey Weinstein did for decades before the #metoo movement exposed his predatory behaviour. In a world where every day, perpetrators are seen and heard saying all the wrong things, we desperately need the voices of perpetrators who do the opposite. Who own up to their actions, who denounce sexual violence and are willing to do everything in their power to become a part of the solution, as opposed to being a part of the problem. We need them, not least because we need other men to open their eyes to this grave issue, which remains the biggest threat to the lives of women and children around the globe.

Unfortunately, the tendency to blame victims for their perpetrator's actions is still alive and well, and it effectively prevents many from breaking their silence. As a result, being a rape survivor who told her story publicly, choosing not to be anonymous, was a lonely place to be in. It's easy to become disheartened in times of adversity, when the wind blows in your face. That's also when it's important to remember that only when the wind is blowing in your face, not at your back, your kite can rise to the sky.

Many people commended me for my bravery, although I didn't feel particularly brave to use my privileges as a white, educated, Western woman to voice experiences that many of my fellow survivors around the world are ostracized, punished, or even killed for speaking up about. But I understood where the compliments came from, because shedding the shame and silence that continues to be attributed to survivors worldwide is still a rare thing to witness. That is, until a five-letter hashtag changed everything.

After #metoo, I have now been joined by millions of survivors around the globe who have broken their silence. Much like me, they believe in their right to shed the responsibility wrongfully attached to them, and return it to their perpetrators. They refuse to feel ashamed anymore, embracing the truth we've known deep inside all along, that the burden of shame was never ours to carry.

Many perpetrators also followed Tom's footsteps and owned up to their actions after #metoo. It underlined how responsibility for abuse can indeed be taken, but also how this is a delicate balancing act that cannot be justified if it only serves the perpetrator's feelings, at the cost of the survivor. How we, as a society, respond to such confessions is also crucial. If we react with condemnation, perpetrators are less likely to admit the wrong of their ways, even to themselves. If we react with compliments, we're adding insult to the survivor's injury by applauding their abusers. It is important to find the middle ground, where we can create the space for necessary conversations to be had, while withstanding the temptation to make it about our own feelings.

Sports have sometimes been heralded as the most successful

activity when it comes to bringing together the human race, across borders, religion, class, and ethnicity. The late, great Nelson Mandela once said: 'Sport has the power to change the world. It has the power to inspire. It has the power to unite people in a way that little else does. Sport can create hope where once there was only despair.'

In January 2018, I was on an international flight, flying out of Iceland where I'd recently accepted the Person of the Year Award on behalf of the #metoo movement, which I helped manifest in my home country. Seated next to me was a man whose face I remembered from the news. I knew he was a famous athlete and that I'd seen him compete in various international sporting events, but I couldn't remember his name nor the sport he played. As a result, I decided to pretend I didn't recognise him rather than risk making a fool of myself. Later on in the flight, I had to use the lavatories and he got up from his aisle seat to let me pass. When I returned, he smiled brightly and said: 'Oh and by the way, congratulations on the revolution!'

That's when it struck me that #metoo and its worldwide achievements rival any major sports event. When human rights unexpectedly storm the field and score a goal, all of mankind wins. To quote Mandela, it inspires, unites, and creates hope where once there was only despair.

We still have a long way to go, and the wind will continue to blow in our face. But that is also when our kite can fly higher than ever. If we dare to aim high enough, I believe that we can one day wake up in a world free from sexual violence. It's going to take all of us to get there. #Youtoo.

This book is an invitation for you to join me on a journey that forever changed my life. My hope is that, together, we can change the world.

Thordis Elva, Stockholm, January 2018

From : Thomas Stranger
tomsstranger@hotmail.com
Sent : Saturday, 21 May, 2005 5:38 AM
To : thordiselva@hotmail.com
Subject : words for you

Thordis, I don't know where to start. When I saw your name in
my inbox, my spine went cold. My memories are still as clear
as day. Please believe me when I say I have not forgotten what
I did, and how wary I have to be of myself.

I don't know how to reply. I want to call myself sick (but
I know I am not), I want to say that you are so strong, so
strong to be able to write to me and recall the events and my
actions. I want to thank you for not hating me, although I'd
like you to. It would make it easier for me.

Without looking for a scratch of sympathy, I want to tell
you that the events and emotions I was party to in Iceland
have replayed in my head many times, usually when I am
by myself for any length of time. They flash past me, vividly
accurate, and then, shortly after the denial and positive
character reinforcement, comes the question: 'Who am I?'
It is a dark part of my memory. I've tried to suppress it.

But this is not about me. Whatever I can do or offer you,
I am more than willing. The question is where to go from here.
You tell me.

Tom.

Seven years and five months later

My heart beats fast, in sync with the blinking cursor on the computer screen. My fingers tremble slightly as I type the name of my hometown into the empty field. *Place radius by location name: Reykjavík, Iceland.*

Radius: 11,000 km.

Enter.

Without delay, the United States, Europe, and nearly all of Asia are covered in a green layer, along with most of South America and Africa apart from their southernmost peninsulas.

Inhaling deeply, I delete Reykjavík from the field. After a moment of hesitation, I write the name of his hometown: *Sydney, Australia.*

Radius: 11,000 km.

Enter.

Another green layer covers the opposite part of the world: the southernmost peninsula of Africa and South America, along with Southeast Asia. Fear gives way to curiosity, and I lean closer to the computer screen, fascinated. I knew we lived worlds apart, but it's still remarkable to have it confirmed this graphically.

Between the green layers is a thin strip on the world map, right in the middle between him and me. It nudges the toe of South Africa before arching across the Atlantic and South America where it embraces parts of Uruguay, Argentina, and Chile. Zooming in, I read the names of the cities in question.

With clammy hands, I click back to the window with the half-written email. *I suggest we meet up in Montevideo, Buenos Aires, Santiago* … After pausing to hold my breath for a second, I add: … *or Cape Town.*

The following day, a reply awaits in my inbox. 'I've always wanted to go to South Africa,' it reads.

OK.

Time to take fear by the horns.

Day One

The taxi picks me up at a quarter to five and takes me to the bus station, where I'm booked on the fly-bus. The grizzled taxi driver, hoisting my suitcase into the trunk with a smooth manoeuvre, asks me where I'm going.

'To South Africa.'

'Oh, really? To Johannesburg?'

'No, to Cape Town,' I reply, still in disbelief at my own words despite the time I've had to adjust to the idea. It would be an understatement to say that the proposed meeting has been on my mind. It's reverberated in every step when I've gone out for a run; it's been in every breath of cold winter air that scraped the insides of my lungs; it's soaked the wet washcloth I used to clean my son's sticky fingers. And I've tried my best to push it out of my mind when making love to my fiancé, enjoying his warm skin against mine.

After all, that would be a highly inappropriate time to be thinking about it.

From the moment the destination was set, I adapted to a new calendar — 'before or after Cape Town'. The last time I bought deodorant I automatically deduced that I wouldn't have to buy another one until 'after Cape Town'. Yesterday, when snuggling down with my three-year-old son to do some painting together, spending quality time with him 'BC' momentarily appeased my guilt for leaving him for ten days to travel halfway across the globe to face a man from the past — without any guarantee of the outcome.

Something tells me that parents of young children are not meant to take such foolhardy decisions. That's the reason I gave up my dreams of parachuting when I fell pregnant with my son. Then again, throwing myself out of an airplane at seven thousand feet carries less emotional risk than taking a trip down memory lane with the man who turned my existence upside down. Because it wasn't an unknown lunatic who tore my life apart all those years ago. Who turned down the offer of medical help for me, even though I was barely conscious and vomiting convulsively. Who decided instead to rape me for two endless hours.

It was my first love.

Check in goes smoothly, but I don't trust my suitcase to follow through to my final destination. In the past, it's proven to be an adventurous traveler that jets off to Bali instead of accompanying me to respectable conferences in Finland, for example. *Don't even think about it*, I mutter, and give my suitcase a stern look as it disappears behind the check-in assistant.

On the other side of the window, an airplane takes off and fills the dreary morning with a thundering rumble. Ever since my son was a baby, he's had a fascination with airplanes, peering up at them through his long eyelashes, and drawing contrails in the sky with white finger paint. Unsurprisingly, it was the only thing he wanted me to paint for him yesterday. I produced something that looked more like a disfigured penguin than a plane, but my son was pleased. He pointed at the painting and stated proudly: 'Uncle is in an airplane.'

A pang of guilt shot through me. My brother is, in fact, studying overseas, but since my son doesn't understand the concept 'abroad', it was easier to tell him that his uncle is 'in an airplane'. And that's the explanation he'll be fed while I'm on the other side of the globe seeking closure instead of being in the bosom of my family, organizing the Easter-egg hunt, and wiping chocolate dribbles from my son's and stepdaughters' chins.

Oblivious to my inner turmoil, my son, who has recently begun to confess his love to me, grabbed my face with paint-smeared hands. Tenderness welled up in his eyes as he uttered in a silky-soft voice: '*Dearest* Mommy.'

My heart ballooned inside my chest. 'Yes, love?'

Gazing at me through his blonde eyelashes, like butterfly wings, he said: 'Never lose Halifra.'

Although he's reached the age of three and a half, he's still prone to talking about himself in the third person, using the mispronunciation he invented when he was still too young to say his name — Haflidi Freyr — properly.

Swallowing hard, I wrapped my arms around him, buried my face in the crook of his neck, and whispered that I'll never lose Haflidi Freyr, never ever. It was the most honest love confession to ever escape my lips.

Loosening my grip reluctantly, I forced myself to look him straight in the eye. 'You know, Mommy will be getting on an airplane soon.'

His big eyes grew even wider, the dimples bouncing on his cheeks. 'CAN I COME WITH?'

For a moment, the cat had my tongue. I'd anticipated a tantrum or even tears, but not the genuine hope that lit up my son's face like a beacon on a winter's night.

'No honey, not this time. Maybe later, huh? You can come with Mommy on a plane later.' I hugged him tightly. He pouted, his little arms dangling moodily from my grasp.

He'll get over it, I thought to myself.

I was wrong. My son was unnerved and fussy for the rest of the evening and broke down crying when his father, Vidir, had the nerve to gaze lovingly at him and call him 'munchkin'.

'I AM NO MUNCHKIN!' he screamed, tears of wrath spurting from his eyes. 'I'M JUST HAFLIDI FREYR!'

Last night, as Vidir helped me finish packing my suitcase, the wailing from our son's bedroom was so relentless that we decided to let him sleep in our bed, between us.

That is how I fell asleep on the eve of my trip to Cape Town: with my nose buried in the hair of a little boy who clutched my finger tightly and sobbed through restless dreams. I could barely make out Vidir's silhouette in the dark, lying on the other side of our sleeping child. The last thought that went through my mind was how I had to be careful out there in the great, big world so I could return home to these two gems.

Safe.

I'm waiting in line for the airport security screening when the double standard hits me. *One failed attempt at a shoe bomb, and we all dutifully take off our shoes to ensure each other's safety.* Meanwhile, the average day greets enough perpetrators of rape to fill thousands of jumbo jets, according to global statistics. Yet there are no official security measures in place to fight *that* pandemic. *To be fair, it's not as easily solved as screening someone's boots*, I admit to myself.

My seatmates on the plane to Norway, the first layover on this mammoth trip, are an exceptionally well-behaved five-year-old girl and her mother. The chances that Haflidi would sit nice and still on a three-hour plane ride are non-existent, and I reward the girl with an encouraging smile. She hides under her mother's arm, shy. It reminds me of my own mother, whose approval I desperately wanted before embarking on this journey.

Yes, I am aware that I am thirty-two years old.

It doesn't change my childish need for my parents to bless my endeavors.

My mother's eyes flew wide open when I told her that I was traveling alone to South Africa to meet up with the man who raped me when I was sixteen. She strung together a series of hair-raising worst-case scenarios before letting out a sigh, looking at me with loving reluctance, and adding: 'But I know it's pointless to try to talk you out of things you've set your mind to, dear.' Shortly thereafter, my dad interrupted my packing when he dropped by for a coffee. Despite my attempt to break the news to him in the gentlest manner possible, it didn't prevent him from freaking out. He lectured me in a thundering voice about how I was jeopardizing my life for an utterly ridiculous idea.

'But I have to finish this chapter of my life,' I said softly. My cheeks were on fire.

'Finish this chapter?' he repeated, appalled, and jumped out of his chair. 'You don't need to travel across the globe to finish anything! This whole idea is a big pretentious drama, that's what it is!'

His words hit me right where it hurts.

'You'll have no control over anything. Nothing but your thoughts! Nothing else!'

'What do you mean?' I asked, confused. 'I'll obviously control my actions and whereabouts.'

'No you won't, dear,' he hissed. 'You can't always. If you could, then *that* wouldn't have happened.'

We both knew what he meant by 'that', even though we've never talked about the incident that changed everything. In recent years, I've spoken widely and publicly about my status as a rape survivor — yet my father and I have never discussed that fateful night. He has never asked, and I've always assumed he doesn't want to know.

I sat up straight, aware of my glowing cheeks. 'If you reduce me to victim and him to perpetrator, I can see how this seems incomprehensible to you. But we're much more than that, Dad.'

He scoffed loudly before storming out of the kitchen.

I leant against the wall and let the air out of my lungs slowly. *Goddamn it.* I knew this would be hard, but bloody hell.

My father appeared again in the doorway, pacing up and down with frustration I knew was fueled by fatherly love. 'How can you be sure you'll finish anything with this nonsense? This may just as easily be the start of something else entirely!' The distress in his voice made it sound like a threat.

I sat alone in the silence my father left behind him and watched the dust settle. In a way, I think we're both right. This trip will surely mark an end to a certain chapter of my life. What sets me apart from my father is my belief that in the next chapter, I won't be the victim any more.

The seatbelt lights have been switched off, and I use the chance to unbuckle. While stretching my back, I'm met with my own reflection in the screen on the seatback in front of me. On the outside, I've always been fierce. During my college years, the word most commonly used to describe me was 'intimidating', something I was told by countless schoolmates in various stages of inebriation during parties. Unbeknownst to them, a part of my survival strategy was to project fearlessness. This was underlined by the safety pins I proudly wore, my willingness to try anything once, and my unwavering motto that 'if a guy can do it, so can I.' At the age of twenty-one, I'd moved to a different continent by myself, gotten a tattoo, and dated girls. However, the most effective way to hide my brokenness turned out to be overachievement. As a result, I aced everything, including the college education I completed in the States in English, my second language. I'd long realized that nobody suspects the valedictorian of leading a double life, especially one who also excels in all things extracurricular, represents students on the School Board, and holds a part-time job. Being insanely busy had the added advantage of leaving me with no time to dwell on the past.

I turn on the in-flight entertainment system and browse through the TV programs. One of them is about a police unit that specializes in sex crimes that are, without exception, committed by armed and dangerous lunatics. Uninterested, I continue browsing. *I'm done with that myth.* When I was sixteen, my idea of sexual assault was of something that took place in dark alleys and was carried out by knife-wielding psychopaths. I'd watched enough TV that I didn't question the stereotype. When it came crumbling down in my head later, and I realized that I had indeed been raped, my perpetrator was already on the other side of the planet, leaving me with the only option of bottling up my pain. It came at a cost. At the age of twenty-five, after nine years of keeping up appearances and suffering in silence, I hit rock bottom. I'd struggled with eating disorders, alcohol, and self-harm. Despite my shining achievements, I didn't trust my judgment after having it fail so horribly in my first relationship. This led me to doubt everything: my career choices, my romantic choices, my self-worth. I was at war with the world, never really sure who the enemy was. As my past was still a secret that I didn't trust anyone with, I found myself increasingly channeling my grievances into writing. Diaries turned into poetry that transformed into plays, and, before long, I was making a name for myself as a playwright. It was nothing short of liberating to make up characters that were free to speak all the words that I myself choked on. And everybody respected it as art, so I wasn't bothered with uncomfortable questions, either. Simply put, it was perfect. Or as close to perfect as any profession could be for the deeply divided person that I was at the time.

Regardless of my inner turmoil (or rather, *because* of it), my repertoire grew rapidly and my career started to take off. In May 2005, I received an invitation to attend a distinguished conference in Australia for the world's most promising young playwrights. I went cold. The country of *his* residence — the man who had violated me when I was sixteen. A wild hope was born. *Could this be a chance to step out of my cage and make him own up to his crime?* My heart backed into the innermost corner of my chest, scarred from a previous time when I'd tried to word out my past with disastrous results. I collapsed into my office chair and spent days staring at my computer screen, weighing my options. Finally, I mustered the willpower to fire off an email: a short and polite explanation of how I was visiting his homeland in July, followed by the question of whether he'd be available to see me during my stay. Nervously pacing around my apartment, I envisioned everything from his grateful acceptance to his outright rejection, settling for the likeliest possibility of getting no response whatsoever. After all, it'd been almost a decade since he came to Iceland as an exchange student and he could very well have changed his email address. To my relief, his account turned out to be active, but once I clicked on his reply with trembling, nicotine-stained fingers, my relief shifted to sharp disappointment. As he was living on the other side of the country and was stuck with work obligations, he explained he couldn't see me. The courage and hope came wheezing out of my deflated heart. That was it. I'd have to surrender to the cage.

Unbeknownst to me, my subconscious started rattling the bars.

A few weeks later, I wandered into a café on a dreary afternoon, sobbing and reeling after a fight with a loved one. I asked the waitress for a pen while digging a small notebook out of my bag, hoping that doodling in it would calm my nerves. To my surprise, I watched the doodles cohere into letters that in turn became sentences, and shaped themselves into the most pivotal letter I've ever written, addressed to my perpetrator. Along with an account of the violence he had subjected me to, the words 'I want to find forgiveness' stared back at me. *Where on earth did that come from?* Forgiveness had been the last thing on my mind. The suggestion to meet up with him had been based on my wish to give him an earful of withering words that would eat their way into his brain, becoming the first and the last thing he'd think about for the rest of his days. That was the reality he had forced on me. But *forgiveness?* As much as they astonished me when streaming out of my pen, the words were like a healing balm, soothing the sting in their truthfulness. Following my bewilderment came the magnificent discovery that I had found the key to my cage. Just when I'd stopped looking.

This was uncharted territory. For the nine years that had passed, I'd adopted a zero-tolerance policy for people who abused my trust, resorting to such militant measures as sending shit in a shoebox to a man who'd let me down. And confrontations of this kind weren't recommended by specialists in the field of sexual violence and survivor support, either. Many of them spoke favorably about writing to the perpetrator in order to give voice to the hurt, only to then destroy the letter rather than send it. Yet I found myself typing the letter into my computer when I got home. A part of me was in shock that I'd even entertain the idea of sending it, thinking it highly unlikely that its recipient would be willing to take responsibility for the violence it described. As a result, I prepared myself for all kinds of outcomes: being told that I was misremembering things; being accused of lies; a downright denial of the whole ordeal. However nerve-racking and unappealing, all of these possibilities seemed more desirable to me than the alternative, which was to silence my newfound voice after it had made such a daring appearance. Given that I had nobody else's footsteps to follow in, I decided to follow my heart.

Despite all my careful predictions, the only outcome I didn't prepare for was the one that I then got: a reply with a typed confession full of hot regret that disarmed me with its candor.

Although I've come a long way in recent years, and talked publicly about my experience of rape, this part of my story is still secret, even to my loved ones. What my father didn't know, when he stormed out of my house after having deemed my mission ridiculous, is that the scribblings from the café that day in 2005 spurred eight years of correspondence, covering page after page with brutal honesty. He doesn't know about the exchange of searing questions and even thornier truths that sometimes had both sender and receiver doubled over the nearest trash bin. He doesn't know that I put the blame where it belonged firmly and unapologetically; nor does he know how it was received — wholeheartedly and unwaveringly. He doesn't know about the healing miracles that dotted our computer keyboards with tears at ungodly hours of the morning, or how our correspondence was terminated on two occasions when we'd gutted each other with the serrated past. Both times, some life experience shed a new light on the incident, rekindling the exchange. And somewhere along the way,

I let go of my anger. It launched me through the turbulent troposphere and up to the stratosphere of my mind, where there are no winds to disturb the peace. The clear skies within unclouded my vision.

However healing it was, our correspondence didn't bring about closure for me. Perhaps because the email format didn't feel personal enough, perhaps because it's easy to be brave when hiding behind a computer screen ten thousand miles away. Too easy, in fact, to resonate with my heart. 'As a result, I'm going to South Africa to seek final payment for the costliest night of my life,' I whisper to myself as the steel-gray city of Oslo emerges out the plane window. Enough of haunting memories. Enough of self-blame. I want to face the man who snatched away my innocence in 1996 and absolve myself from the guilt I wrongfully carried for him for all too many gut-wrenching years.

I want it to end.

My mission might be crystal clear, but the same cannot be said for my expectations of this journey, which have peaked and plummeted like a cardiogram lately. On good days, I've found the thought of it encouraging, inspiring even. I imagine finding peace with my demons when faced with my perpetrator, whom I sometimes picture strolling around the streets of Cape Town with me, or squatting down on a beach and gazing at the Atlantic through pensive eyes.

On bad days, I've panicked at the very thought of this journey. When it comes to the prevalence of sexual violence, statistics point to it being more common in South Africa than in many other countries where comparative data exists. The same can be said about child rape, with victims as young as infants. Unfairly or not, Cape Town is sometimes dubbed Rape Town. I know this because when it comes to sexual violence, I accidentally became an expert despite having had very different plans for my career. The course was set in April 2007, when a 19-year-old girl asked a stranger for directions to the bathroom in a hotel in Reykjavík, Iceland. The stranger followed her inside, shoved her into one of the stalls and, locking the door behind them, proceeded to rape her. Terrified, she experienced a form of rape-induced paralysis that rendered her unable to fight her attacker until the pain became excruciating, jolting her into defensive mode.

The Reykjavík District Court reached the conclusion that the sexual activity had, without a doubt, taken place without the girl's consent. Nevertheless, the court acquitted her attacker, pinning the blame on the girl instead for not having fought her attacker with enough vigor. Icelandic law states that 'he who uses violence, the threat of violence, or other means of unlawful duress to force another person to have sexual intercourse is guilty of rape'. Because the perpetrator had not needed to resort to such measures, he had not committed rape, in the eyes of the law.

At the time, I was simultaneously working as a magazine columnist and a playwright. The pay was a joke in both areas, but I was inspired, ambitious, and in love with the arts. My secret correspondence with the man who'd raped me had lasted two years by then, and had lifted some of the shame I'd wrongfully shouldered, but I was still haunted by my past. Unsurprisingly, I identified strongly with the girl in the hotel rape case. Outraged by the acquittal, I felt compelled to write an open letter to the papers condemning the verdict. It's outrageous to claim that there's a 'correct reaction' to being raped and that it includes 'fighting back with vigor'. Fighting back can even prove to be deadly, if it prompts the perpetrator to apply more force or violence. Some survivors freeze, others dissociate in order to survive the attack. There is no such thing as a standard reaction to rape, I argued. To make sure my arguments were bulletproof, I studied the law, read hundreds of rape cases, and interviewed lawyers, doctors, and survivors.

As I had far too much to say to fit into any newspaper, the letter never came into being. Instead, I ended up with a 270-page book. Overnight, it elevated me from being a chain-smoking bohemian to a respected specialist on sexual violence, surprising nobody more than myself. Meanwhile, in private, I was in an ongoing dialogue with the man who brutally introduced me to the subject.

During the writing of my book, I realized that silence is one of the major obstacles in the battle against sexual violence. Although unsure, and light-years away from my comfort zone, I decided to include my story about being raped at the age of sixteen. I left my perpetrator's name out, not to protect him, but because ironically it was safer *for me*. A survivor who stays silent about the perpetrator's identity can still be scrutinized and defamed, but she will be spared the public condemnation and fury of those who would otherwise side with the perpetrator. Women are attacked, even killed, for less.

My perpetrator was protected by distance, living on the other side of the planet. I protected myself with his anonymity.

On occasion, worried women I knew pulled me aside to ask me about his identity. I saw the suspicion in their eyes and realized that they were afraid someone close to them was a rapist — *my* rapist. Their fear is not unfounded, as statistics from the UN and various human-rights organizations suggest that at least one in three women is raped or beaten by a man close to her at some point in her life.

Fear is a hard thing to unlearn. No matter how much I'd raised myself to be strong and courageous, the thought of going to Cape Town prompted a knee-jerk reaction, not just in the violence expert I'd become but also in the girl I once was. I, like millions of other women, was taught to scream and go for the eyes or groin if I were attacked. I was taught how to make my keys stick out of my fist so I could inflict more harm to my attacker. I was taught to avoid badly lit areas and to learn where the rape-crisis phones were located on my campus. I was taught never to leave my drink unattended, never to accept a ride from a stranger, never to go on a date without letting someone know who I was meeting, and never to look strange men in the eyes if on my own in a public place. Don't get too drunk, don't dress provocatively, don't flirt too openly, and, above all, don't show fear when being catcalled or followed.

In short, I, like millions of other girls, was taught from an early age how dangerous it is simply to be a girl.

At the end of the day, none of this guidance helped me. Most rapes don't take place in the circumstances we're taught to avoid. Most of them take place in the privacy of our homes, and are carried out by people we're supposed to trust — relatives, spouses, friends.

If I let fear be the deciding factor in whether or not I go to Cape Town, that would be defeat, I reasoned with myself. The 'rape capital of the world' would surely be the ultimate testing ground when it came to conquering a fear related to sexual violence. And where better to exercise forgiveness than in a country that built an entire institution around truth and reconciliation? Where the nation's leader, Nelson Mandela, forgave his tormentors after twenty-seven years of captivity and made peace with them in order to build a better society?

No matter how I looked at it, I couldn't think of a place better suited to prove to myself that violence can't destroy my life or control my choices. Not then, not now, not ever.

Oslo airport greets me with preposterously expensive sandwiches and coffee. At least the Wi-Fi is free. I glance at the clock and wonder what Vidir and Haflidi are up to. By now, they should be preparing lunch, enjoying their Easter break at home. Vidir proposed to me recently, after almost five wonderful years together during which neither of us felt the need to tie the knot. Together, we successfully navigated the minefield of putting together a stepfamily, with me striving to earn the trust and friendship of his daughters: Hafdis, now fourteen years old, and Julia, who is nine. They live with their mother but spend holidays and weekends with us. After we came to the decision that marriage would be a practical move for both the kids and our joint finances, Vidir still managed to propose in a way that was hopelessly romantic and unforgettable. Despite finding the idea of this trip of mine uncomfortable for many very understandable reasons, he wants nothing more than to be supportive. When we started dating, I was in the middle of writing my first book, and he had to endure my rants about sexual violence for days on end. Nobody has a better understanding of how much this trip means to me.

Due to work, stress, and a general lack of time in the days leading up to this trip, we haven't discussed it as much as we would've wanted to. Then again, something tells me that we'd still not feel prepared, even if we had talked ourselves blue in the face.

'Check your email,' I tell him when he picks up the phone. 'I just sent you something.'

Aware of the worries that have infused his every sigh lately, I'm hoping he'll feel more at ease if he can envision my whereabouts in South Africa. I listen to him start up his computer and open the email I sent him with the address of my hotel. Together, we tramp up and down the streets of Cape Town on Google Earth. I'm eager to show him how good the security is in the area where I'm staying, despite having described it to him at length when I booked my accommodation. 'Look,' I say encouragingly. 'Security cameras on every other corner and barbed wire on top of foot-thick walls surrounding the hotels.'

The line is silent. 'Imagine what horrors it must take for people to resort to such measures,' Vidir says in a quiet voice.

His words make me flinch, but I put on a brave face. To my relief, Vidir plays along. I'm grateful to him for not rubbing my nose in the recent news about Anene Booysen, the 17-year-old girl who died after being gang-raped and disemboweled in a village near Cape Town. May she rest in peace.

'Don't take any risks, my love,' he gently urges. The irony seems to hit him immediately, because he clarifies: 'I mean, don't take any unnecessary chances. Stick to registered taxis. Just ... just come home safely.'

I close my eyes and concentrate all the love I have for Vidir and Haflidi into two simple words: 'I promise.'

After hours of sitting in the Oslo airport, I straighten my stiff limbs and decide it's time for a drink. In a thoughtless haze, I wander out of the Duty Free with a six-pack of beer in a bag. Though I'm only planning to enjoy one, I'm secretly pleased that the whole thing cost me less than a single drink would've cost in a Reykjavík bar. As I exit the store, things get tricky. Where can I kick back and enjoy a quiet drink? I quickly conclude that the waiting area, full of families and breastfeeding mothers, is not the place. Walking around in circles, I'm losing hope by the minute. *Why oh why didn't I just find myself an airport bar, like a civilized person would do?*

Ten minutes later, I've locked myself in the ladies' room with my laptop on my knees and a can of beer in my hand. This has got to be one of the most incompetent moments of my life. In order to type on the keyboard, I have to rest the beer on the edge of an automated sink that is activated by the motion, startling me every time. I can't help but smirk, point my mental lens at myself, and file this ridiculous scenario away in the memory bank. *Cheeeeeeese.*

Still in the realm of complimentary Wi-Fi, I read over a list of safety recommendations in a traveler's forum for South Africa. *Don't flash your valuables in public. Avoid deserted places after dark. Don't leave your drink unattended.* No problem there, as I've abided by these rules my entire adult life. The irony is overwhelming, and I slump against the wall when I realize that this decades-long training will serve me well in a country known for high levels of sexual violence, to which I'm traveling so that I can meet up with a man who raped me.

I put the beer on the edge of the sink and almost jump out of my skin as the water begins to flow loudly yet again. After regulating my heartbeat, I open the folder on my laptop where I've saved the emails we've exchanged for the past eight years. What do I know about his life, anyway? Having no desire to become his pen-pal, I always set a rigid frame for our exchanges, keeping them strictly analytical and focusing exclusively on that fateful night in the hope that dissecting our past would help us better understand our present. As a result, I have few details of his day-to-day life and have given him close to no information about mine. I recall him writing about having a degree in some kind of social work. I know he's a nature buff — the kind who loves to challenge himself by climbing mountains or taking long, difficult hikes into the wilderness. I wonder what his state of mind will be? To soothe my nerves, I find myself seeking answers in one of his emails:

> I still don't like myself. I like my life, I don't like my body. I love what I do, I hate what I've done. I reward myself for hard work, and then beat myself up with alcohol and cigarettes. If people ask me 'So, how are you', my stock standard straight-out-of-the-box response is usually 'If I had two tails they'd both be wagging'. I know I am the luckiest person I know. I live in the richest city on the planet, I have a pristine beach at the end of

my road, I'm healthy, not ugly by western standards, young, single, supportive family, I've got a beautiful circle of friends who support me in all I do and think the world of me. Last week I swam with dolphins and seals ... the list of riches goes on. Some days I can be listening to music and skating to work and I tingle all over with happiness. Other days, I sit on my verandah, drink coffee, and take to myself with a heavy bag full of regrets and criticism.

I work as a Youth Worker at a drug rehab for young people. I've analyzed at length my reasons for choosing such a career, and have concluded there is no hidden guilt or hope of redemption in working with young people in need of help. I don't know how to put into words what I have witnessed. Some of the disclosures these young people have come to me with are ... beyond comprehension. Self-harm, mental health issues, suicide ideation, out of this world drug abuse. What shook, no leveled, me most, Thordis, was a young woman burning her t-shirt in front of me. She had been raped in this garment. She asked me for the lighter. I watched her and then went straight to my office and ... fell apart.

You asked me how I coped with what I did to you. I think I've done my best to detach myself. Unsuccessfully. Evidenced, I think, by my periods of drinking and constant movement from place to place. Also in my relationships, I've never let a partnership evolve into something committed or stable. The longest I have lived with a girlfriend is two months.

Dark secrets don't go so well with loving, trusting relationships, I think as I meet my own eye in the bathroom mirror. *I should know.*

I don't think I have let go of anything. I've managed to forget at times and commend myself briefly for who I am, but I remember I've still got my personally designed label on my back. I'm sure I identify myself as 'marked'. As somebody who once did something horrific to somebody they later found out they loved.

Loved.

I close my eyes and am swept back to a cold winter day in Reykjavík sixteen years prior, just a few days before the night that changed everything. My hand in his hand. My heart racing inside my chest. My insecure teenage self, smiling and asking: 'Why me? Why did you decide to hit on me?'

Shamelessly fishing for a compliment, really. With his handsome looks, exotic accent, and worldly ways, he could've chosen from a big group of admirers at our school.

He replied: 'It was the first time I saw you. You were wearing that red sweater. I can't resist a blonde wearing red.'

Opening my eyes, I look down at my bright-red coat. For years, I avoided this color. I reach for the beer and make a toast as the water gushes loudly from the tap. *The color of love, passion, blood, and fire: Here's to taking it all back.*

Day Two

Day Two

28 March 2013

During the plane ride to Turkey, I cry over a film about a boy who loses his family in an accident at sea and is forced to share a lifeboat with a ferocious tiger. The airport in Istanbul smells of spices and cheap soap. Stagnant perfume hangs in the air and 'Macarena' seeps out of the speaker system in the Duty Free, where I munch on a chocolate bar before boarding yet another plane, this time to Cape Town.

By the time Johannesburg flickers by at a wild velocity below me, I'm squirming with unease. The questions pile up at the same speedy rate as the distance between us decreases. *What am I going to say?* Work kept me so busy in the last few days that I hardly had time to breathe, let alone think. I wonder if the lack of time for proper mental preparation was a good or a bad thing. Am I perhaps as prepared as I can get, after half a lifetime of reflection?

Outside the window, breathtaking mountains rise out of wispy clouds. Incisive thoughts tear holes in the cloudscape. *Should I tell him how deeply he hurt me?* I've avoided going into detail about that in our correspondence. Dwelling on the pain is hardly helpful when trying to close the wound. On the flipside: Can I reach forgiveness if I avoid illustrating the full consequences of his actions — and in turn: how can he own up to something he isn't even aware of?

Relax, I tell myself. *This was your initiative and nobody but you is pushing this envelope. Now let go and undertake the journey. Meet up with the man who changed everything and see what it leads to.*

But where? In my mind, we meet on a beach, under clear African skies. Our past is ugly enough, no need for our surroundings to be dreary too. As Cape Town approaches at five hundred miles per hour, my rosy ideas turn more realistic. Perhaps it's smarter to ask him to meet me at my hotel, instead of me trying to find my way to the beach alone in a strange city?

I break out in a cold sweat when I realize that I don't know if I'll even recognize him. It's been thirteen years since we last saw each other, when he returned to Iceland in the summer of 2000. After our brief relationship ended in 1996, we went our separate ways without exchanging so much as one word about the dark deed that had preceded our breakup. I'd surrendered to the thought that we'd never see each other again and that the truth would never be uttered out loud, which is why my heart pounded wildly in my chest when the phone rang four years later and a familiar, husky voice on the line told me he was coming back to spend the summer. *Could this be our chance to confront the past?* That hope seeded a twisted, broken interaction between us. My rationale muzzled my rage, because I wanted to get it right. I wanted a chance to explain in grueling detail how he'd hurt me and what the consequences had been, placing the responsibility squarely on his shoulders where it belonged. My own personal trial, of sorts. So I waited, planned, and calculated. After years of suffering in silence, this was too important to be furiously spat in his face on some heated spur of the moment. Despite my best efforts to the contrary, that's exactly what happened. One August night, on a weekend trip with friends to the Westman Islands, it all came boiling to the surface in thundering fury. Four years of toxic silence got the better of me and I shoved the past in his face, only to have him drown my truth in the Atlantic Ocean, blind drunk and covered in blood. The disappointment cut so deep that it took another five years and a conference invitation to Australia before I gathered the courage to break my silence again.

I balance my laptop on the tray in the seatback in front of me. The folder with our correspondence is still open when I turn it on. Following my train of thought, I find myself searching for the words 'Westman Islands' in his emails, coming up with the following match from June 2007:

I've resorted to running again. Because facing up to that mountain of evil ... is at this stage still too much. This point is where I traditionally turn inwards, cut all ties without regards to the damaging outfall, and run. It gives rebirth to the feelings I had in the Westman Islands, and that is a place I never wish to revisit.

The current relationship I have with myself is tainted with self-hatred and detachment, which is manifesting itself in some pretty damaging behaviors. Perhaps once I can separate myself from my actions that night, without disowning them in any way, I can address the void in myself that looked to fill itself by stealing from you.

I skim through my reply, noting how I broke off the correspondence by saying that I couldn't invest so much of my heart in something that sent him running off in the opposite direction without warning. It was too big an emotional risk for me and made further healing impossible. *It took years and life-altering events for us to get in touch again, and here I am cruising at 550 mph towards another event that will most likely be life-altering too.*

My father's words echo in my head: 'You don't have to travel all the way to South Africa for some symbolic gesture.'

And yet I've always known, in my heart, that I must. There are things that can't be handled in writing, things that shouldn't exist in print. Vaporous things that are best whispered into the dusk, in a strange country where they can be dispersed by the desert wind.

The screen in the seatback in front of me shows a blinking plane over a map. According to the timer, Cape Town is just twenty-nine minutes away. The butterflies in my stomach nosedive, as the time seems way too limited considering how many questions are left unanswered. *Goddamn it, what if I can't forgive him? Am I ready to let go? If the answer is no, will a week suffice to find peace with the rape that changed my life?*

Frustrated, I scroll through the folder on my laptop, searching for something to calm my nerves. I was levelheaded enough when I suggested this trip, wasn't I? In an attempt to recover my faith in this risky undertaking, I read through my own proposal:

> You may need a lifetime to forgive yourself for what you did to me. That is up to you and you take however long you need, independent of anyone else.
>
> I, however, am climbing a different mountain. And I am getting very close to the top.

I propose that in six months' time, we meet up with the intention of reaching forgiveness, once and for all. In person.

It is the only proper way for me to do it, I feel. No letter can ever compare with face-to-face communication. And after all we've been through, I think it is the most dignified and honest way to finish this chapter of our story.

I sound so calm, so fucking *reasonable*. How is it possible that this was written by the same person now hyperventilating in a plane 30,000ft over South Africa, full of nerve-racking doubt?

Reading through his reply, I'm somewhat comforted that he, too, felt conflicted:

I'll admit that I was floored by your request to meet up. Fearful, anxious, cautious, paranoid. You name it, it all came swarming in. But you've asked, and you sound like you are making vital ground towards something very special for yourself. So of course I'll agree to see you. After much thought I do think it will be beneficial, and an opportunity for myself to air, face to face, some long held words and for us both to look to close some doors.

I want it for you, Thordis, as you seem strong, open, and ready to see me and move forward. I want it for me because I'm so very sick of being sick and seeing myself as unlovable, and believe I can move on if I could just look you in the face, own up to it, and say I'm sorry.

Forgiveness is the only way, I tell myself, *because whether or not he deserves my forgiveness, I deserve peace.* Because I'm doing this for me. The way forgiveness has been hijacked by religion and turned into a sanctimonious concept by the keepers of the moral high ground infuriates me. *What a load of conscientious crap.* My forgiveness is not selfless, not sacrificial, and certainly not heroic. It doesn't come with an angelic chorus and a fuzzy feeling, nor does it offer the other cheek. My forgiveness is white-hot from the whetstone, and its purpose is to sever the ties because if I can let this go, once and for all, I'm certain that my overall wellbeing will benefit greatly. Self-preservation at its best.

I close the laptop as my seatmate leans shamelessly over my lap to admire the fast-approaching landscape out the window. Staring at the back of his head, I decide to surrender to the questions because there are no answers. The only way to find out what lies ahead is to shove my thoughts aside and enter the present.

When the plane bounces on the landing strip in Cape Town, I take a deep breath. *No turning back now.*

My back is throbbing after thirty sedentary hours as I stumble into the airport. An agitated bank clerk exchanges my Icelandic krona for South African rand. Counting the bills, I realize that the exchange rate did me no favors, but I can't be bothered with that now. All I want is to check into my hotel room and take a hot shower. *One step at a time.*

The sky above Cape Town is overcast. Clouds cover the smooth top of Table Mountain and spill over the slopes like a fluffy tablecloth. A mist of rain hits my face as I climb aboard a downtown bus. It starts with a grunt and I look out the window, mesmerized by strange vegetation like the Icelander I am. Pretty much every country in the world beats Iceland and its measly vegetation. As a result, an Icelander with a thing for trees is like a kid in a candy store on foreign ground. I look at the giant creatures rising out of the ground with majestic canopies swaying in the wind and think: *Amazing. I really am in South Africa.*

I'm dutifully sending out text messages that I've arrived safely in Cape Town when the bus stops at the Waterfront, the famous shopping area by the harbor. Having trotted around these parts in Google Earth until my feet actually felt tired, the place feels familiar. As I struggle with my suitcase, armed with a belt pouch stuffed with crispy bills, I feel like a decidedly vulnerable tourist target. Taking a deep breath of fresh ocean air, I send out a silent plea for a taxi. *And make it fast.*

'Ma'am, do you need a cab?' someone yells from the other side of the street. Mumbling thanks to the universe for instant delivery, I wave.

The voice belongs to a man in his fifties, sitting behind the wheel of an old Toyota. I read the sticker on the side of the car, trying to remember if it's one of the trusted taxi companies. My first friend on South-African soil doesn't beat around the bush and walks up to me with a smile, ready to help me with my luggage. I feel torn. *Should I try to find a taxi recommended by the tourist sites?* My doubt disappears as I see a uniformed traffic conductor strike up a friendly conversation with my new buddy. As I climb into the backseat, he takes off with a well-rehearsed tourist speech about the lookouts on Lion's Head mountain, which towers over us. I'm in the midst of thanking him when a uniformed bellboy from the Ritz hotel pulls my suitcase out of the trunk. Signs welcome me in English and German as I walk through the black revolving doors of the hotel at half past three local time. The 34-hour long journey is starting to take its toll and the marble floor billows beneath my feet. Much like my laptop and cell phone, I'm dangerously low on battery.

My hotel room turns out to be on the twelfth floor of twenty-one. It's spacious and bright, its double bed adorned with a silver blanket. I throw everything on the bed, kick off my shoes with a relieved sigh, and walk straight to the window. Sheer curtains obstruct the view and

I pull them aside. My heart skips with joy at the discovery that the ocean is visible from my room, even though the glass is smudgy with sea salt. I lean against the cool windowpane and drink in the view. The garden stretches out below. Rain beats down on deserted tanning chairs, which look like little matchboxes scattered across the lawn. A neon-blue swimming pool cuts through the gloom. The wind carries faint squawks from seagulls.

Closing my eyes, I take a deep breath. *All right, Cape Town. The game is on.*

My phone beeps and I pick it up, certain it's from my beloved who is relieved to hear I've landed safely. I catch my breath when I realize that the text isn't from Vidir. It's from *him*, the man I've come here to meet. An army of butterflies hatches in my stomach, hijacking my heart and flying it to the back of my throat. I sink down on the bed. The text asks whether I've arrived safely at the hotel and when I'd like to meet up.

Okay, focus. It's raining outside. You don't know the neighborhood.

'Let's meet up in the lobby of the Ritz at five o'clock,' I type with trembling fingers.

Moments later, the reply arrives.

Sounds good. See you there.

One hour to go. Baby steps. *Now take that shower and remember to breathe.*

Instinctively, I check if there's a keyhole on the bathroom door while an echo of muffled moans seep through a keyhole in my mind. I automatically start to hum, drowning out the dreaded noise in my head while concluding to my relief that there is a simple latch on the door. *Breathe, Thordis.*

As I undress, a rock falls out of my pocket and bounces on the carpeted floor. It's still warm when I pick it up. He gave it to me years ago, in a moment of uncomplicated bliss, before everything changed. The rock, he explained, has special needs that call for its return to its natural habitat, on Australia's shores. 'Now I've guaranteed that you'll come to Australia one day,' he added, and the teasing look on his face made my knees go weak.

Nine years later, when attending the Australian conference for young playwrights, I took the rock with me. I'd accepted the fact that the desired face-to-face confrontation wasn't going to happen during my trip, but I still wanted to leave something behind in his country, something that was symbolic of the hurt I wished to separate myself from. Filled with mixed emotions and heavy memories, I walked down to the beach one night. The moon was full, sprinkling silver on the foamy waves that were frothing between my toes. When I tried to leave the rock on the shore, I realized that I couldn't, I wasn't ready. Funny. In reality, a rock is nothing but weight. If life is a journey taken on foot, one would like to keep the baggage at a minimum. Harboring negative emotions such as anger or resentment is like walking through life with a bag of rocks. For years, I held onto his rock, allowing it to weigh me down until I discovered that it isn't my burden to carry. *Time to unburden*, I tell myself.

After a long-awaited shower, my hair gets to hang free and my makeup is barely there. Contrary to what I had hoped, Cape Town is chilly today, so I put on a cardigan over shirt and jeans.

It's 5.02pm, and I'm pacing in front of the hotel elevator. I reach for the elevator button only to drop my hand again, my heart pounding. After calming myself, I press the button. Seconds tick by. Finally, the elevator arrives and the doors slide open. My stomach churns as if I'm staring down a cliff, not into an empty elevator car.

Whoa.

On second thought, I'll take the next one.

The elevator glides back down, without me. I muster the courage to press the button once more and pace the floor while I wait. The elevator comes to a halt and opens, standing before me a second time like a chrome-plated cell.

Come on now.

I breathe deeply and take a step forward, but before I get any further my feet take a sharp and unexpected turn to the right.

The doors slide shut and the cell glides down again without me. *Shit.*

Every minute that passes feels like a file rasping across my nerves. If I don't get my act together soon I'm going to be embarrassingly late, with my accompanying tendency to begin the conversation by apologizing. And wouldn't that be typical? Having waited sixteen years and traveled thousands of miles to face a man and hear him say 'I'm sorry' — that I should beat him to it by saying, 'I'm sorry I'm late'?

NO, bloody well no.

The elevator opens a third time and I walk straight in. As the backlit digits count down the floors, my heart climbs the opposite way up my ribcage and into my mouth. When the doors finally open, I'm regretting it all. All I want to do is run back to the airport and board the next flight home. Why oh why didn't I just get myself a therapist and a bottle of vodka like normal people do?

I hold my breath and scan the lobby. There's a small souvenir shop opposite the elevators. Cheerful chatter fills the air. So far, I can't see him. I feel like the boy in the film that I watched on the plane, stuck in a rowing boat on a sea of hopeless ideas. On his way to meet the tiger with whom he'll be forced to share the boat for the coming week.

I steel myself and walk towards the desk, where I give the receptionist a mechanical smile and ask if I can borrow a power adaptor for my laptop. And then the man who changed my life forever emerges from the west wing of the hotel.

Our eyes meet. Time builds a suspension bridge between us, with steel cables that stretch sixteen years over the Atlantic into a darkened bedroom, a stolen kiss, a shattered moan.

The smile freezes on my lips. I indicate that I need a moment and turn back to the receptionist, who is bending over a box of plugs. Every hair on the back of my neck is standing on end. Shaking her head, the receptionist looks at me and advises me to go to the corner store where they sell converter plugs. Acutely aware of his presence, I can barely make out what she's saying. His presence. After all those emotions, all those letters, all that goddamn counseling, all the pain — here we are.

Thomas Stranger and I.

I take a deep breath and turn round. Tom has moved over to the sofa by the exit. A convenient spot from which to beat a hasty retreat, perhaps? Trembling from head to toe, I make my way towards him.

'Hi,' we say in unison. His cheeks and ears are glowing red and he appears just as unnerved as I am, though we're both trying to hide it as best we can. My God, he hasn't changed a bit. Those blue eyes. That blonde hair. The beard, all as it used to be. It's really him.

'Wow, it's you,' I blurt out.

'Yeah, weird,' he says, appearing equally thunderstruck. 'Surreal. I had no idea what this would feel like.'

'Me neither.'

We stare at each other for a moment.

'It's raining. You're wet,' I note.

'It's not too bad.'

'Did you bring an umbrella?'

'No.'

'Me neither.'

His voice is husky, just as it was in the old days. The sense of familiarity is overwhelming. So much so that I cling, in desperation, to practical matters. 'I need to buy a converter plug. Perhaps we can find an umbrella somewhere, too?'

'Sounds good.'

Relief washes over me as we move towards the door, no longer nailed to the floor with half a lifetime weighing on our shoulders. He seems equally relieved as we walk out of the Ritz and down to Main Road.

In the corner store, I catch myself glancing at Tom, still finding it hard to look directly at him. He's wearing a checked shirt, gray trousers, and leather shoes. His posture is stiff, like he's walking on eggshells. Or maybe it's just my presence? Enviable tan and straight, white teeth. Obviously in good shape. The blonde locks are still in place, long in the front and shorter in the back. Deep inside me, a crack opens and a silent scream escapes. *HIS BLOODY HAIR IN MY FACE ...*

Inhaling sharply, I regain my balance and back cautiously away from the precipice. *Breathe, Thordis.*

The assistant rings up my converter plug and tells me that they don't sell umbrellas, which is no longer an issue because it has stopped raining. Our little errand was nonetheless a brilliant way to break the ice, giving us a mundane task to share, blissfully unrelated to our past.

Moments later, we're standing in colorful shell sand facing the ocean. A paved walkway, aptly named Sea Point Promenade, lines the seaside. The sky is overcast and the clouds seem close enough to touch with an outstretched hand. I take a deep breath and realize that although my heartbeat has calmed down, my insides still tremble.

'I attempted to imagine you here, when I came here yesterday,' he tells me.

'I had a similar idea. That we would meet up like this, by the sea.'

'I was worried that my feelings would overflow when I'd see you,' he says, and looks away. 'That I'd turn into a teary, blubbering mess.'

'I had doubts. About this … mission.'

'I did too. It just seemed so overwhelming …'

'… almost unthinkable …'

'… after all these years.'

He concurs with a nod.

'Have you been to Africa before?' I ask him.

'No, but it's a place I've always wanted to travel to.'

'I did too, but I've never traveled this far away from home — well, apart from for work — and I don't know if I ever will again. Which is why I wanted to meet you here, in a place where I know we could leave our past behind for good.'

'I agree. This is the right place.'

We stand in silence, observing the city that will hold our secret. The street is lined with high-rises and hotels facing the ocean. A barrier made of stacked rocks separates the promenade from the beach. Apart from a couple walking a black dog, and a panting jogger, we're the only people around. Tom bends over and picks up an empty plastic cup from the sand. He then reaches for an empty bottle, and I realize he's collecting trash.

He hesitates before asking: 'What does your family think about you being here?'

'They're not thrilled about it.'

'And your partner?'

'Vidir? He supports me wholeheartedly.'

'Nice to hear, that's comforting. Vidir, that's his name?' He says my fiancé's name cautiously, as if he doubts his permission to speak it out loud.

'Yes. It means willow in Icelandic, like the tree. What about your family?'

'My parents know I'm here. After this week, I'm flying to Western Australia to spend time with friends there. My friends in Sydney think I'm going to Western Australia for two weeks. My friends in Western Australia think my holiday is only a week.'

'So nobody in your group of friends knows you're here?'

'No, this week is not accounted for anywhere, really. To complicate things, my friend who I'm about to visit in Western Australia is South African and he has spoken about Cape Town so many times. He'd be hugely upset if he knew I came here without him,' he says awkwardly, dumping a handful of trash in a nearby bin.

'I know this isn't easy, for you or me. I've gone in infinite loops with this myself. But I'm convinced it had to be this way. Us meeting up in person.'

He nods. 'Yes. You can only come so far on paper.'

Dry seaweed crackles beneath our feet as Tom asks: 'So do you imagine ceasing the correspondence after this week?'

The question is laced with fear. Our correspondence has been an important stepping stone for both of us. It spans eight years of failed relationships, lifestyle changes, college degrees, jobs, child rearing, joy, and sorrow. In a way, we've accompanied each other through all these phases, even though they were never the topic of our conversation.

'Well, yes,' I tell him. 'I'd like to get as much work done as possible here, in Cape Town. What about you?'

'I was hoping we'd never need to write another word about this,' he replies.

I flinch at his words. So much has been invested in this, so much time, energy, money, and emotion has gone into our exchanges that even the tiniest rejection feels like rubbing a blister.

'So what do you want to do today?' he wonders.

'Get reacquainted, perhaps?' *Half a lifetime separates the teenagers we were from the adults we've become*, my mind adds. Aware of my habit of forgetting to eat in stressful situations, I suggest: 'And find food somewhere, maybe?'

'Sounds good.'

As we walk along Sea Point Promenade, still stiff and self-conscious, I don't know which is more surreal: the distance between us being less than a meter or the fact that I'm halfway across the world from home. In the same hesitant manner, Tom recounts how he had spent the previous day exploring the Waterfront, where he enjoyed a lovely performance by a men's group. 'They were brilliant, really stirring,' he tells me.

'You didn't feel nervous walking around by yourself at night?'

'Somewhat. It feels like you need your wits about you. I've avoided eye contact with people I've walked past. So, nervous, yes, but not particularly unsafe. But there is an air of ... desperation, it feels like.'

A magnificent tree growing out of the sidewalk catches my attention. It's got irregular white and brown patches, reminiscent of a cow. The robust trunk is split into two boles, stretching their crooked branches towards the sky. I find myself running my hand along the smooth bark, smiling to myself in fascination.

When I realize Tom is watching me in surprise, I state the obvious: 'I'm such a tourist.'

'A tree-hugging tourist?'

'And not ashamed of it.'

We smile at each other. All of a sudden, it's back. The old surge, the magnetic pull between us. My body identifies him as the source of pleasure, pain, and everything in between. The discovery shoots through me like an electric current, and suddenly I feel incredibly naive for not having foreseen this. Of course. I should've known there might be an attraction, even after everything we've been through.

My mind races back in time, to 16 November 1996. The night I lost my virginity.

It started with a birthday party at one of Tom's friends'. He had invited me along, and it was our first outing as a couple. I was sixteen and over the moon, my feet barely touching the ground.

After the party, we went to my place. With my parents and siblings' rooms on the ground floor of our house, I enjoyed the luxury of having the entire basement to myself, complete with a separate entrance that guaranteed discretion and 24-hour privacy.

Our mission was to 'bake a cake'.

Right.

I don't know where that joke came from. We must've thought it was a hilarious idea to bake a cake in the middle of the night. We laughed a lot, all giddy about it on the way to my house.

By the time we got there, the joke was growing old. We changed the plan to 'watch a video'.

Right.

I didn't even have any videos. In the end, we settled for my little brother's copy of Disney's *The Little Mermaid*. We both knew we wouldn't be doing any watching, anyway.

Then we started kissing. Petting. I was wearing a Bart Simpson t-shirt; a testament to my youth, the childhood I was about to shed. We made up wonderfully lame excuses to take off our clothes. 'Man, I'm feeling so hot, I better take off my pants.'

Right.

We made out for six intense hours before we decided to go all the way. It felt natural. We wanted each other. I didn't feel pressured. I was ready.

I remember trembling with excitement as he busied himself with the condom. Could this really be happening? Was I about to take a leap into womanhood? Would it show in the morning?

And then we made love.

It didn't hurt at all, to my surprise. It was just ... wonderful. Respectful, intimate, and beautiful, born of passion and free will. A delicate frame around which a first love could blossom.

Later on, the memory of that night would haunt me like a recurring nightmare. How could the same man be gentle and yet so unfeeling? How could he make tender love to me one night and rape me the next? Why did he decide to rob me of something I'd given him freely before?

This incomprehensible contradiction rendered me defenseless when it came to trusting people for years to come. If even those who claim to love me are capable of violating me so deeply — whom can I trust?

The question echoes in my head as I stand by the patchy tree, breaking eye contact with Tom. None of it matters any more. I'm in love with Vidir and no memories can threaten what he and I have.

Tom doesn't seem to have noticed anything. 'A week in Cape Town,' he says with a deep breath. 'To work on forgiveness.'

I regain my composure before adding: 'And manifest it.'

'Manifest it?'

'To me, forgiveness isn't something you just say, it's something you do.'

I find myself coming to a halt, turning to face Tom. 'Once upon a time when you were in Iceland, you gave me a rock. You said it had to be returned to its natural surroundings in Australia. You entrusted me with this task. Do you remember?'

He wrinkles his forehead. 'I think so. Is the rock grayish and oval-shaped?'

'Yes! Yes, it is.'

'It was from a beach near my house. I was down there taking some time the day before I was due to fly to Iceland. I remember picking it up and taking it with me after sitting down on a rock shelf and trying so hard to capture in my mind that bay that I love, to take it with me. But I think I settled for the rock instead when I wasn't successful.' He shakes his head. 'I'm sorry, I don't remember giving it to you.'

'Well, years after you did, I was invited to attend that playwriting conference in Australia, remember? I'd been doing my best to forget what you did to me but the invitation shocked me back into reality. It all felt fated somehow, as if I was being sent to the other side of the world to face my past. But you couldn't see me, so that was the end of that.'

He nods. 'I remember where I was living when you came to that conference, and I remember my excuses for not flying to see you. Some were valid, I guess. I was just starting my youth-work course in Perth, and I remember I was a poor student again. But I think there were other reasons, or hesitations maybe.'

'Anyway,' I continue, 'I took the rock with me and walked down to the beach one night. But I couldn't return it. The time wasn't right.' I look him straight in the eye. 'I think it's because I needed to give the rock back to you, Tom. Face to face. But I don't want it to end there. The whole point of forgiveness is letting go of the burdens, not passing them onto another person, even if it was theirs to carry in the first place. It'd be meaningless if the rock only changed hands and continued to nurture a vicious circle.'

'Yes,' he concurs in a quiet voice. 'You know, I'm not sure if I was ready to take that rock from you in 2005. And I agree, it'd be a pointless exercise to have me just take on the burden and continue the hurt.'

'Which is why it needs to be removed from the equation altogether. When the time is right, you should rid us of it, Tom. Where it can't weigh anyone down any more.'

He nods, and I reassure myself that I'm on the right track. Based on my knowledge of domestic violence, I know that continued communication between perpetrator and survivor can lock them in a destructive pattern. *This is different*, I tell myself. I'm not entering into a relationship with Tom. I will have nothing to do with him in the future and we're not even going to be living on the same continent. I have a family and a life that I'm hoping to set free from the past and its unfinished business, once and for all.

It's close to seven o'clock when a waitress shows us to a table at a Thai restaurant. Suddenly, I become acutely aware of what our situation looks like and it makes my skin crawl. I'm bursting to tell everyone that Tom and I are not on a date, envisioning myself storming around the place, removing everything that's even slightly romantic; blowing out candles and emptying flower vases into the trash, before turning my chair backwards, straddling it like an old mobster, and grunting in a deep voice: 'So whaddya say, think they've got anything to eat in this joint?'

I bite my lip and swallow my nervous discomfort. Our situation is strange enough without me behaving like a character from *The Sopranos*.

Shortly, the waitress returns with steaming chicken noodles for me, and a bowl of tofu for Tom.

'Are you vegetarian?'

'For twelve years now, I think.'

'Why?'

'Numerous reasons.'

'Like, ethical?'

'The main reason is ethical, I guess. After learning about the sentience of animals, the factory farming and treatment of them … also for environmental reasons. It takes a thousand liters of water to produce one kilo of beef. I tried it for one summer after reading a book by Peter Singer and just ate fish. The transition wasn't hard and I've just stuck with it,' he says. It's clear that he has no need to argue his lifestyle choice further. I take a sip of my drink and decide to respect that, even though a part of me is jumping up and down screaming about the leather shoes he's wearing. *Seriously, Thordis, shut up. Pick your fights.*

'So how are you doing, in general?' His words break the tension between us as he digs into his tofu.

I give it some thought before answering: 'I have no idea where my life is going, I have no clue where my next pay check will come from, and I've never been more content with it all.'

He raises his eyebrows. 'Wow. Just going with the flow, eh?'

'In a sense, yes. My work is project based, which means that I do short and intensive periods. It's everything from writing plays to translating novels, shooting films, and doing public speaking. Luckily, the work is diverse and there's been enough of it to pay my bills. Sure, a steady income would be nice, especially now that I have a family with all the accompanying costs. But you can't have it all. I feel very lucky to be able to make a living from projects that I love and that serve the ultimate goal.'

'And what's the ultimate goal?' he wonders.

'Changing the world.'

A smile flashes across his face.

'And you?'

'I'm still a youth worker and case manager at the refuge. I work a few shifts every month in a store that sells outdoor clothing and gear, too. One job is emotionally demanding and the other not so much. I'm also involved in an organization called Responsible Runners.'

Despite being too high-strung to have much of an appetite, I manage to work my way through the noodles as Tom tells me how he was out jogging on the beach one night six months earlier when he saw a guy with a headlight and a plastic bag picking up trash from the sand. Together they filled four big trash bins in two hours. 'This fellow then organized for others to join in with us and now it's grown into a weekly meeting of people wanting to clean up their beach. It's turned into a bit of a movement, operating in eight places in Australia. Together we've collected three tons of plastic and trash so far.'

This explains why he collected trash almost compulsively on the beach earlier, I silently conclude. Raising my glass, I say: 'To changing the world.'

'Cheers.' His eyes narrow as he smiles.

The moment is interrupted by a loud sizzle, coming from the kitchen. A husky chef is cooking over red-hot pans. Sweat drips from his brow as the open fire licks the ceiling.

'I'm still pinching myself to make sure this isn't all a dream,' Tom says quietly. His eyes convey that he's not talking about the chef.

In the following two hours, we paint a picture of our day-to-day lives, something we've avoided doing in our correspondence. It's strange but relieving to take a break from the strict dissection of the past and enter the present. The portrait of Tom is slowly revealed on the evening's canvas through his descriptions of work, hobbies, and interests. At the age of thirty-five, his love life has had its ups and downs and he's recently broken off a relationship, as a matter of fact. 'She's one of the most incredible people I've met … and the time together has been lovely … but unfortunately the "fireworks" weren't there,' he tells me.

I accept this casual explanation with a nod, although I can't help but be reminded of his words about feeling unworthy of love altogether. *As a result of what he did to me.*

'You seem happy,' he says.

My mind goes to Vidir, the kids, and my work, and a genuine smile lights up my face. 'I am. I'm lucky. I'm loved.'

'I'm happy to hear that,' he says warmly. Despite being hyper-aware of all the things that can go wrong in the days ahead, a strange bliss spreads through my chest: a mixture of release, humility, and gratitude towards the universe. *Thank you for letting me experience this. Thank you for helping me find the strength to face the most corrosive part of my past, no matter how senseless doing so may have seemed.*

When we exit the restaurant, it's already dark, and insects in nearby trees are praising the African night. All of a sudden, Tom stops and points to a sign ahead: 'Look!'

The sign is an advert for one of the daily newspapers in Cape Town. The headline screams at us in capital letters: 12-PAGE BOOKLET ABOUT RAPE WITH TODAY'S PAPER.

I am yanked back to reality. The beautiful, generous country in which we find ourselves has one of the highest prevalences of rape in the world. And the man beside me gave a face to the crime in a way I'll never forget.

'I want a copy of that,' I whisper.

'I do too,' he says. 'That's what we're here to discuss, after all.'

The truth quivers in the air, strung between us like a spider web. It is evident that we need to steel ourselves to be able to go where we're headed in the next few days.

Under the scab.

Although adrenaline has given way to jet lag, I find myself suggesting that we have a nightcap. A part of me doesn't want to leave until I've proven to myself — and Tom — that we're here to talk face to face about the night that changed our lives. A moment later, we're seated on the patio of a bar around the corner from the Ritz, which cuts through the darkness like a flaming torch. The beer bottle is cool and moist between my fingers, and Tom uses the opportunity to blow cigarette smoke into the night. Just as I'm about to break the silence, a toothless fellow in a dirty sweatshirt comes rushing up to us, asking us to take pity on him as he could really use some change. As much as I'd like to help, I'm painfully aware that nothing we do here and now will solve his problems. Tom shakes his head no, and, as the man gives up and disappears into the night, I stare quietly at my hands, the weight of my privilege like a metal blanket in my lap.

'You OK?' Tom asks.

'Yes. I'm just negotiating with my comfort zone. We're going to have to spend a week together in this town. Better find a way to adjust.'

'Indeed.'

I squint into the darkness. For a moment, neither of us says a word.

'One of my jobs taught me to master the art of stepping out of my comfort zone.'

'Which one was that?' he asks, drawing back on his cigarette.

'News reporting. Before I started working as a reporter, I would feel intimidated by people I respected or felt were in a position of power. Inferiority complex is the first thing you need to rid yourself of in reporting. By the end of it, I had toughened up to the point where I'd already talked to half of the Cabinet and it wasn't even lunchtime yet.'

He nods. 'Fear can be so toxic and paralyzing ...'

'... until you realize that the other person is just as afraid as you.'

Our eyes meet. The ember of his cigarette hovers above his lips like a firefly. He nods. Instinctively, I look away.

'You've changed,' he says.

'I know.' I'm no longer the impulsive, self-destructive girl with the cracks running down her entire existence; this much I'm aware of. Yet I don't know what he's referring to, or even if it's a compliment. 'Is that good or bad?'

'Good,' he answers. 'You're not the same girl I remember from when I returned to Iceland in the summer of 2000.'

'You, however, are exactly the same.'

'I am?' he asks, surprised.

'When it comes to your looks. Either you sleep in formaldehyde or all that vegetarian food has done you good.'

'You too.' He strokes his beard. 'I guess from the outside we look pretty much the same?'

Gravity is pulling on my limbs with unknown force, and the bench feels like granite beneath my thighs. Realizing that I don't have the energy to tiptoe around the subject any more, I pull the little orange notebook out of my handbag and place it on the table between us.

'What's this?' he asks.

'Square one,' I say, and flip through the scrawled pages, past shopping lists, doodles, and unfinished poems until I find the original letter to Tom. 'Look, there aren't even corrections or strikeouts,' I say, pointing at the handwritten pages. 'It just came out perfectly, even though I'd never thought consciously about writing it. I guess my subconscious had been working on it for a while.'

He studies the book, running his finger across the ballpoint scribbling. The pages are spread before him like white sheets and somewhere in between them, I'm sixteen years old and sprawled on my back. Suddenly, it feels like Tom is leafing through my soul, and I find myself yanking the notebook out of his hands, surprised and frustrated at my reaction. *Haven't you come further than this?*

Wide-eyed, he hesitates before asking: 'If it's possible, do you think I could read it one day? As it is the original.'

'Yes. One day,' I reply, stuffing the notebook back in the bag with trembling hands.

A little while later, two exhausted people are standing in front of the Ritz, deciding to meet up the following morning. After pulling an all-nighter by Australian time, Tom's complexion has turned sickly gray. Having watched him disappear into the night, I turn around and walk into the lobby. Here, one of the most fateful moments of my life took place mere hours ago, in front of dozens of people who had no idea that these two anxious individuals were about to rewrite their history.

My shoulders tense up at the thought that I still don't know if I'll succeed in finding closure and forgiveness this week. Taking a deep breath, I remind myself that as far as breaking the ice goes, it went well. I may not have been as cool-headed and prepared as I would've liked, but I still managed to conclude the night by broaching the subject we came all this way to discuss. It'll be tempting to avoid the difficult subjects in the days to come, but giving in to that temptation would be the ultimate betrayal. *No more running*, I think, and my stomach responds with a pang of anxiety. *No more hiding*.

My plans to talk to Vidir on Skype before going to bed crumble when the receptionist tells me that they've run out of access codes for the Wi-Fi. 'But we'll be getting more codes tomorrow,' she quickly adds.

'Really, on Good Friday?' I can't hide the skepticism in my voice.

She nods enthusiastically. I swallow the lump of disappointment in my throat and send Vidir a text explaining the situation while riding the elevator up to the twelfth floor. I close my eyes and try to remember his scent. I miss burying my face in his neck and listening to him breathe. *My God, what am I doing here?*

Moments later, a disappointed but understanding Vidir replies with news that is both comforting and crucial in its banality: a trip to the swimming pool, grocery shopping, and macaroni soup. Haflidi, he tells me, is managing pretty well considering that his mommy is alternately lost or stuck in a plane, depending on how he's feeling.

A bittersweet sting floods my heart. *Dearest Haflidi Freyr.*

'Tell him that his mommy will NEVER lose him. Let's talk tomorrow. Love you,' I reply, blinking away the tears.

The time is 11pm South African time when I pull the blanket over my shivering body. I let out a loud sigh of relief as I am finally in a horizontal position for the first time in two days. My chest harbors a whirlpool of emotions, and I don't know whether to be overwhelmed at the thought of the upcoming days or elated about the small victories so far. My last thoughts before sleep takes mercy on me are about a teenage betrayal that morphs into a bowl of macaroni belonging to a blue-eyed toddler holding my heart.

From Tom's diary

Thursday

My new room has glowing ironed sheets and the crispest, brightest white towels I can recall. I left the backpackers this morning and checked in at the villa, and there is a small sense of guilt around having this pristine, manicured, and private room to myself. Not the typical back of a sandy van or a friend's futon. It isn't particularly large, nor opulent by contemporary standards, but there is still something distinctly ... excessive and mature about having this space all to myself.

The justification for staying here was simple — I knew meeting Thordis would be hard, and I'm sure we'll be walking our way through some strained and thickly guarded places. I knew I'd need a padded space to return to each night, a short walking distance from her hotel.

I unpacked my bags and took a walk down to Three Anchor Bay after checking in, just trying to relax and get some ocean. But when walking back, my nerves jolted when my phone vibrated in my pocket.

She'd arrived. And she was on a bus from the airport.

Some deep slow breaths, spliced with nervously organizing my belongings. I sat down and rubbed the soles of my feet on the polished timber floors, just needing to earth myself and let go a little. The anticipated anxiousness duly arrived and I readied my light long-sleeve shirt and plain thin trousers, items chosen well in advance so as to be cool and not show any sweat marks should I have one of my panic 'attacks'. I don't like the powerlessness of the word 'attack' and have always tried to word out my episodes internally as something else, like a 'wave' or even a panic 'spike', so that I'm assured it will swiftly pass. The weather today was thankfully blustery and cool.

I had my coffee early, smoked my last cigarette an hour before I showered, and even drank half a glass of wine with lunch just to safeguard myself against any undue rushes.

I hate the fact I've just rekindled the old dusty habit of smoking. I'm not a smoker, this I know. I haven't smoked in a long time. But with the gravity of this week, I can understand why I am again.

Blended with a bit of frantic was a bit of surrendering. We've put so much into this, we know so much already, and so much has been exposed and disarmed. There is also the foundation of unmistakable intent laid beneath us, and I felt confident that any tremors and wobbles would pass. Plus, I know her ... albeit from years ago.

I left with ten minutes to spare and, as I'd walked past the Ritz the day before, I figured I had plenty of time. Two hundred meters down the road, the skies opened so I jogged back to my room and grabbed my jacket. I then had a few minutes less than expected and it was enough to quicken my step and rattle my planned composure. I remember thinking: *more deep breaths, slow down the exhalation and lengthen it. It will tell your body there is no threat and it can relax.* I was trying to focus on the cool breeze hitting my face, or noticing the texture of the paint on the fence. Anything to slow down my pulse.

I thought it was going to happen on a beach … I thought there would be privacy and space for emotional outcomes, perhaps salty air and horizons to focus on, and now it was a foyer with the possibility of other people around.

I walked up the hill and a flight or two of stairs before reaching the rotating doors. It was 5pm exactly. Instead of stopping to measure the moment and practice my calmness, I let the nervous momentum urge me straight into the foyer. Scanning the place, I was satisfied that I didn't recognize her in the faces present. She hadn't arrived yet. I dashed into the toilet to dry myself from the rain and steal a few more slow breaths. Looking in the mirror and leaning on the washbasin with both hands, I reminded myself, *I've come such a long way for this.*

When I left the men's room and looked across the foyer I saw her. She was speaking to the receptionist and hadn't seen me yet.

Long hair. Casual colors and dress. Jeans.

Jesus.

It's truly her.

I felt like I was looking at an apparition. A chimerical person who had spoken to me in a dream.

As I walked towards her, my lung capacity was halved and time became weirdly visceral. I felt impelled forward by a bending, internalized history that took no notice of the windy doubt pushing around me.

She looked at me and motioned with her finger that she needed a moment to finish up with the receptionist.

She was … Exactly. The. Same.

A small scar inside my chest received the first bit of blood flow it had had in years and I acknowledged a partially expected yet still surprising jabbing feeling.

The couch was empty. Perfect. I sat down and tried to imagine what my calm self looked like so that I could produce exactly that. I could feel heat moving up from my thumping heart and into my neck, and thought to myself, *it's okay. Be nervous. She probably is too.*

Shit. Here she comes. She looks so calm!

Just say hello.

I did. And so did she.

A momentous first day. Dangerous and thorny, but some ground was made. I didn't think I'd be so very tense around her, but I'm hoping that will ease this week.

When we sat down on the patio tonight it was getting cooler and she had a longer coat on, but I still had an urge to offer her my jacket. I held back though, as wouldn't that smack of some kind of chivalry and be grossly misplaced? *Too intimate.*

She spoke of having to 'spend a week together', and that such a prospect was on the edge of her 'comfort zone', which kicked off a string of questions for me, and when that gate was opened my mind sprinted.

Had I done something wrong just now? Was she scared of me?

I noticed she was composed but obviously ruminating and working her way through something. In an instant she became the familiar strong survivor and voice of our emails. I recalled learning about her PTSD, her numerous trials with psychologists and therapists, the symptoms and side effects of the trauma. I know so much about her, but at that moment I was learning something new.

While watching her there was a slow shift internally, and I became aware of an unclean feeling in my belly.

The sunken black box flipped open and a connection was made:

novel and complex. *I'm* the one responsible for what she's experiencing right now. *I'm* the individual who lies at the root of her fear, and *that's* why she is having to strengthen and monitor herself right now. I was violent with her, and her body remembered me.

Have I been too hopeful? Did I really think she'd be relaxed around me?

How on earth are we going to talk things through this week if she seems to be affected by just being near me? Growing out of that worry is the familiar weight of the old chain connected to me, quietly producing its dull metallic sounds as it tensions itself between me and the events of that night.

I momentarily fall out of love for myself.

Day Three

29 March 2013

A barking dog wakes me from a dreamless sleep. I feel blindly in the dark for Vidir, only to sit up with a start when I realize I'm alone. *That's right. South Africa.*

The first sunrays of the day color the curtains with a golden tinge. My phone on the bedside table tells me that it's six o'clock. For the following hour, the African sunrise strengthens the outline of the room little by little while I convince myself that I'm not completely insane and that this trip isn't my own version of 'mission impossible'. *Stay focused. Trust your instincts.*

Out of old habit, I reach for my laptop to read the morning news, but alas, no Wi-Fi. Fiddling absentmindedly with the keyboard, I open one of Tom's emails.

There is an internal minefield of 'whys' to be stepped through, and lots more meditating and revisiting that time in my life, and that horrific night. I don't doubt I will reach a point whereby I will get some perspective, some insight into my choices. But ... I can't promise you I'll cleanly or quickly find my way through this, and wouldn't dare to. I know this is not what you are asking me for. But in saying this communication could 'bring closure to both of us', I'm cautious of it being tied in part to me freeing myself, and you assisting me with this.

I sincerely hope this sentiment doesn't offend. I guess there is also an element of me that doesn't want to feel helpless, and wants to offer you something in return. In short, I'm hoping there is a two-way flow, and that this is mutually beneficial, and not dependent upon one side's healing. I know this has been spoken of before, but it still concerns me and I wanted to be honest with you.

Just reading what I've written ... I can see I'm also uncomfortable with the strength I read in your emails, and the vulnerability I display in mine. As uncomfortable as that is to say, it's apparent. As I'm sitting here pondering, I believe that is due to me wanting to divulge all I can, apologize endlessly and pour out the shame that I feel in the hope that that might make amends. But you don't need or want for that. You're stronger than that, and on some unsettling level, I have an issue with that.

I feel uneasy after communicating that. It reads like I need for some part of you to remain vulnerable. Or like I'm 'needed' on some level for your recovery, as if you require my help.

I quietly contemplate if there is a grain of truth in Tom's insecure writings. Did I need him to validate my hurt? No, I would've found another way to acknowledge my wounds. Not doing so would've killed me, of this I'm sure. But had I never contacted Tom again, a part of me would have been beset with relentless questions. I'd wonder whether he realized what he'd done. If he cared. If he was sorry. If he'd done it again to someone else. It would've eaten away at the oxygen around me like an open flame. Whether I'd like to admit it or not, his regret was as soothing as aloe vera on a burn wound.

After a quick shower, I put on a long skirt, a tank top, and the cardigan, which turns out to be very useful to combat the chilly winds of Cape Town. The dining room on the first floor attracts hungry guests, neatly lined up in a queue for fried potatoes, bacon, and scrambled eggs. At the end of the line, a cook with a hairnet custom-fries eggs with friendly gusto.`

Not ready for anything fried this early in the morning, I fill a bowl with yoghurt and raw fruit. The door to the garden is open and a fresh breeze blows through the dining room, along with a pigeon that struts confidently between tables until a man shoos it away with a sandal-clad foot. The pigeon cocks its head coolly, as if to say: *you think you can ruffle my feathers, you tourist? I was hatched in this garden.*

I pour myself some coffee from a jug on a hot plate only to swiftly conclude that it tastes like earwax. Although less anxious than I was yesterday, I still steel myself as I walk down the stairs to the lobby, where I'm meeting Tom for the second time in less than twenty-four hours.

He seems aware of the repetition too. 'It was a whole lot easier to walk in here today than it was yesterday,' he tells me. Our interaction is self-conscious and awkward, in spite of yesterday's rendezvous. Thirteen years' worth of separation doesn't dissolve overnight, nor does our awareness of the unspoken truth between us.

With neither of us eager to take the lead, we walk hesitantly into the souvenir shop opposite the elevators, which turns out to be a small travel agency, to get advice from someone with no strings attached to the delicate power balance between us.

A massive oak desk is the first thing we see, decorated with a brass sign that reads TRAVEL DESK. African crafts adorn the walls, along with framed magazine articles about the must-see places of Cape Town. To the right are two leather chairs, and between them is a rack with tourist brochures. The overall feel is tidy and organized, much like the man who greets us. He's wearing a white, well-ironed shirt and black slacks. His face is clean-shaven and radiates health. *And good moisturizer*, I note internally.

'Hello there, my name is Nigel,' he says, pointing happily to his name badge. 'What can I do you for?'

We have no particular plans for the week to come except for talking, which in our case is enough of a task. There's nothing to say these talks can't take place at some of Cape Town's interesting destinations. In fact, I'm sure that beautiful surroundings can only help open up our hearts and minds. As long as it's affordable, of course. My finances have taken quite a hit due to this trip, and I'm already aware of how broke I'm going to be in the months to come. Shoving my worries aside, I take a seat in one of the leather chairs while Nigel makes a few enquiries for us. Tom follows suit and his legs catch my eye as he stretches them. Every cell in my body is aware of his presence. Its effect is like that of a strong espresso — a sharpened focus and heightened senses.

Nigel hangs up the phone and turns to us. He is so accommodating that I wonder whether we're expected to pay for his assistance. He gives no such indication when he informs us that the afternoon tour to Robben Island, where the great Nelson Mandela was held captive, is sold out. 'I checked with Table Mountain as well, but unfortunately, it's too windy. The cable car is closed.'

Tom and I shrug and thank Nigel for his help. Outside, a day checkered with clouds, sun, and wind awaits us.

'What do you say about walking down to the Waterfront?' Tom asks. 'I explored it the other day, it'd be nice to go down there.'

When I agree, he adds: 'Do you mind if we stop by the beach? It's a bit of a thing, but I like to splash some seawater on my face. It's kind of a daily ritual when I'm near salt water,' he adds apologetically.

'Sure, okay.' I'd be lying if I said I didn't want a bit of sand between my toes. An Icelander abroad is — after all — an *Icelander* abroad.

I follow him onto the coarse sand, which is thick with shells. Smooth brown rocks protrude into the ocean, and large areas of the shore are covered in brown kelp. The Ritz is especially elegant from this point of view, perched next to the Lion's Head like a twin tower. I take a picture to send to Vidir with the subject line, 'My hotel from the beach.' *Anything that can help him envision my surroundings.* I take the photo and look hard at my phone, the sun making it hard to see the screen properly. Even though it's taken from a distance, there's no mistake that Tom is in the picture, walking along the shore. I hurriedly delete it. *Over my dead body am I sending Vidir a picture of Tom strolling on a seductive beach.* I wait a moment until Tom is out of the frame before taking another picture and sending that one to Vidir. Missing him dearly has resulted in an ache, which is soothed by the thought that perhaps I can find wedding rings for us in the country of gold and diamonds, although such a gift seems small compared to his support and understanding of my highly unusual journey.

A little while later, we're back on the street that leads to the Waterfront. The wind uses my skirt to whip my legs, and I fish an elastic band out of my handbag to keep my hair from blowing constantly in my face.

'Tom?'

'Yes?'

'Will you tell me your life story?'

He looks at me and giggles awkwardly. When he realizes I'm serious, the smile on his lips gives way to surprise. 'All of it?'

I nod.

He raises his eyebrows. 'Have you got some time on your hands?'

'I've got six days,' I reply, dead serious. 'Think that'll do?'

He falls silent for a moment, seemingly trying to wrap his mind around the idea.

'Look. I know who it was who raped me sixteen years ago. What I need to know is who I'm trying to forgive for it.'

We're standing on a busy street corner, surrounded by humming traffic, and yet, the whole world seems to stand still until he answers: 'And I also get to learn yours?'

'Only if we switch back and forth, so we don't end up with monologues that stretch out for days.'

'Sounds fair.' He studies me and hesitates. 'Should I start?'

'I asked first.'

He exhales. 'Fair enough. Let me see ...'

While he contemplates where to start, I wonder if it was a stupid suggestion, only to quickly conclude that it's worth a try. I've always wondered what it was that shaped the 18-year-old who violated me. What was his past like? What was it like to subsequently grow up in the shadow of his own wrongdoing? All these years, I've only had one piece of the puzzle, and I've held it for so long that it's become worn around the edges. I'm hungry for the full picture.

Tentative, and obviously mulling over the past, Tom starts his life story at his conception, which was actually against the odds. 'My mother had an IUD when I was conceived,' he explains. 'I wasn't exactly planned, in other words. But I made it past the defenses, somehow. Mum was really worried, as was the doctor, that the IUD would cause serious complications.'

I can't help but wonder if perhaps Tom's life was *meant to be*, given how the odds were stacked against him. This speculation is closely followed by the question of what *my* life would've been like if he hadn't turned it upside down, but the rational part of me instantly shuts down such fruitless mind games.

Judging by Tom's story, the first thirteen years of his life were like a fairytale. 'We lived just out of Melbourne, and then we moved to a small town nearby in country Victoria, while my parents built our house on a small block of land they had bought. It was a beautiful little hobby farm and sat atop a small hill. Dad studied nursing before working at the local hospital, and Mum was a teacher at the local community college. My older brother and I could just roam around the bush and paddocks, and the whole place was like a postcard. We had a few chickens, sheep, ducks, fish in the dam, and a goat at one point. When we were older, my brother and I were given a calf each to feed and raise. We got pretty close to them over the course of a year, but they were then sent to the abattoir, which we, of course, knew would happen.'

That would be enough to plant the seeds of vegetarianism, I can't help thinking.

'My younger brother was born when I was five,' he continues. 'We built cubby houses together, rode bikes, played in puddles; in hindsight, it's the stuff of storybooks. I've always held my childhood as dear, as a time that was slow moving and rich with experiences. When I get nostalgic about it I think of bush camping with family and friends, summers at the beach, wrestling with my brothers. We were outdoors at every chance. And you know what it's like when you're a kid — a tree or trampoline can be transformed into a day's worth of wonder and fun. Holding it up against my later adult years, those times seem simple and untainted … like a bit of a calm before the storm.' Suddenly, he inhales sharply.

In front of us is the Green Point Stadium, built to accommodate the World Cup of 2010. We come to a halt to admire the colossal white doughnut. I can almost hear the roar of a giant crowd echoing down the path that leads up to the stadium, like a red version of the road to Oz. The air is thick with drama from sweet victories and shattering losses. *Not unlike the path we're on,* I think, glancing at Tom from the corner of my eye.

Continuing our walk towards the Waterfront, Tom prompts me. 'Alright. Your turn.'

I search my mind. *Where to start my life story?*

'Well, I was born in Iceland, moved to the States by the age of two, Sweden at four, Iceland at five, Sweden at seven, and Iceland at eleven. My dad was studying medicine, which explains the moving back and forth. My mother studied fine art and graphic design, making a living off the latter for twenty years. Having to say goodbye to my friends and go back to square one on a new school playground, asserting myself in a new language over and over again, was tough at times.'

'I can imagine,' Tom says with the empathy of someone who has had to learn another language, especially a difficult one like Icelandic.

'I don't know if there's any correlation, but there was a period when I was terrified of the dark. Maybe my fear had something to do with all the moving around we did, as a reaction to the rootlessness.' I shrug. 'Maybe not. My sister, who is eight years older than me, has battled alcoholism since she was a teenager. It's affected the entire family, but she has fought it heroically, and I respect her deeply for it. My brother, who is eight years younger than me, was born with a cleft palate and a split lip. He needed surgery, speech therapy, and orthodontics, and he was bullied as a kid, but he grew up to be a respected musician with more friends than I can count. During our childhood, when our problems were weighing down on us, I came to the conclusion that I was the only sibling who was close to "normal", if there is such a thing. I aspired to never add to my family's worries and to — if possible — make up for their trials. So when I was in first grade and my sister started skipping school, my childish logic told me that I could somehow make up for it by striving to get straight As, which led to me becoming valedictorian in every school I ever attended. My brother's facial deformity led to my obsession with being "pretty". By the age of eleven, I had developed an eating disorder that haunted me for the next decade.'

'Man ...' Tom says, wrinkling his forehead.

I clarify: 'Don't get me wrong. These expectations didn't come from anybody but me. I was loved. I was cuddled and had storybooks read to me every night. I received compliments for things I did well, and encouragement to do whatever I wanted. Most days, I was happy. My parents were good people who did their best. More than their best. I could always turn to them with my problems. I just decided not to. I was under the impression that it was for the best. No more worries on my family's already full plate.'

I stop at a street corner. 'Which is why I didn't tell them what you did to me,' I add. 'That's why I told no one.'

'I understand,' he says quietly.

Waiting in silence at the pedestrian crossing, my mind is still on my parents. After years of practice, my habit of protecting them had become so ingrained that when I finally realized that I'd been raped, the natural choice was not to tell them. The seriousness of the matter only deepened my need to shelter them from it. Added to that was my acute awareness of my family's suffering due to my sister's battle with alcohol. Telling them that I'd gotten drunk and danced with the devil felt like the ultimate act of betrayal, the utmost disrespect that I could show my family. To add insult to injury, not only had I gotten myself drunk, I'd 'gotten myself raped' as well. That last, ridiculous idea was supported by the victim-blaming notions that I'd picked up from the public discourse about rape, which also rendered me incapable of placing the responsibility on Tom's shoulders for many years. I glance at him standing next to me and think: *We sure have come a long way.*

When the light turns green, I inhale deeply and step into the present. 'So this is it. The famous Waterfront.'

One of the most popular destinations on the African continent stretches out in front of us as I go through my memory, recalling what I know about it. The harbor was built in the British colonial times and named after Queen Victoria and her son, Prince Alfred. Today, the Victoria & Alfred Waterfront offers everything from fast food to haute couture. The ocean licks at the side of the harbor. Boats secured to moorings rock softly in the cerulean water. An enormous Ferris wheel gives a stunning view of the harbor and the city. The mountain range, with the magnificent Devil's Peak dead ahead, frames the view for a postcard.

Awe-struck, I lag behind Tom. *Wow. This place totally lives up to expectation.*

Seagulls circle above my head, squawking loudly as one of them makes a quick dive to snatch a sugarcoated pretzel. The gulls of the Waterfront don't have to settle for crumbs, thank you very much.

'Coffee?' Tom asks.

'Yes. Absolutely.'

We enter a large mall with shops stretching out on both sides and stalls offering hand-painted ostrich eggs and other memorabilia.

Once inside a cozy café, he pulls out his wallet and asks: 'Would it work if I got this round, and you the next?'

'Deal.'

Our eyes meet and, suddenly, the membrane of time is ruptured. Something in his clear blue eyes turns into acid, burning my corneas. I look away, gasping, as my heart pounds with irrational panic in my chest. *Breathe, Thordis. In … and out …* Muscle memory doesn't adhere to logic, but I try to reason with my mind. Yes, those may be the same blue eyes but the circumstances are different. *You're safe now.*

Tom hands me my coffee, unaware of how time had stopped while a corrosive flashback was injected into the present moment.

'I need to call Vidir,' I say, not looking him in the eye.

'Absolutely. I'll meet you back here.'

After trying unsuccessfully to regulate my heartbeat and climb out of the crack I fell into, I dial the number of the man who never fails to pull me up and out.

Vidir is happy to hear from me, and tells me he's on his way to his parents' summerhouse with the kids so we'll not be able to Skype tonight, unfortunately. He acts brave, but I can hear the worries simmering in his voice.

'You're so far away,' he says, tenderly.

'I know.'

'On the other side of the planet. With a man who …' He stops.

I close my eyes. We've been through this many times.

'But I support you,' he quickly adds. 'You know I do. This whole thing is just so … strange. That's all.'

The part of me that is still hyperventilating from the flashback wants to confess to Vidir that this was a colossal mistake, that I'm getting myself on the next plane and declaring the whole mission a failure. The part that wants to remain strong for the sake of our future scrapes together every last scrap of courage and replies: 'Strange indeed. You know I love you, Vidir.'

'And I love you.'

I concentrate on steadying my voice when asking: 'Is Haflidi's mommy still missing?'

There is a humorous undertone to Vidir's answer. 'Well, if it suits him. If he doesn't feel like doing something, such as putting on his overalls or going to playschool, the tragedy of his missing mommy is recalled with tearful passion. Apart from that, he's fine.' I can hear him grin and I find myself smiling as well.

We say our goodbyes, and the result is evident as I get up from the bench. No crack in my armor is too deep to be mended with the unconditional trust that has grown to exist between Vidir and me.

A quick lunch later, as Tom and I are treading the boards of the Waterfront with our second coffee of the day in hand, I become acutely aware that we look like a couple, complete with to-go cups. Uncomfortable and confused, I slow my step, coming to a halt. Tom keeps walking, unaware. My eyes go to the shop window next to me and discover it's a jewelry store. The thought of finding wedding rings resurfaces, and I jump at the opportunity.

'Mind if I take a look?' I call in Tom's direction. He turns around, and I'm dumbfounded when he intends to accompany me inside. *Well done, Thordis. Now you look like a couple on your way to the altar.*

'I'm looking for wedding rings,' I say to a smiling lady who offers her assistance. 'It's not him,' I quickly add as I gesture in Tom's direction, quietly cursing my own awkwardness.

While the assistant is getting the rings, I realize I'm between two worlds. In one of them, I'm in South Africa with my ex trying to make peace with the past, while in the other world I'm looking for a symbol of love to seal the future with my current partner. My homeland is a geographical wonder where two tectonic plates meet, and yet I've never found myself on a more remarkable border.

After realizing that this jeweler is well outside my price range, Tom and I continue our walk. We pass one of the Waterfront's countless souvenir stores, boasting an eight-foot Nelson Mandela made out of beaded wire. His hands look like rakes with spread, angular fingers. The proportions of the face are skewed, complete with eyebrows that are uncomfortably reminiscent of Jack Nicholson in *The Shining*. He's wearing a gaudy sweater made of beads in at least four shades of neon blue. Mandela's signature white hair covers the head, removing any doubt about the statue's identity. The overall look is radically kitsch, deeply violating my sense of aesthetics to the point where I'm embarrassed that I can't take my eyes off it.

'I'll take a picture of you and him,' Tom offers.

I'm shocked at the suggestion until I realize that he's kidding, judging by the wide grin on his face.

'Ha ha. Very funny,' I reply in an icy voice. *What nerve!*

He pretends he didn't hear me and reaches for my camera phone with feigned sincerity. 'C'mon, just one tourist shot.'

Even though I know full well that humor is a necessary companion on our journey, my ego still crumbles under the first joke he makes at my expense. *Too soon.* A part of me even thinks that *I* should be the one to crack the first joke, not him. I regain my cool, put on a bitter smile, and reply: 'Go to hell, Stranger.'

He shrugs. 'Fair enough. Your call.'

Closer to downtown, the buildings stretch higher and higher until we're surrounded by skyscrapers rising proudly out of the asphalt. Meanwhile, Tom describes how his family moved to a coastal suburb in another part of the country after the fairytale childhood on the hobby farm. His mother was offered a job, and both parents thought it would be a chance to expand the family's horizons. 'I remember the tears my older brother and I cried when they told us; we were both enjoying high school, and we struggled to see the logic of our parents. The first few months were really tough. The adjustment to the new private school was the hardest part, and it wasn't easy to break into friendship groups or to deal with the cultural change. There was a pretty specific mold to fit. If you weren't interested in surfing and rugby, you were either bullied or left out. Surfing I had an interest in, but rugby seemed alien to me.'

'So your love for surfing was originally a means to survive in a town full of bigots?'

His eyes narrow a bit. 'If you didn't make the cut, you weren't one of the "fellas". So yes, I loved surfing, but it was also a bit of an "in".'

I whistle softly in surprise.

'But don't get me wrong, the area we moved to consisted of suburbs stretching along beautiful east-coast beaches. It might have been hard at first, but I got used to the way of life there pretty quickly. Hard not to when you're thirteen and living a block away from a national park and surf beach. There were some really solid relationships seeded in those high school years, too, and some of the people I met at school are still near and dear friends. Speaking of near and dear ones, I should mention a young man that my mother took in before I was born who has been a constant figure in my life. He's older than me — he traveled the world and would write letters to us, telling stories of his foreign adventures. If I had a life mentor, he'd be it. He's been a big influence, and I reckon has inspired me to wonder about what's over that next hill. He's a massive support also, and as adults I consider him a dear friend.'

Listening to his life story, it's obvious that Tom didn't lack brothers to love, learn from, and identify with. I silently ponder how it would've affected him if he'd had a sister too. *Would it have changed anything for me?*

As if he read my thoughts, Tom adds: 'We also had three female exchange students while I was growing up. My parents wanted us to experience other cultures and expand our world views, but having our foreign "sisters" in the family was also a way to develop our understanding of girls.'

Listening to Tom's story, I note that central Cape Town is a ghost town today. Capetonians must be eager travelers during Easter, much like Icelanders who flock out of town on bank holidays. Wherever we go, we're met with closed doors and quiet businesses. In spite of the missing hustle and bustle, the city is far from empty. On every street we encounter the homeless citizens of Cape Town. They watch us closely and the attention isn't always friendly. Turning a corner near the train station, we walk into a group of people gathered around a ghetto blaster. A haggard man wearing a dirty baseball cap points at me, and the group by the ghetto blaster turns to face us.

'We should get going,' I whisper, quickening my step.

'I agree. Should we take a taxi?' He nods towards a taxi waiting beneath a row of trees that are swaying in the wind.

The relief that floods my veins as we get into the backseat is accompanied by the feeling that we narrowly escaped trouble. It's closely followed by guilt and distaste over my own whiteness, my undeniable privilege. Tom climbs in next to me and for a split second, his knee brushes mine. It's an innocent touch, and it doesn't trigger any fear in me, nor an involuntary flashback. Leaning back into the seat, I celebrate this tiny victory, having worked too hard for too long to go limp with terror over trivial activities like buying coffee and sharing taxis.

The driver takes us to the South African National Gallery, as suggested by Tom, who had read about it in a tourist brochure over breakfast. We're blown into the foyer of a majestic neo-classical building from the 1930s, praising our luck that the museum is open on Good Friday. The current photography exhibit marks one hundred years since the cruel Land Act was passed. The Act allowed black citizens to own a total of just 8 per cent of South Africa's land, despite making up 80 per cent of the population. Justified by the apartheid policy, an increasing number of areas were declared to be for whites only, leading to the uprooting of black people and the destruction of their homes. *Some of whom are still roaming the streets,* I think. The photographs capture devastated people who had their life savings wrenched out of their hands. A photo of a shell-shocked woman with a goat on a leash and crying children hiding in her skirts is instantly etched into my memory.

I catch myself clenching my fists, furious at the injustice that took place in this lush country, the echoes of which reached far beyond its borders. Photograph after photograph depicts the turmoil caused by the forced relocations of black South Africans. The poverty in the government-assigned 'black spots' was abysmal, with no infrastructure or job opportunities, light years away from the quality of life that whites allotted themselves. My heart sinks as I read the dates. Some of the photographs are taken after I was born, in the '80s. The systemic discrimination lasted until the historic elections of 1994, when blacks were allowed to run for office for the first time in a South African democratic election.

'I'm ashamed of the privilege people of my race acquired by stealing from others,' I hiss.

Tom nods, upset. 'The cruelty is unfathomable.'

After gazing at hundreds of photographs documenting the inhumanity of racism, my mind starts to ponder the dehumanizing effects of labels; when people are no longer people, they are 'whites' or 'blacks', 'oppressors' or 'the oppressed'. I turn my head to look at the man I flew here to meet, the 'perpetrator' who cast me in the role of 'victim'; the labels that shape and separate us. My thoughts bounce off the walls, off the country's history, our history. Suddenly, I'm overwhelmed. All I want is a chance for my thoughts to settle in private, away from Tom. My feet carry me into the next room — and into a horror scene.

The space is small and closed off. I am met with three terrifying creatures sitting on a bench. Their skin is pale and lifeless; their eyes black, without pupils. Instead of ears, they have holes below broken horns that protrude from their hairless heads. Their noses and mouths are covered with coarse skin. Deep incisions line their bodies from the throat down to the navel, like they've been dissected. My fists are still clenched in anger towards apartheid when I realize that I am looking at its embodiment. *Of course*. Only when people cut out their hearts, rip off their ears, and sew their mouths shut can they condone hatred. Yet these demons are sitting relaxed on a bench like they're killing time, much like cruelty. Cruelty also relaxed on a bench for half a century, nonchalantly crossing its legs while forming the backdrop to South African existence.

A quote by a renowned specialist in the field of sexual violence pops up in my mind: *Rape is mundane. It happens every day, every hour, every minute all around the world. As horrible as it is, it's a mundane part of everyday life.*

Tom's voice pulls me back into the present. '*Butcher Boys* by Jane Alexander,' he reads from a sign. 'I can't even look at them. Holy shit that's creepy.' He shudders and turns away, marching quickly into the next room.

Watching him, I can't help but wonder if his reaction is colored with guilt about his own evils. I look back at the Butcher Boys, who are staring at me through blind eyes, calm as a millpond. In the spirit of true cruelty, they couldn't care less. Nothing is as coldhearted as perfect indifference.

When we exit the museum a while later, the wind welcomes us like an eager dog, tearing playfully at Tom's shirt and blowing my hair into my mouth. A gorgeous garden stretches out before us, complete with sculptures and ornate fountains. I stop to look at a statue of a late leader. The bronze has turned blue, and yet I know that the leader's skin is white and his gender is male. South African colonial history in a nutshell.

As we settle down in the grass, an oddly shaped cloud hovering over Table Mountain catches my eye. Wrapping my cardigan tighter around me, I vaguely recall reading that certain types of clouds foreshadow stormy weather. I wonder if there is a storm upon us, in more ways than one.

'One of my favorite films is about the struggle against apartheid in South Africa. It's based on a book called *The Power of One* by Bryce Courtenay. It's a family favorite,' Tom tells me. Before I've had a chance to respond, a beggar appears. After he illustrates his hunger and misery, Tom reaches into his bag and hands him a prickly pear. The act is so effortless and spontaneous that I classify it as genuine kindness, not as a play to impress me. I frown, filled with distaste at how judgmental I'm being. *What does it matter? Am I not scrambling to put on my best act too?*

While I'm battling my thoughts, Tom pulls a folded piece of paper out of his bag. 'Can I read something to you?'

'Please do.'

He clears his throat and starts reading a chapter from a book that argues how masculine stereotypes have made it harder for men to embrace things like humility, sincerity, and forgiveness throughout the years. His hands tremble slightly, and although nothing in the text comes as a surprise, I'm still moved by his effort. A warm certainty is born in my soul. *There's no play going on, just well-intentioned sincerity.*

'Thanks for sharing,' I say when he looks up from the paper.

'Thanks for listening,' he replies, flushed. The sun is about to set, and the shadows stretch their long, cool fingers across the lawn.

'I need to tell you something,' I say when we're seated in a sushi-train place, walking distance from Sea Point. The last rays of sunlight draw Tom's outline in shimmering motes of dust as the wind shakes the palm trees across the street.

'What's that?' he asks, grabbing a piece of avocado maki off the conveyor belt.

'I've been working on a play about forgiveness for four years now.'

He raises his brows and I add: 'The reason I didn't tell you before is that I didn't want you to think that I was using you as some sort of guinea pig for my theatre experiments. I'm done writing the play and it is in no way about us.'

He nods. 'Geez ... four years is a long time. You've certainly gone deep into looking at forgiveness.'

'I discovered so many things. You know, people are always apologizing without even noticing. We bump into someone at the supermarket — we're sorry. We step on someone's toes in the elevator — we're sorry.'

'Yes, but "sorry" and "forgive me" aren't really the same thing, are they? I'd say that "sorry" carries a lot less weight.'

'I agree. "Sorry" is the diet version. "Forgive me" is reserved for when you've really hurt someone.'

He nods and takes a sip from his beer.

'I think I had this rosy idea of forgiveness before I learned more about how it really works. One day, I interviewed an 84-year-old woman who radically changed my outlook when she claimed that people only forgive when they have to.'

He looks me in the eye. 'How ...?'

I put down my chopsticks. 'Imagine that you stop at a gas station, only to get shitty service from a rude clerk. What would you do the next time you need to take gas?'

He gives it some thought before answering: 'Go to a different gas station, I suppose.'

'Exactly, because you have a choice. When people have a choice, most of them choose not to forgive. However, if it were the only gas station in town, you'd be forced to find a way to deal with this incident in order to keep getting gas, right?'

'Right.'

'If a family member hurts you and you hold onto the anger, the atmosphere at home gradually becomes unbearable. That's why people usually find a way to forgive their loved ones, because the alternative comes at too high a cost. It's not as easy to change families as it is to change gas stations. Sometimes, the pivotal factor is not the proximity to the offender; it's the gravity of the hurt. If it cuts deep enough, life can slowly become unbearable despite the offender being miles away, or even dead. Which, in turn, can make forgiveness seem like the only way out.'

'That would explain why people can forgive some heavy stuff while still holding a grudge over small, petty things,' he says thoughtfully.

I feel my face light up: he understands what I am trying to say. 'Precisely. For example, I'm still pissed off at that asshole classmate of mine who accused me of cheating in a game of bingo in sixth grade, while I've already forgiven ...'

Tom watches me closely as I search for the right example to finish my thought. Suddenly, I realize he might be nurturing a false hope.

'… other things that cut much deeper,' I quickly add, and lower my stare into my wine glass.

He nods and reaches for another piece of sushi. I don't know if I'm imagining the disappointment on his face or not. Suddenly, the moment is paper thin, much like the translucent shreds of salmon the cook is slicing in front of us.

'Speaking of meaningful experiences, where were you in your life story?' I ask, relieved to change the subject.

'Let's see …' He puts down his chopsticks and gives it some thought. 'We had moved and I was in high school. I was fifteen when I had my first taste of romance. She had curly hair and an incredible talent as a singer and dancer. We all knew she'd quit school sooner or later to go professional, that's how good she was. We kissed and made out, but that's as far as it went. Around the same time, I started experimenting with booze. For one party, a few of my friends and I planned to either steal liquor from our parents or get our older brothers to buy it. We then went down to a secluded spot on the beach and started a fire. Shortly after that the drinking began … and then it turned into somewhat of an … orgy.'

I choke on my wine. 'An orgy?!' I splutter.

'It's difficult to explain, but relationship or not, people were just making out with anyone. Some went down on others … it was a mess.'

'What about you?'

'No, I didn't go that far. Well actually, I made out with a girl who wasn't my girlfriend. But that was OK, because my girl made out with someone else too, or at least that's what I remember.'

'Wow, what a strange case of mob mentality.'

'Yes, it was a freaky night, to say the least. The consequences for the guys and the girls were very different. We boys had a disgusting brag circle about who had gone the furthest that night, received the most head, and so on. The girls were given horrible nicknames that stuck with them for a long time. But the boys boasted about it, of course.'

'Of course,' I mutter. 'I can't tell you how sick I am of the notion that sex turns girls into sluts and boys into men.'

'Couldn't agree with you more. I still hadn't had sex though, not until I met the girl I lost my virginity with. She was slender, loved running, and had a bit of a reckless streak like me. We were together for around eighteen months, but it was something of a distant relationship. We spent time together but didn't develop a ... closeness. I wish I could say that our first time was romantic and beautiful, but it wasn't. Frankly, it was ... well, awkward. There had been drinking, and we were at a friend's parents' place. In the dark, we fumbled about, neither of us took off our clothes completely, she just lifted up her dress and I pulled my pants down. I didn't know what to do with the condom and somehow got it on inside out. The experience was, I think for both of us, terrible,' he says with a grimace.

Listening to his story, I wonder if I feel he's allowed to use a word like 'terrible' to describe an incident that took place with both parties' full consent. I wonder if he's ever experienced real terror in sex — would he then phrase things differently?

Tom takes a sip from his drink before continuing. 'I was fortunate enough to be offered to do an exchange overseas the last year of high school. I applied for an exchange program and was offered Jamaica. My friends were green with envy, and I was over the moon myself. But then I was told that I was too old for the Jamaican educational system. I was offered the chance to go to Russia instead, but my parents, as well as the headmaster, said it was too much of a risk, as I'd be part of the first ever group to go. Eventually, I was sent a brochure with pictures of snowy mountains and stocky horses and told that Iceland was the only option left.'

Peering through the sliding doors of our lives, I can't help but wonder who I would be today if Tom had gone to Jamaica or Russia. *Who would have been my first love? Who would I have grown up to be?*

He interrupts my thoughts. 'I received a letter from my Icelandic host family — that's what we called them. My host sister and I started a correspondence, exchanging pictures. When I got to Iceland, I had to spend a few days at an orientation camp before I met my host family, whom I was very excited to see. The last day of camp, I went swimming in Reykjavík. And guess who was sitting in the pool? My host sister. I didn't believe my own eyes, I mean, what are the odds of me going to a public swimming pool and bumping into my future host sister?'

'They're quite good, actually,' I say with patriotic sarcasm. 'We're talking about Iceland, here. In a nation of three hundred thousand, you're bound to bump into someone you know at the pool, whether you like it or not.'

'Anyway, I mustered the courage to talk to her. We laughed at the coincidence and chatted a little before she said goodbye and left for the showers. I was a bit nervous about the showers, considering I wasn't at all used to being butt-naked around strange men. Given that I didn't understand the signs on the doors, and I was nervous as hell about stripping off again, I walked straight into the women's showers and the first thing I saw was my sister-to-be. Naked.'

I gasp in horror. 'Nooooo!'

'Luckily, she didn't notice me so I didn't have to worry about having humiliated her. But how do you think I felt the next day? Meeting my host parents and shaking their hands, all "Hi, I'm Tom, the exchange student who hasn't even moved in yet but has already seen your daughter naked".'

We share a giggle at the awkward scenario.

'My host family was truly amazing. I was incredibly lucky to be placed with such a caring family; there was a lot of love there. They went out of their way to take me on camping and hiking trips, and I was welcomed in by the whole extended family. They helped me get a grasp on basic Icelandic, to the point where English was banned in the house, as I think I've told you. I still have a picture of them on my wall, and yeah, I miss them a lot.'

'Cheers to good families,' I say, raising my glass.

'Cheers,' he replies. 'And then I met you, in school,' he says over the edge of his glass. 'I'll never forget when I signed up for the school play and first saw you. You were jumping down from the stage, wearing that red sweater I liked so much ...'

'... that belonged to my dad,' I tell him.

He stares at me and I can see the sweater losing much of the charm it held in his mind. 'That belonged to your *dad*?'

'It shrank in the washing machine.' I can't help but grin.

He shrugs. 'Your turn.'

I resume my life story at the time when I moved back to Iceland from Sweden. 'My self-imposed assignment of making up for the wrongs around me was quite the formula for perfectionism, unsurprisingly. When I was eleven, my 19-year-old sister fell pregnant, doubling everyone's worries about her addiction. She gave birth to a son whom my parents ended up raising and loving just as dearly as they did my siblings and me. However great it was to get another family member, the added responsibility only strengthened my resolve to "get it right".'

Tom shakes his head and lets out a soft whistle. 'Quite the responsibility you took on ...'

'I tried my best to stay out of people's way and obsessed over my grades in school. Never breaking the rules, never taking risks; being absolutely crushed if I made even the smallest of mistakes. Heaven forbid that I'd do stuff normal teenagers do, such as being out past my curfew or sneaking off to smoke cigarettes during lunch breaks. For this and various other reasons, my classmates left me out. I spent most of my time alone, reading books and developing an interest in things that were either plain weird or well beyond my age. As a testament to what a nerd I was, I even taught myself how to write in runes. So, you can maybe imagine how uncharacteristic it was for me to get drunk like I did that night at the Christmas dance. The guilt afterwards for having "strayed" like that was huge, laying the groundwork for the self-blame I carried for years and years afterwards.'

Tom's eyes say it all when he gives me an empathetic look, and I'm glad that he doesn't try to complement my story with sympathy or wit. *Sometimes, being heard is more than enough*, I think. Grinning at the memory, I add: 'Being a nerd had its upsides, as I could make my diary incomprehensible to my younger brother. Come to think of it, I wrote about my crush on you in runes.'

When we exit the restaurant, darkness is upon us and Cape Town dons a shining evening gown.

'My villa is just over there,' Tom says. 'Would you be comfortable coming in for a bit?'

I hesitate. *Do I want to be alone with him in such a personal setting? Is it inappropriate, even?*

As if he read my thoughts, Tom adds: 'Or we can sit in the garden. I can lend you a jacket if you need one.'

My teeth are already chattering, now that the sun has set. Shoving my doubts aside, I accept Tom's offer.

The guesthouse is located half a kilometer from the Ritz. A white wall with an electric fence encloses the house. Inside, the furniture is made of hardwood and bamboo. An old-fashioned fireplace lends a cozy atmosphere to the sitting room. 'When I get back here at night, there are always some words of African wisdom lying on my pillow. A quote, you know?' he says, pleased.

I gratefully accept his jacket, only to be filled with mixed emotions when I slip it on and catch a whiff of the first man I fell in love with. *How hard I worked on forgetting this scent.*

The chairs in the villa's yard are colorless under the dark skies. Astounded, I watch the wind grab massive palm trees and bang them against the bamboo fence as if they were rag dolls. A pool is located in the middle of the garden, water gushing over the sides. Clouds eclipse the moon as we sit down on wooden lawn chairs. The garden is surprisingly sheltered from the weather. I'm amazed at the sight of a large cluster of bananas swinging from a nearby tree.

'Wow,' he says, following my line of sight. 'It just seems surreal. All of this. And the fact that we're sitting here together.'

I nod.

'I admit that I'm surprised how physically comfortable you are around me,' he says, looking away.

My mind goes to the precipice within and how I've found myself on the edge without warning. With no need to pretend or play hero, I say: 'There have been moments in the last two days where I haven't even been able to look at you. They pass by quickly. But I still have them.'

Selecting his words carefully, he asks: 'Next time it happens, will you tell me?'

'Yes.'

'Thanks. I'd like that.'

Somewhere nearby, a frightened animal wails in the wind.

'I've been thinking about "the now", a lot,' I tell him. 'Of allowing myself to just be. I've come to realize that one of the most destructive effects of trauma is that it chains you to a certain point in time and demands that you constantly revisit it. That *fateful night*, that *particular moment*. I know this is true for both of us, strange as it sounds. We can't erase what happened, of course. But we can find ways to gain control of our time travels, becoming willing travelers who go on short trips to the past to make a conclusion or a discovery, instead of being involuntary victims who are dragged back there kicking and screaming every time something in our environment triggers a painful memory.'

'I agree,' he says, resting his eyes on the churning surface of the pool. 'And on that note, there's something I'd like to discuss, Thordis. I want to talk about the night you celebrated your birthday, during the Westman Islands weekend in 2000. Will you help me recall it?'

My mind goes to the trip I took with a group of friends to a renowned music festival in the Westman Islands. Tom spent the summer of 2000 in Iceland, and as he knew some of my friends who were going, he came along to experience the festival. It was the week I turned twenty, which is the legal drinking age in Iceland. 'It doesn't get much cooler than celebrating your twentieth with thousands of other partygoers at the Westman Islands festival,' I say with a faint smile. *Little did I know about the agony we were in for.*

His face has gone a strange shade of pale. 'I remember how excited we all were — you, your friends, and me. I'd even brought my fire stick—'

I repeat in disbelief: 'Your *fire stick*? That was your *fire stick* that you set alight and swung around over the heads of innocents and mortals sitting on the grass? I always thought that was a branch you'd picked up from the ground somewhere!'

'It's an Australian festival thing,' he answers, shamefaced. 'You'd see people doing it at music festivals and I'd made my own before ... and thought I was kind of decent at it. Trying to impress you, I'm guessing. Drinking horrible amounts of straight vodka from somebody else's bottle probably didn't help the situation.'

A joyless laugh escapes my throat. 'Well, you sure made it something to remember. I spent half an hour trying to talk the police out of arresting you. I told them you were just a drunken foreigner who didn't know any better and that we'd make sure you'd stay out of trouble for the rest of the evening.'

He looks away. 'I remember I wasted no time breaking that promise. As soon as I got a chance, I sprinted away from you. There are empty blanks in there. I'm not sure of the order of events but I remember running down a slope, falling, and hitting my head.'

'You were out cold.'

'I was?' He shakes his head. 'Shit …'

'That's when we took you to the medical tent. You couldn't walk, so my friend and I had to hold you up between us. The whole ordeal took an hour and a half: the wait for the doctor, the time it took to stitch your head up. My friend gave up and took off, but I stayed with you, sick to my stomach, watching the needle go in and out of your scalp while squeezing your hand. I begged you to behave so I could enjoy the remainder of the concert.'

I pause in frustration and take a deep breath. Tom sits still and stares into the stormy night.

'Can you tell me what happened next?' he whispers.

'As soon as we got out of the medical tent, you tore away from me and prepared to disappear into the night, bleeding and drunk. Once again, I'd be forced to chase after you, ruining my chances at having even the slightest bit of fun on what was supposed to be my birthday trip. So I lost it, simply. That was the first time I'd ever said it out loud: "How dare you treat me this way? After raping me!"'

He nods, transfixed. 'And I broke down crying and rambling

about how I wanted to ... bleed for you. God, that gives me such a sick feeling in my stomach,' he adds with dismay.

'You just looked at me with this bewildered expression on your face, and a moment later, you were gone, without responding in any way whatsoever to my colossal charge. I didn't have the energy to chase after you this time. But I notified the coast guard. They found you on the beach later that night, soaking wet and passed out.'

The wrath and bottomless disappointment that marked the start of my twenties comes washing back over me with surprising intensity. In hindsight, I know my anger served a vital purpose. Had I not been so furious with Tom, I doubt I would've worked up the nerve to put the violence he subjected me to into words.

I turn to Tom, who is squirming over this bleak recollection — treading the murky waters of shame with me watching him from the shore. It's a pattern I know all too well from our correspondence, and I'm not having any more of it. Yes, he needs to own up to the fact that he raped me, but there's nothing to be gained from dwelling on the drunken dramas that followed. The only purpose it serves is to feed Tom's self-pity, for which I have zero patience, and to tilt the power balance between us by placing him in the dirt and me up on a pedestal I've repeatedly tried to climb down from. And I think I know just the right story to break the cycle.

'So what?' I ask in a harsher voice than I'd intended. 'You think you're the only one who's ever had a bad night out?'

He looks at me in surprise. 'Well, I'm pretty sure it's hard to find a bigger asshole than I was that night in the Westman Islands. One of the blackest times of my life.'

'Don't be so sure of that,' I tell him dryly. 'I once ditched a prestigious peace conference, stole eight liters of hard liquor, and went skinny dipping in the pool.'

He stares at me for a second. 'You did what?'

'Because I had graduated top of my high school in Iceland, I was offered a scholarship to study in the States along with ninety other gifted students from all over the world. A few months into our studies, we were invited to a peace conference in a fancy hotel in Florida. I was twenty-one years old and naive enough to think that the conference would actually be about peace. So I read everything I could about the current state of affairs in the conflict zones of the Middle East and Africa. Much to my disappointment, the hot shots who showed up, including Bush's brother and a Nigerian prince, were only there to strengthen their business ties. The only thing I remember being remotely linked to peace was when we foreign students were made to dress up in our national costumes and sing Andrew Lloyd Webber's 'Love Changes Everything' while the moguls feasted on steak. I was young, rebellious, and outraged by the whole thing. So I rallied a few students, let them into the drinks suite, and emptied the bar, taking all the liquor to the poolside.'

'How come you ended up naked in the pool?'

'Well, we had no mixer and nothing to pour the stuff in. The other kids didn't feel so good about drinking vodka straight out of the bottle because they were, after all, honor students who didn't normally engage in risky behavior, right? So I tried to show them how it's done by taking a few big gulps, Icelandic style. That wasn't such a good idea, considering I hadn't eaten anything. A little while later I was so revved up, I decided it was time for a pool party. Conveniently, I was wearing my bikini under my clothes after a sunbathing session earlier that day. When in Florida, right? Well, in an attempt to boost the morale, I started telling jokes while I was undressing. However, I was so consumed with my own wit — not to mention drunk — that I accidentally took all my clothes off including the bikini. Then

I announced that the pool party was on, jumped butt-naked in the pool, and wondered why nobody would join me.'

He shakes his head and lets out a chuckle.

'The best part is that I have no idea how I dried off. I sincerely hope I didn't walk stark naked into the conference room and ask a random world leader for a towel. Or use the nearest table cloth.'

This time, he laughs out loud. It's the sound of relief.

'So don't you dare think you're the only person who's had a bad night of drinking and lost face. Strangers from every continent have seen me naked,' I say, sipping my wine. 'It's a matter of finding a way to laugh about it and carrying on with your life.'

He nods. 'Thank you, Thordis.'

'No need to thank me, I didn't do it for you. I'm fully able to get into trouble of my own accord, you know.' I raise my glass. 'Now cheers to never being young and stupid again.'

'Cheers,' he says with a grateful smile. 'From now on, we'll just be stupid.'

We sip from our glasses, and I wrap the jacket tighter around me. 'Now that you mention it, the day after I celebrated my birthday in the Westman Islands I was walking around the festival, furious with you. I ran into a girl I knew, who told me she'd spent the last two hours listening to some wasted Australian complain to anybody who would listen about this girl and how he'd fucked things up with her. He even had the poor girl's initial tattooed on his ankle, she told me.'

Taken aback, he stares at me. 'You're kidding?' He bursts out laughing. 'So all these years you've thought I'd tattooed myself with your initial?'

Suddenly, it's my turn to be sheepish. 'Well, I don't know, I'm just telling you what she said ...'

He shakes his head. 'First, I don't doubt I was that drunk rambling asshole your friend ran into. What a horrendous coincidence! Second, I have the protective rune Thurisaz tattooed on my ankle. The uncle of my host family gave me a necklace with a Thurisaz pendant as a goodbye present when I moved back to Australia in '97. Once I got back home, I wanted a tattoo and that symbol happened to have meaning for me.'

I'm confused. 'But ...' I begin, only to have the sentence die on my lips.

'Being absolutely wasted and dramatic in the Westman Islands, I probably found it very fitting that Thurisaz looks like your Icelandic initial, and I can imagine myself going on about it in a drunken ramble. But I swear that originally, the tattoo had nothing to do with you.'

Having reclaimed my cool, I exclaim: 'To think that all these years I believed that somewhere out there, an ankle was dedicated to me,' in a curt voice that makes him laugh again, and I chuckle along myself.

'I've never discussed this with anyone, let alone laughed at it,' he confesses. 'The shame was too overwhelming, I suppose. Yet hardly a day has passed where I haven't held my breath for fear of being discovered. I imagined that someone had overheard us in the Westman Islands. Or that someone saw me at the Christmas dance and put two and two together when you went public with the events of that night in your book, though you didn't name me. My worst fear was that my host parents in Iceland would find out what I did while living under their roof.' He shudders and I know it has nothing to do with the weather.

'I've told you, I have no intention of revealing who you are.'

'I know.' His eyes are glazed with anxiety. 'Still, my fear tells me it's just a matter of time. One fine day the secret will be out and it will sail across oceans to find me.'

I can sense his hopelessness, and for a moment it drags me down into a black pit. In a knee-jerk reaction, I say: 'Well, beat them to it, then.'

He looks utterly lost.

'If the world finding out about this is the worst thing that could happen, you should take matters into your own hands, Tom. Instead of waiting for someone else to break the silence, break it yourself. Don't live in that goddamn fear all your life.'

He remains silent, his eyes on the trees dancing about in the wind.

'When you read stories where people have regretted their actions and done their best to make up for them, do you sit there and judge them? Do you think to yourself: *Man, what a shitty human being?*'

'No, that's not what I lean towards.'

'Exactly. On the contrary, do you think to yourself that everyone deserves a second chance if they truly regret their mistakes?'

'Yes, I guess I do.'

'Then be that guy.'

We let it sink in for a moment. My heart beats eagerly in my chest as I add: 'There's something I'd like to tell you—' but he interrupts me.

'Do you mind if I run inside and grab my cigarettes? I'm dying for one …' he says apologetically.

'No, go ahead.' Biting my lip, I watch him run up the stairs and disappear into the building. It was probably a bad idea. Better be equipped with a clear head, not an exhausted one, when we edge into the minefield.

Moments later, I see the ember flicker through the dark. He takes a deep drag from the cigarette and resumes his seat on the lawn chair next to me.

'So what was it you wanted to tell me?' he wonders.

'It's nothing,' I reply, trying to sound casual. 'The moment … blew out of my hands.'

'That's a shame,' he says in a disappointed voice. 'Sorry to cut you off.'

'We'll get to it later,' I say, and stretch my stiff legs. 'Truth be told, it's too cold and too late to be sitting here anyway.'

He invites me into the sitting room, where the night guard calls me a taxi. I'm two steps ahead of him up the stairs and realize that I've been two steps ahead of him all day — in and out of the mall, the gallery, the restaurant ... The symbolism strikes me because, in essence, I've been the one to instigate and lead our way for the past decade. *By the end of this week, I hope neither one of us will need any navigation,* I think.

'Please text me once you're back at the hotel?' Tom asks as the taxi stops in front of the villa. I'm so consumed with thoughts about today's discoveries that I forget to ask the driver to turn the meter on. Half a kilometer later, he pulls up to the Ritz and charges me a quadruple price. I'm boiling with rage as I cross the marble floor of the Ritz lobby. *If only young women like me could walk the fuck home at night like Tom has done ever since he got here.* Not to mention the bloody fucking injustice when shady taxi drivers exploit this fact to further screw me over. I want to hack the patriarchal system down with a machete. *Whooosh!*

Despite my seething fury, patriarchy suffers no sudden setbacks when a bald guy leans casually against the bar as I buy myself a beer and yells questions at me. 'Where are you from?' he barks repeatedly. 'Hey cutie, where are you from?'

'I heard you the first time,' I hiss with such frigidity that the room temperature drops a few degrees. 'Now if you don't mind, I'm trying to place an order.'

The bald brute scowls as I walk past him, my head held high. *Over my dead body am I letting another man mess with me today*, I think as

I push the elevator button and take a sip of my African beer. *Kiss my Windhoek.*

The air in the room is stagnant and smells vaguely of mold. Fishing my phone out of my pocket, I text Vidir good night. Before I put my phone down I notice an unread text. It says:

You OK? Dad.

My heart lights up. My father may be unhappy with his daughter's vagrancies, but he's far from indifferent about my wellbeing. I text him back, describing strong winds, good sushi, and pretty wedding rings. It seems we have a silent agreement not to mention Tom. A moment later, I receive a reply:

Good. Careful, precious, careful. Dad.

The windowpane quivers in the storm, much like the thoughts inside my head. Standing by the window, I rest my eyes on the shimmering cityscape. Despite having made progress, Tom and I still have a lot of work ahead of us. The hardest conversations are yet to come and the toughest questions are still unanswered.

I take a seat by the desk and start up my laptop, lost in thought. How much should I show Tom of the damage he caused me? Does forgiveness only look ahead, not over the shoulder? Would we be better off if he got to look under the carpet and see everything I've swept there throughout the years?

My mind goes to my late teens, when I was wading up to my knees in hate, declaring a war on this so-called 'love' that had turned out to be a cruel joke. I lacked the insight to see Tom's crime against me for what it was, but there was no denying the destruction he left behind.

Without understanding, I had the rage but nobody to direct it at. I felt the pain but couldn't reason with it. I wanted nothing more than to slay the enemy, but ended up hacking away at my own shadow. Life was a senseless mockery, and I found myself dangling from the ledge of a high-rise during a thunderstorm, raging against the Almighty and daring it to make me fall. Attempting to reclaim the power that was stolen from me by faking intimacy with people I didn't love. Couldn't love. Mustn't love. Numbing myself until nothing felt real and slicing myself open was the only way to experience any sensation at all. Warm and trickling. Pooling in seconds that I compulsively counted. *One, two, three …*

I crawl out of the memory, shuddering at the bleakness of my lost years. My fingers rest on the keyboard and I find myself double-clicking on a poem I wrote shortly after waking up on my eighteenth birthday, feeling ancient and worn down. That is when it dawned on me; the fact that my parachute hadn't opened on my first jump over the land of love. Blood-red capital letters paint a vivid picture of my crash landing: pinned down by Tom's weight on the asphalt that was my bed. The sheer vehemence in the poem hits me so hard that I gasp. Tears streak my cheeks and dot my lap.

Holy shit, this still hurts like hell.

Moments later, a depleted woman curls up in bed, while the wind scatters her scarred emotions and finally rocks her into a deep, dreamless sleep.

From Tom's diary

Friday

I've just made myself some peppermint tea, and sniffed the fresh steam rising from my cup. I'm taking some time out on one of the cane loungers in the reading room and I'm so glad it's quiet here.

I've wanted to broach it, but I still wasn't looking forward to it — revisiting that weekend on the Westman Islands — purely because of its bleak heaviness. Even its mention mortifies me. What I remember of that weekend has always felt like tar; stuck to me and impossible to clean off. That's why it was one of my few imagined goals this week, to talk to Thordis about that weekend, and somehow scrub myself clean of it.

Now I have a kind of chronology from the night she celebrated her birthday. She let me in on some truths and helped me add detail to some of the mysteries. Now the vodka gulping, firestick twirling, icy water and blood, tears and stitches all have their proper place. I can understand why I ran away when she screamed at me.

Such a perfect storm of emotions.

I did, however, hold back. I wonder why I didn't come clean with the details of that weekend that I do actually recall? I asked her to remind me what happened that night, but I kind of made it sound like I have no memories of the entire weekend. It felt like the conversation then quickly moved into her relating a story of her own drunken night. But I also went quiet. *Why didn't I speak up?*

Maybe because my memories are messy, confused. Misplaced. Irrelevant, even.

These things I remember. Laughing when we were all half drunk and trying to set up the tents in howling winds. The first band playing on the main stage. Those huge purple sunglasses Thordis wore. Reminding myself that drinking spirits from a bottle was too much for me, and yet accepting the offer from the crazy girl in the orange overalls.

I also remember the next day, when I was piecing my head together and had just fallen out of my tent. Thordis asked to speak to me, and then walked ahead of me through rows of wind-damaged tents, leading us to a vacant patch of grassy hillside.

I was panicking. *Shit. She seems angry with me. What the hell happened last night?*

She sat down and was looking straight ahead. I was waiting for her eyes to meet mine as I approached, but they didn't. I sat next to her, crossed my arms over my knees, and turned towards her. She slowly turned towards me and finally looked me in the eye. I remember being surprised by her expression.

Determined and calmly furious.

She said that she'd never hated anyone before.

'But right now, Tom, I hate you'.

I felt her disgust and sat there solemn faced. Questions were squealing in my head.

What did I do?

I drew blanks. Nothing. But I knew that I must have done something heinous, and whatever strange connection we'd had was now gone.

Run ... I just want to run.

And I did.

I waited until Thordis and the others passed out that afternoon. When they were asleep in the tent, I stuffed clothes into my backpack and ran off into the grassy hills. I made my way to the islands' airport and got the fuck out of there. I think it was days and not weeks before I booked my flight and left the country altogether.

I remember the months after getting home. I couldn't sit still, chased distraction, drunken parties, and far-away jobs. I did my utmost to not remember. It was a time of an even more masterful rejection. Before going back to Iceland in 2000 I had 'redesigned' the past. I'd engineered it so that I didn't have to remember what I did to Thordis, and I didn't have to admit to myself that I had caused so much hurt. Such understandings and words were completely outlawed in my mind. Even when I was on that plane back to Iceland in 2000, I didn't see myself as going back there to address a crime.

On that trip, when I added a drunken night of unknown consequences, my policing of my thoughts had to be even more stringent. I had to also keep *those* events mysterious and forbidden, lest I actually think them through.

My system of avoidance, for the most part, held up. Of course it did. I don't think anyone has a vested interest in obsessing over shame, and besides, I was working hard, camping, surfing, drinking, young, and so frustrated with what I was learning about the world.

It was only when I was reminded of her, or Iceland, or the Westman Islands, or when something insignificant sparked a significant memory.

That's when that festival weekend would crawl through me, because I *did* give myself some license to store those vague drunken memories.

What kind of weight do I put on the selectiveness of my memory? A part of me understands it as involuntary self-preservation, but another part argues that it's a wicked convenience that doesn't deserve a defense.

Where would I be if I'd been honest with myself?

When she sent me that email in 2005, explicitly naming what I had done to her, my deceitful trickery eroded like a sandcastle does when the tide comes in. The truth washed in with that email, and I recall frantically wondering how deep I would be standing in it.

That's where it really began ... for me.

And that's why any minor blanks in my memory have felt like they are weak structures, just waiting to be filled in with inevitable truths.

Urgh. Such leaden feelings. My cup feels heavy in my hands just sitting here.

At least, now these feelings have a place. They're not clunking around in a locked box, after she helped me give an order to things. Now that I really know what happened that night on the island, the cringing has been disarmed ... just a bit.

Day four

30 March 2013

I fall through a black divide and land in my body. The smell is unfamiliar, the mattress beneath me harder than I'm used to. Raising my head and peering through one eye, it hits me. *Africa. Tom.*

Oh shit.

I forgot to text that I'd gotten home safely last night. I reach for my phone and discover that I have three unread texts, two of which are from a worried Tom.

Sorry, I totally forgot to let you know! I'm a dork. All is good.

My phone beeps a minute later.

Phew! Thank you. See you shortly.

I refrain from dwelling on the irony of partaking in this ritual imposed on women to let their safety be known, especially when the biggest threat to women's safety is men who betray their trust. My heart expands in my chest as the third text turns out to be from Vidir.

Hi love. We just saw the most magnificent northern lights I've seen in years. I'm putting Julia to bed, everyone stayed up a bit late tonight. Can we talk tomorrow? I think the internet reception here is pretty bad, but we can give it a shot. Hope you and Tom did well today. What the two of you are doing together is beautiful and important. Thinking of you.

Beloved Vidir. My best friend and the only man on earth that I trust not to freak out when his fiancée goes across the planet on a strange and unpredictable mission. I text him back that I'm looking forward to chatting with him later today.

The bald brute is having breakfast when I enter the dining room, and we practice the art of ignoring one another. It's half past nine when Tom walks through the doors of the Ritz on this windy Saturday morning. Standing by the rail overlooking the lobby, I wave to him. He looks up and meets my eye.

'Sleep well?'

Given that I fell asleep in a fetal position with a head full of muddy darkness, I decide to shrug off the question. 'Can't complain. You?'

'Well, thanks. I woke up to someone singing. It turned out to be the delivery boy. We're not talking about a quiet hum here, this guy was belting it out,' he says with a genuine smile. 'I keep seeing people singing their heart out here. It lifts you ... it's something special about this place.'

'Have you been in touch with your family since you got here?'

'I've texted my parents and just given them an update on how things are going,' he replies. 'Have you heard from Vidir?'

'They're out in the countryside, enjoying the northern lights. Vidir wishes us good luck. He thinks what we're doing is beautiful and important.'

Tom's eyes grow larger. 'He said that?'

'Yes. I told you he supports us wholeheartedly.'

'Still. That's quite huge of him.'

'Yet another reason why I love him. That, and how unimpressed he is by me.'

'Unimpressed?'

'It's ... hard to explain. He loves me in this down-to-earth way that is ... unfazed by outside influences, somehow. Since our relationship began I've won a few awards and gotten media attention for some of my projects. He's happy for me but also somehow ... unaffected. He's as much of a loving rock for me to lean on whether I'm off winning victories or having a bad day.'

Tom nods. 'He sounds like someone who knows himself well, who's comfortable in his own skin.'

'Indeed. I had been through a tough separation eight months before I met him. He got to know me in all my broken, reeling, spend-all-day-in-my-sweatpants type of glory. The fact that he had two children from a prior marriage terrified me, so letting go of that fear took a while. Today, my son and stepdaughters are the foundation of my wealth.' I open a silver locket around my neck and show a picture of Vidir and the children to Tom.

'Good-looking bunch,' he says with an approving look. 'I've always been in awe of those who choose the path of parenthood.'

I close the locket. 'Nothing makes you laugh as sweetly nor cry as bitterly.'

Nigel, who is as smooth and tidy as before, reserves a ticket for us to Robben Island on Monday, two days from now. According to him, the cheapest way to travel around Cape Town is by buying a day pass to a sightseeing bus. 'The price is just a fraction of what repeated taxi rides would cost,' he says, all smiles and good service.

Grateful for a chance to save some money, we take his advice and decide to catch the next sightseeing bus, enjoying the view of the city while we continue our talk. The wind greets us heartily as we step outside. A double-decker tourist bus drives past us a couple of hundred meters down the road, next to the ocean. We take it as a sign to start walking in that direction.

'Mind if we stop by the beach again?' Tom asks.

'Not at all.'

I follow him down the steps leading to the beach. We're met by the pungent smell of sun-dried seaweed just as another sightseeing bus drives by. Watching it disappear into the distance, Tom shrugs. 'At least we know they come every few minutes.' Both of his hands are already full of trash. I attempt to pick up a few cans and plastic cups but stop when I realize that doing so doesn't come naturally to me. I'm passionate about many causes, the environment being one, but I don't feel the need to prove it here and now just to impress Tom.

I'm sitting in the sand, resting my eyes on clouds that look like ragged cotton candy, when he takes a seat next to me. As a result of his daily ritual, his face is wet from the ocean.

'Do you want to see my tattoo?' he asks.

'You mean *my* tattoo?' I reply with a smirk.

He cocks his head. 'Ha ha. You're funny.' Pulling up his pant leg, he reveals a red and yellow rune with a black outline. I recognize it as the letter Thurisaz.

'What's that?' I wonder, pointing at a round tattoo above the rune.

'I got that one on my second trip to Iceland, in 2000. At one point I had a silly idea of getting one for every continent I'd traveled to. Thankfully, I've dropped that idea.'

Looking at the Iceland trips that decorate his ankle, I realize that the past is written on my skin, too, albeit in a different way.

'Look,' I say, showing him two scars above my left ankle.

Quietly, he asks: 'Did you do that?'

'Yes.' Deep inside, a whisper stirs. *Your tattoo, Tom.*

He knows. Not only did he see some of my scars himself when he returned to Iceland in 2000, but I also told him about my self-harm in our correspondence. It had been a desperate last resort after I found myself unable to break the silence about being raped. For many years, I despised the girl I used to be — for having done something as futile as cutting herself — until I realized that the truly futile thing was to bash the broken teenager I once was by judging her reactions to being brutalized by someone she loved. That's when I apologized to her, took her in my arms, ran my hand across her dyed hair, pierced ears, and bandaged limbs, and forgave her with the words: *you were alone in a hard situation and you did your best.*

Now I'm sitting on a South African beach, discussing my scars like another part of my body, like your average tattoo. After all, tattoos are nothing but colored scar tissue.

'I remember the big one on your shin.'

'This one?' I ask, pulling my pant leg further up, uncovering an almond shaped scar.

'Yes.'

'This one looks like an eye, kind of,' I say, studying the scar. 'They become more visible when I'm tanned.'

For a moment, we sit in silence, and it strikes me that in a way, we've got each other's initials forever carved into our skin.

'In the first email you sent me, along with confessing to your deed, you said you wished I just hated you.'

He responds with a solemn nod.

'To be honest, there were moments where I did just that. In between loving memories, I found layers of scathing hot hate. But hate was a treacherous ally that always ended up turning on me. In the end, I hated my own guts for caring so deeply for someone who devastated me the way you did.' My mind goes to the rock he gave me. 'Hate — now that's a heavy rock. It's the biggest millstone there is.'

'And a hot, caustic one, at that. So is regret.' He narrows his eyes and looks into the distance. 'I've been in this … communication with you, primarily in the hope that it would result in healing for you because I didn't hold much hope for myself. As you know, I've enjoyed self-crucifixion and flagellation, and you've had to endure years of me saying that I'm not worthy of forgiveness, let alone a self-love that might sustain happiness. There were times where I think I would have put my hand up from a place of punishment and screamed "it was me! I raped her and shamed my family, please make an example of me." Dramatic, but I felt that could have been a deserving sentence that would have fit the crime, considering I've never been charged. I live half a world away and was never sentenced. Shit, if I chose not to talk with you, I could have hidden from my past deed quite well, roaming around Australia like I have been unless you ran a campaign to locate me.'

'You're right, you could've chosen to hide. Similarly, I could've chosen not to acknowledge what you did to me. But I would've lost so many other things in the process. Denial is a cruel master.' Looking at my scars, I add: 'Who knows if I'd even be alive by now?'

He nods. 'I think I'd have beaten myself to death with that stone if I'd turned away from your offer all those years ago. Your time in that café, your hand scribing out that letter — it was beyond pivotal, in your world and mine. A moment that certainly changed it all.'

We let this simple yet powerful truth sink in while sipping on water from a bottle I fish out of my bag. When the third sightseeing bus whooshes by, we look at each other and roll our eyes.

'Come on,' he says, and throws his backpack across his shoulder.

The next bus stop turns out to be by Green Point Lighthouse: the oldest beacon in South Africa. Beyond it is nothing but open seas. The wind makes it clear that we're in its kingdom by unleashing its entire cavalry on us. We're saved by a red double-decker that stops and invites us aboard. The driver presents us with earphones and a day pass in exchange for crumpled bills. The peace and quiet inside the bus comes as a relief and yet I follow Tom to the windy upstairs. After all, the silence downstairs makes us vulnerable to listening strangers.

Tom gets in the inner seat next to the railing. Settling into the seat next to him, my knee brushes against his. This time, a wave of heat shoots through my body. I quickly withdraw my leg, cursing to myself. *Why couldn't you just be an unknown attacker?* a bitter voice inside me screams. *Why did you have to be my first love?* I instantly grab my self-pity by the throat. Violence is always horrid, no matter who perpetrates it. And the only love that matters to me today is the one that I share with Vidir.

Just as sarcastic jokes about 'stranger danger' are forming in my mind, Tom Stranger breaks my cycle of thought by muttering: 'This has got to be the most "touristy" thing I've ever done in my life.' Judging by his stories, I know his idea of a trip means hiking into the wilderness, bathing in creeks, sleeping under open skies, and surviving run-ins with wolves and bears. It certainly doesn't involve package deals, hotels, and — God forbid — a campy sightseeing bus.

'Don't worry, cowboy,' I mutter back. 'Your secret is safe with me.'

The tourists sitting in front of us all have their earphones plugged in, consumed by an audio guide about the wonders of Cape Town. I'm quietly amused by the fact that neither Tom nor I did as much as unwrap ours.

'I suppose this is as good a time as any,' he says, unfolding a piece of paper in his hands. Suddenly, a particularly nasty gust of wind throws gravel in our faces and I scramble to cover my eyes. All around the bus, the restaurant owners of Cape Town are fighting to contain chairs, tables, and signs from being scattered all over the place.

'The wind. It's almost as if it's … angry,' Tom says in a flat voice, putting the piece of paper away in his bag again. Despite my curiosity, I say nothing and respect his decision, knowing from experience that sometimes the moment is simply blown out of one's hands.

'I've been thinking about that,' I say, looking at the city through narrowed eyes. 'About anger.'

'What about it?'

'I've never shown you my anger.'

He waits patiently as the words form into sentences in my head.

'Right from the start, in my very first letter to you eight years ago, I spoke of wanting to find closure and forgiveness. But that's obviously only a fraction of the story. It'd be wrong of me to paint a picture of myself as some kind of stoic Buddha who moved effortlessly from rape to forgiveness. On the contrary, it was one hell of a venture and I often found myself crawling on my knees. But if we're serious about closing this wound once and for all, it'd be wrong of me to censor those feelings.'

'If I can request, I'd like for you to not spare me anything,' he says quietly.

'I justified it by telling myself that it was pointless and flat-out harmful to detail the pain you caused me. It wouldn't help us,

I reasoned. But somewhere deep inside, I suspect that this attitude stroked my ego; being the mature type who doesn't dwell on things. Who doesn't want to get her hands dirty with messy feelings and hurt. It's obviously a load of crap. And cowardly, to be honest.'

I pause, looking myself in the eye in Tom's reflective sunglasses.

'It created a power dynamic between you and me that was in my favor. I got to sit up on a pedestal while you groveled in the dirt. But I'm sick of it. I want us to be on equal footing. In all our messy human glory.'

He nods. 'I'd like that.'

'So you want to see my anger?' I ask in a low voice.

'Yes,' he answers without hesitation. 'I want to see you.'

Our eyes meet, and I feel anxiety spring open like a switchblade in my stomach. Truth be told, I'm not sure if this will be harder on him or me. I shudder at the thought of the toxic bitterness that consumed me when I read the poem last night. *That's exactly why you need to go there,* I think. *Until it doesn't hurt any more.*

'Let's get off this bus soon,' I suggest.

'Should we check out the famous Long Street?'

'Absolutely. I could use a cup of coffee.'

As soon as we're off the bus, a friendly guy walks up to Tom and offers him weed to buy. He politely declines. Two minutes later, a passing guy with a rastacap asks Tom with a stoned smile: 'Hey man, want some grass?'

'No man, I'm good,' Tom replies as we continue walking. 'What?' he asks, insulted. 'Do I look like a weed smoker?'

My eyes go from his unshaved cheeks to his long locks to his hippie shoes. 'Yes. Yes, you do,' I answer straight out.

'Ouch,' he says. 'Caffeine withdrawal makes you ruthless.'

'Lucky you weren't around when I quit smoking.'

A little while later, we find ourselves in a small café with old-fashioned teapots suspended from the ceiling like a British tea party frozen in time. I've almost succumbed to the idea of yet another cup of bad coffee when the first sip carries me through to coffee heaven.

'Good, eh?' Tom asks, eyeing me over the edge of his cup.

'Divine.' The coffee fanatic in me memorizes the name of the place like a creed: Café Mozart.

We continue our walk with to-go cups in hand, and I'm pretty sure that the world is a better place. Even the wind is more bearable. *We have everything we need to carry on with our life stories now,* I think. Neither one of us has picked up where we left it, in our thorny teens. When faced with the choice of basking in an exciting city or dissecting a painful past, procrastination is understandable. Ineffective but understandable.

I open my mouth to speak, only to close it again, unsure of how to approach the subject. Just as I'm about to give it a try, we're surrounded by pushy peddlers offering us safari hats and animal statues made of scrap metal. Although playing the carefree tourist has its upsides, a part of me is hyper-aware of how we're avoiding the things we came here to talk about. *If only we could find a way back …*

And suddenly, my prayers are heard.

We see it at the same time. Stopping dead in our tracks, I feel how Tom freezes up next to me.

In front of us is a church. What makes it special, or unique rather, is not the arched windows or the elegant spires but the message that reads across it on a two-meter-long, bright-yellow banner:

Women & men are equal in God's eyes. So … in whose name do men rape?

For a moment, neither one of us says a word. Instinctively, I hold my breath. Without looking at him, I ask: 'Do you have an answer to that?'

'Your own name,' he answers, his voice barely a whisper. 'You only do it in your own name.'

Sometimes, help comes from the unlikeliest of sources. Ten years before I went to South Africa, I was diagnosed with abnormal cells that seemed to be rapidly developing into cancer. Luckily, my immune system overcame it, but the nine months of uncertainty were absolutely terrifying. To make matters worse, I was doing theater studies in the States at the time, far away from my family and friends in Iceland. Advice like 'look on the bright side' and 'just breathe' did less than no good. Instead, I called my father and asked him to play me the 'Flower Duet' from the opera *Lakmé*. Dad didn't ask. He called me back when he'd found the duet that played regularly throughout my childhood. White-knuckled, I clutched the phone receiver, curled up in a ball on the floor of my ratty rental while the otherworldly soprano voices nursed my soul with their ethereal beauty.

Now, a decade later, help arrives in the shape of a message that seems tailored to Tom and me — as if the Almighty is listening. I don't consider myself religious by a long stretch, but I can't help feeling that someone is on our side, helping us write the script that'll lead us to the truth.

'You realize we have to go in there now?' I start crossing the street without waiting for an answer. The first entrance I try turns out to be locked, but I know we're meant to go inside. It's just a question of finding the right door.

The church is modest on the inside. Cream-colored walls and light-gray doorframes lend it a warm atmosphere. A stocky priest with silver hair and glasses studies us with an inscrutable look on his face. Something unsaid hangs in the air until I notice a homeless man sleeping on a nearby pew. His possessions are in a plastic bag between his swollen and cracked feet, which are resting on the ground. His mouth hangs open in his peaceful face. Filtering through a stained-glass window, the sun gives his cheek a prismatic kiss. It is obvious that he is sleeping there with the priest's permission, who studies us as if he's waiting to see if we'll disapprove or not. *Aren't we all children of God?* I think as I smile to the priest. Relieved, he smiles back.

My traveling companion, on the other hand, seems to doubt his right to enter the house of God. Tom's face and poise speak of hesitation, but I walk straight to one of the pews, sit down, and close my eyes. Having been to church often enough in my childhood to know the etiquette, I automatically mouth a standard prayer for the wellbeing of my loved ones. Honoring the strange journey we're on, I add a prayer for Tom and me, and ask for guidance in the days ahead. Last but not least, I pray for the family of Anene Booysen, the girl who has recently become a poster-child for the horrendous violence that some women and children in South Africa are subjected to. *May they find strength in these trying times. Amen.*

The peace and calm of the church seeps into my mind. One feeling rises above the others: a strong sense of gratitude that I'm in the right place at the right time, serving the right purpose. Although I've never doubted the existence of unconditional love, I've always had a hard time giving a name to it. *Thank you*, I repeat in my mind. *Thank you, Holy Spirit … thank you, divine love … thank you, God.*

Suddenly, I hear music. My eyes fly open. I must be imagining things. *Can it be? Yes … it can!*

The 'Flower Duet' from *Lakmé* starts to play over the church's sound system in all its delicate glory. The exquisite sopranos intertwine, braiding me a chaplet. Smiling, I look up to the sky and add: ... *and thanks for the song request too.*

My chest expands with genuine joy. I turn my head to look at Tom. He is sitting on the pew, near me. His eyes are closed, tears streaming down his face.

A magical moment later, we both get the impulse to stand up. We pay our respects to the priest while putting money in the collection box. 'Excuse me, I was wondering if you could tell us the story behind the banners outside?' Tom asks.

'It was a joint decision by a few of our ministers, who had it made and put up two weeks ago, after the murder of Anene Booysen,' the priest replies. 'May she rest in peace.'

On the way out, I light a candle in her name. Tom lights one too, and we stand in silence, watching the flames. When the doors close behind us, the homeless man is still asleep, unaware of the enchanting moment two foreigners had under the roof of his dreams.

The world seems different when we step out into the busy street again. The wind sings louder in the treetops and the sun feels warmer on the skin, now that the heart is wide open. The same goes for the stomach, suddenly growling with severity. Due to my newfound loyalty to Café Mozart, I suggest that we eat there. Tom agrees and a little while later, we're sitting on the second floor of the café that serves the best coffee in Cape Town, in my humble opinion. A cheerful waitress who finishes every sentence with the word 'darling' recommends the roasted vegetables and goat's cheese on rye bread. I take her advice.

'That banner on the church. I'm at a loss for words,' Tom says when Darling disappears down the stairs to the kitchen.

'And the music ...'

'... so beautiful,' he concludes with heartfelt sincerity.

Self-conscious, I again have the realization that we're surrounded by people while having a very private conversation. Automatically, I lean over the table and lower my voice. 'It's weird, going from never talking about this to talking about it all the time, everywhere.' Our conversation about anger springs to my mind and I add: 'Even on the windy roof of a double-decker bus.'

'Yes, but nobody can hear us there anyway. Everyone has headphones. Come to think of it, it's probably a perfect place for a private conversation.'

'True, but there are still things I wouldn't say. Especially not when it's so windy I'd have to scream for you to hear me.' I give him a knowing look.

Unsuspecting, he shakes his head. 'I can't think of anything you couldn't say.'

His incomprehension renders me speechless. For a moment, all I can do is stare at him. Then I blurt out: 'So I could scream RAPIST at you on a bus and you wouldn't care?'

He gulps as if I just smacked him. Shocked at what I just said, I cover my mouth with both hands. My words still hang in the air.

All of a sudden, we both convulse with laughter. It pours uncontrollably out of us until tears are streaming down our faces.

'I can't believe you said that,' he manages to squeak between fits of laughter.

'And I can't believe we're laughing at it,' I moan, hysterical.

Our awareness of how inappropriate it is to be laughing only adds to the hilarity. We can't even look at each other without prompting another spasm. Eventually, I excuse myself to go to the bathroom, hoping that a temporary separation might break this uncontrollable fit. As I return to the table, still sniffling, Tom is letting the last giggle out. Behind our hysterical reaction are years of difficult discussions. Tom's identification with the word 'rapist' was so extreme that it held him back from seeking help, making friends, and having meaningful relationships with other people for a long time.

'For a while there, as we both know, I was what I had done,' he tells me. 'And that was swallowing up my sense of myself and indeed my outlook. The label of rapist stuck to me as if it were my profession, one that was right up there with my name, where I was born, and how old I was — the basic fundamental facts that I saw as defining me and the part I had to play in this world. The label would flash in front of me when I was idly chatting with friends. I'd think "here are these folks laughing with me. Little do they know they sit with a monster".'

I clench my jaw in discontent. There's a fine line between feeling sorry for having made a mistake and feeling sorry for *yourself* for having made a mistake. In my opinion, Tom crossed this line a few times in our correspondence, which left me feeling pressured to take pity on him for being the horrible, unworthy failure of a person he felt he was. Not only have I always found it ridiculous and out of place for me to pity Tom, but I also believe that if people settle into the idea that they're beyond salvation, it hinders them from doing constructive things with their lives. And I have zero interest in enabling either. 'You know how I feel about this "big, bad rapist monster who doesn't deserve forgiveness/friendship/love" mantra,' I tell him.

He smiles faintly. 'Yeah, I know, I remember you getting frustrated with me once and telling me to quit the "pity party". But as you well know, self-blame is a familiar warm blanket that I've got a nice tight grip on. I've come to realize that it's an emotional pattern to which I've become addicted. Playing the victim, even with you. Talking of my "hardships" to try and get understanding and attention. Isolating myself from my loved ones so that I can come back and be appreciated and admired for being so hardy and self-reliant. But all the while dodging responsibility for myself, for my emotions and my accountability. It was a real relief to finally identify that pattern and begin to eradicate it. As with a drug, I suffered withdrawal symptoms. "The Story of Poor Me" has been the main feature playing in my mind for a long time, and I'm so very tired of it. The "big, bad rapist" indeed.'

'I suppose I could refer to you as a "rapist", at the very least "my rapist". But it wouldn't be true — hell, it wouldn't even cover a fraction of the truth about who you are. I've drunk myself into oblivion. That does not make me "an alcoholic". I have lied on occasion. That does not make me "a liar". I've been raped. That does not make me "a victim". People do good and bad things throughout their lives. My point is that I'm a person. Not a label. I cannot be reduced down to what happened that night. And neither can you.'

Our conversation comes to a halt as our food arrives. Tom seems lost in thought, and when Darling leaves, I find myself awaiting his next word.

'When I encounter the frequent reminders of sexual abuse all around us, whether it's news of yet another gang rape of a teenage girl at a party, or some semi-naked female celebrity on the cover of a men's magazine, or a joke in a TV comedy about Rohypnol, I give myself a sharp stab of guilt. Right in the stomach. I know this is self-pity, at its best. And I think I, along with my greedy ego, like it. You say you are infinitely more than what "happened" to you, and I emphatically agree. However, I on the other hand didn't have anything happen to me. I had a choice. I did something that I need to refrain from viewing as my defining characteristic.'

'Do you realize what you just did?'

He gives me a quizzical look.

'First, you listed numerous things that underline how widespread and normalized misogyny is, such as sexual violence, rape jokes, and objectification of women. Then, you say that you "didn't have anything happen" to you. Well, patriarchy happened to you. It happens to all of us. But you're right. You had a choice that night. Nobody made it for you. I don't believe that sex offenders are born that way. If it were some inherent male instinct, all men would be potential rapists and molesters. I find the mere notion of that an insult to men. I refuse to believe that my son has a natural inclination towards sexual violence. On the contrary, I think he is born without values and beliefs, and installing them is my greatest task as a parent. But he will also be shaped by outside influences. The answer to why men violate women lies in social structures, in the very attitudes we have towards one other. You felt a sense of entitlement that night. You've said so yourself.'

'You're right, patriarchy is a system I grew up surrounded by, and it soaks into so much of Australian culture. We've promoted the objectification of women so well that the majority of it isn't hidden, but is up on prominent city billboards, in children's books, and thick within our language. I'm just not sure if I can lend it too much responsibility in my situation. The choice to abuse you was mine — I think that has been established. But what I want to question is how I could have made such grossly selfish decisions when the role models around me practised and preached respect, accountability, and equality. I went to wonderful co-ed schools and had as many female friends as I did male. I have not been able to consider myself somebody who degrades women. I *have* been unfaithful in relationships, yes. Do I view women as lesser beings? I know I don't. Do I objectify women? ... I think I could have been found guilty of this in the past. What I'm trying to say is I have been exposed to so much education, so much love, and so many positive females in my life ... and yet I could still commit rape.' He shakes his head. 'I prefer your viewpoint, Thordis, I do. I don't think rapists are born. We are all beautiful clean slates when we enter this world. I'm only trying to explore this uneasy feeling I have.

There is a dichotomy that separates us. You are not a victim, can't be reduced down to such a term, and have moved so very far away from such an idea. But for myself, I've still felt the need to identify myself as somebody who's been sexually violent ... and not in a past tense if you know what I mean. Saying "I was once responsible for raping somebody" seems ... ill fitting. I guess I'm still unwilling to burn that label.'

I let his words sink in and decide to not probe any further. After all, I have no right to define Tom's view of himself.

After settling the bill, we order coffee to go. I'm determined to have more of that caffeinated delight.

'Can I ask what went through your mind in the church?' Tom wonders.

'Gratitude, mostly. I was grateful for my health, my family, this trip ... this moment. You?'

'I thought about how glad and grateful I am that ...' — he searches for the right words — '... that you're happy and healthy and loved ...' His voice breaks and to my surprise, tears well up in his eyes. Suddenly, it dawns on me: his ability to forgive himself is intertwined with my ability to find happiness *in spite of what he did to me*.

Placing my hand on top of his, I whisper: 'I am. I am all of those things.'

He dries a tear from his cheek and nods.

There's a fine line between laughter and tears. When the heart is open wide, they can even merge into one and the same thing.

Once back onboard the sightseeing bus that huffs and puffs up the side of Table Mountain before returning us to Sea Point, I drink in the magnificent view over the city. In the mouth of Table Bay, a lonely ship is sailing on the turquoise ocean. The bus passes a row of flagpoles that sing a loud, clanging song in the wind. For a split second, the sound morphs into the metallic banging of the bedpost against a wall. I glance at Tom, but he doesn't seem to have noticed it. *Are there any smells, sounds, or sensations that pull him under the surface of the past?* I wonder. *Does he ever find himself gulping for air?*

The further up we climb, the stronger the wind gets, until we're forced to seek shelter on the lower deck. Inhaling deeply, I muster the courage to say: 'It's been a whole day since we paused our life stories, just when we were getting to the hard part. Avoiding it won't make it any easier.'

'That's right,' he says with a somber expression. 'You want to continue now?'

My stomach takes a nosedive but I answer: 'Yes. I want to rip the dressing off.'

'Alright. Let's do it,' he replies. I can see how he clenches his jaw, the muscle flexing underneath his beard.

We exit the bus about half a mile from the Ritz. The wind captures the raging surf and blows it like powdered sugar onto the beach, where it blends with a whipping sandstorm. A laughing woman tries to stand upright as her friend takes a picture, her orange skirt strung tight in the wind like a sail. Suddenly we're slapped, literally speaking, by a gust of wind with sharp, sandy claws. As the weather builds up to a frenzy and disperses our conversation, my mind revisits the anger Tom claimed he wanted to see. The air between us is thick with unspoken words and bottled-up tears, rustling like the grass that billows around us in shiny green waves.

It's seven o'clock when we buy ourselves a drink at the hotel bar and sit down by a table facing the garden, readying ourselves for the hard talk. The windowpane clatters loudly, and an endless stream of staff crossing the room distracts me to the point where I give up. 'What do you say about us finishing this conversation in my room?'

He looks at me, shocked. 'Are you sure? You're comfortable with that?'

'I'm sure that it'll be easier to have this talk if we get proper privacy. It's tough enough as it is.'

Tom radiates ever-increasing anxiety as the elevator climbs closer to the twelfth floor. Unlike him, my emotions have calmed down. Almost serene, I step out of the elevator. *There's no turning back now.*

He buries his hands in his pockets as I fish my key out of my bag in front of my hotel room. Putting my hand on the doorknob, it morphs into the white plastic door-handle with the keyhole that haunts my dreams. Within me, everything falls silent. *Ready?* I ask myself.

Without hesitation, I turn the key.

Tom follows me inside my room, takes a look around and smiles nervously. 'Not bad.'

'Sit wherever you like. I'm going to make some tea.'

He sits down on the edge of the bed while I busy myself with the kettle. From the corner of my eye, I notice him closing his eyes and straightening his back, as if he's steeling himself. When the boiling water hits the teabag at the bottom of the cup, Tom begins the story in a hoarse voice. 'I wore my golden shirt that evening. I didn't know it was customary to get dressed up for a dance in Iceland, and I didn't have anything fancy. The son of my host family took me to an exclusive store and helped me choose the shirt. I thought it was the peak of cool, at the time. The striped trousers were a present from my host sister.'

He accepts the steaming teacup from my hand and stares into it for a moment before continuing. 'I remember how excited I was when I bought the ticket. I remember that I was with my friends Carlos and

Ben when we met you outside the dance. You were pretty drunk when you arrived.'

'It was the first time I'd ever tasted rum,' I tell him. 'I didn't know how to drink alcohol. Nor did I know how to smoke, even though I took a drag from the rolled cigarette you handed me. I just wanted to impress you.' *And after the ensuing wild cough, I wondered if perhaps that wasn't a cigarette,* I remind myself.

'I lost you the minute we stepped inside,' Tom continues. 'Carlos and I went straight to the dance floor. I remember feeling happy and carefree in that sweaty pile of people. Then someone told me you weren't well, you were in the ladies'.'

My mind replays the awful scene from the bathroom stall. The stains on my new dress. My hair wet from hugging the toilet. My fear and wonder as one spasm after the other wrung my body out like a dishrag. The repeated promises that I'd neither drink nor smoke again if I were only allowed to survive this night. And finally, the desperate wish for my mom to come save me. *I fucked up, Mom. I'm sorry.*

Tom frowns. 'I felt it was my duty to go and check on you. So I went in and climbed over the partition, into your cubicle. I held your hair back while you vomited, and I thought I was going to be sick as well. Then you flopped to the ground and lay there, motionless. I remember carrying you out.'

He pauses and looks away. Before I have a chance to tell him how grateful I was when he appeared like my mother's incarnate to save me from an untimely death on the bathroom floor, he grimaces bitterly. 'Then I couldn't be bothered to look after you, Thordis. I dumped you on Ben and left you with him. You were slumped on the chairs outside the bathrooms and he stood there, stooped over you, as I went back to the dance floor.'

I look at him in surprise. 'I thought you'd taken me straight home.'

He clenches his jaw. 'My only thought was that this was the only Christmas dance I was going to experience in Iceland. I was selfish and didn't have any concern for you. In the end, I felt guilty that some other guy was looking after my girlfriend. So I scooped you up in my arms and carried you up the stairs, in a foul mood because I had to leave the party.'

'And the security guards stopped you on the way out because they wanted to call an ambulance for me as I was dangling from your arms, foaming at the mouth. They thought I had alcohol poisoning.'

'I'd forgotten that ... moment ... but I don't doubt it,' he says in a low voice.

'I remember that part vividly because for a second there, I thought you'd take their advice,' I respond, looking down into my cup. 'That Mom and Dad would get a call from the hospital saying that their 16-year-old daughter was lying there with alcohol poisoning. I imagined being grounded for life.'

'I'd known for three years by then what it is to drink to excess, and I'd seen many of my friends at various stages of drunkenness. I just thought you were wasted. I didn't think you were in real danger,' he says.

'Whatever it was, it had me paralyzed and unable to speak. But I heard you loud and clear as you refused the offer of an ambulance, telling the security guards that you knew me and would see me safely home.'

He nods, his complexion strangely pale. 'The taxi was white, I recall. I told the driver your address ... I remember letting us in to your house. But what I don't remember is what I did with you while I struggled to unlock the door.'

'You draped me across your shoulder while you rummaged round in my bag for the keys.'

He raises his eyebrows. 'Really? Like a sack of potatoes?'

I nod.

He swears at himself quietly. 'And I remember your entrance hall, the shoes on the floor. From memory, past the coat hooks there were some stairs on the left, leading up to the kitchen and your parents' area. Your room was through on the right.' He stops and swallows. 'I remember taking your clothes off.'

I remember it too. My gratitude when he removed my vomit-stained dress. My relief at having my feet freed from the high-heels. My frustration for not being able to utter a word of thanks. My lack of understanding when he continued to remove my underwear. *Why my panties? Why?*

My stomach muscles reflexively tighten as I prepare for the blow.

He stands up, moving restlessly, and walks over to the wall opposite the bed. 'I undressed you completely. I remember you lying on the bed under me, naked. You were lying at an angle across the bed ... I didn't even bother to take my shirt off.' He falls silent and hangs his head. 'I don't remember how long it took, but it was a long time.'

'Two hours,' I say tonelessly. 'You laid me on the bed so I was facing the alarm clock, which glowed in the dark. Even though my head had cleared my body wasn't obeying me, so I couldn't shift or turn over. The only thing I could do was count the seconds until it was over.'

The wind howls pitifully outside the window.

'There are 7,200 seconds in two hours,' I add.

Tom begins to cry. 'I wish I could tell you why I did it, Thordis.'

'Did what?'

'Raped you,' he says, quietly.

I blink in disbelief that I heard him correctly. 'What did you say?'

'I raped you.'

His words hang in the air, sharp as a razorblade. I want to reach my hand out and touch them. Having read his confession on paper does nothing to lessen the impact of hearing it spoken out loud like this, to my face. Suddenly, the dam within me bursts and I double over on the bed.

'I'm sorry,' he whispers.

'Are you sure that's how you want to put it?' I whisper back.

'No, I meant forgive me. Forgive me for raping you, Thordis.'

I'm in a hotel room in the middle of a tropical storm, listening to a weeping man utter words I've longed to hear for half of my life. Words I've craved like a cure, a crutch, an antidote. I've imagined how I'd react, envisioning the moment and how I'd welcome forgiveness wholeheartedly. Instead, I feel stunned, with a bad taste in my mouth and blood rushing in my ears. Without warning, I hear myself hiss: 'Your goddamn hair was in my face the entire time and what it did to me ... To this day, there's a certain shampoo smell that I can't fucking stand. I can't have anybody's hair hanging in my face under any circumstances.' The words dart between my teeth like bullets. 'I can't even describe the pain ... At first, I honestly thought you'd sever me in two. That my body would be ripped open from my crotch to my chest, that's what it felt like. Little by little, I went numb between my legs but your bloody hipbones, how they dug into the inside of my thighs over and over again, do you have any idea how much that hurt? It was like being punched in the thighs for two hours straight. I was black with bruises down to my knees for weeks afterwards, you know?' I whimper, furious and hurt. 'Shit ... Do you *even know?*'

He shakes his head in desperation. 'I knew it was wrong, even though I was just an 18-year-old kid who'd only been with one woman before you. Hell, even my ten-year-old self would've known that that was wrong. I've searched my soul for years trying to find the answer to how I could betray you like that, Thordis,' he says, and looks away. 'That's the least of what I owe you. But I haven't found anything. I have no answers.'

'You had no regard for me. It's simple as that. You just … took what you wanted.'

He turns to face me. 'Yes, that sounds right. I took what I wanted.'

'That answers it for me, Tom. I don't need to dig any deeper than that.'

Leaning over the sink in the bathroom, I splash cold water on my face. My body is exhausted, as if I just ran a marathon. When I come back out, Tom is huddled on the floor. I sit down on the bed. For a long while, neither of us says a word.

'Two days later, when I was still limping, you dropped by my house to end our relationship. The rape tied me to a block of cement and the following rejection pushed me over the edge. I sank like a rock. The shame and confusion made me withdraw from my friends and family, who thought I was simply suffering my first heartache. My misconceptions about sexual violence and my childish ideas about relationships made it impossible for me to identify what you'd done to me as rape, despite my physical and emotional wounds. As weeks turned into months of senseless misery, I realized that I'd slit my wrists if I carried on this way. In an attempt to give voice to my feelings, I wrote a disgustingly violent poem and read it out loud in class. The only result of that was a good mark from my teacher. One night, when I had the knife to my wrist, I called the suicide line, but they told me they were closing and that I'd have to call back later. In a final attempt to get help, I tried to open up to my sociology teacher. When she realized what I was struggling to tell her, she promptly said that it was too much for her. She took me to her car, drove me to the office of a strange psychologist, and left me there. It did nothing but confirm my worst fear: that I was crazy. I couldn't utter a word for the fifty-minute session until the psychologist announced that the time was up, but I'd still have to pay. I gave her all my pocket money, cried tears of hot shame on the bus, and cut myself to bloody shreds when I got home.'

Wrapping my arms around my stomach, I lean forward, covered in cold sweat. To this day, recounting the seventeenth year of my life still makes me feel sick.

After a long silence, he says: 'I don't understand how you can even stand being in the same room as me. Or how you can even look at me.'

I scoff. 'Come on. I don't find you repulsive. I've always held you in high regard.' *Which is why your violence towards me hurt even worse.*

He shudders as if I just said something revolting. 'I don't want you to spare me any more. Can you show me your anger?'

My mind goes to the poem that overwhelmed me last night and a flurry of disheveled thoughts follow. Would it be right of me to share it with him? Doesn't this hurt enough, anyway? *And why the hell am I so scared?*

'My anger?' I stammer. 'I don't know ... I wrote this poem many years ago. It doesn't reflect how I feel today, not by a long shot, but it expresses some of the things I wanted to say to you when I was at my lowest.'

He waits in silence.

Nervously, I prattle on. 'It's not a pleasant read. Brutal, you know, written by an angry teenager. Perhaps it's not a good idea.' *Because deep down I'm petrified of you judging me for the hate I felt for you, after everything we've done to get to where we are now.*

'If you are able to show it to me I'd like to see it,' he says, not breaking eye contact. 'Will you show me?'

Suddenly, I realize that this is about trust. By sharing the poem with him, I'm trusting him with uncensored emotions nobody has been privy to before. *That's* what makes this so difficult. And I want to face this fear head on, even though I'm trembling from head to toe. 'I'll read it out loud to you, but only once. I don't want you to get a chance to memorize it so you can use it to feed future feelings of guilt. Once, and that's it. Understood?'

He agrees with a nod.

My hands are shaking as I open the laptop and start to read:

Spread too thin, stretching my skin until breathing brings pain and patterns the wall behind me with veins like a flashlight against an open palm. Shit stains the sheets from a seeping crack in the back of my head. FIFTEEN MINUTES AWAY FROM LOSING MY MIND rendered down to mute meat at your feet. No one to confide in, talking makes it worse. I know this, you taught me: Trusting is perverse. I trusted you I trusted you I trusted you I trusted you I trusted you and this is what it left me with and now it's all I have. ALL I HAVE LEFT. Just a blade on my skin to scrape off your sin. Need to stand still, need to stay low where nobody can touch me and no one needs to know. Stop it stop it stop it stop it stop it GET OFF ME you're crushing me with your weight. You wore protection I'd like to know WHAT PROTECTS A GIRL from being raped on the second date and what do they mean by safe sex when I'm hooked like live bait. I'm small and weak and I'm going to be sick THERE'S A MASSACRE TAKING PLACE between my legs. What went through your head as you hacked away at me and my tears made my temples sting and my scalp itch DID YOU FEEL LIKE A MAN? It wasn't good enough when I gave it to you so you had to come back and steal it WAS THAT THE PLAN? Swollen shut, pounded numb, was it good, did you cum? An hour later and I'm no longer there. No more betrayal, no more

*despair. You're shoveling away but I'm long gone. Dissolved like
the snow you trample on.*

Putting the laptop aside, I rub my wet cheeks with trembling
fingers, unable to look at Tom. Suddenly, a strange memory comes
back to me — a man I used to live with accidentally walking into an
open cabinet door made of glass. Instead of breaking in the usual way,
the tension in the glass plate made it explode into countless particles
that came raining down all over the room. I was going to rush to his
aid, but something in his face made me stop dead in my tracks. We
locked eyes as the last shards fell to the floor. He looked down at his
naked chest. All of a sudden, he started bleeding. Gaping in surprise,
we both watched how his entire upper body started to glisten with
blood from invisible cuts.

Shell-shocked.

Tom is curled up in a ball on the floor. I'm sitting on the bed,
hugging my knees. Our razor-sharp past hangs in the air, and it
wouldn't surprise me if we both started to bleed.

'Thank you,' he whispers, pale and hollow. 'Thank you for trusting
me with that.'

'You're welcome,' I whisper back.

'I needed to hear that ... what you felt,' he breathes, staring at the
carpeted floor. 'You have Haflidi, now. You have Vidir. You found
happiness, in spite of what I did to you.' Tears trickle down his face
again. 'That's why this story can have a happy ending, Thordis.'

Acting on an impulse, I gesture for him to come over to me.
Clumsily, he climbs onto the bed. The hug is stiff but oh so tight.

He inhales deeply.

Suddenly, I make a remarkable discovery. 'You hear that?'

'What?'

Amazed, I look him in the eye. 'The storm is over!'

The howling wind that has been the constant soundtrack to our time in Cape Town has quieted. On the other side of the window lies a peaceful city with glowing arteries that pulsate through the darkness.

He smiles faintly. 'When I was a kid, I told myself I could control the weather with my feelings.'

'And now you tell me!? We could've ended this storm days ago!'

The howling wind is replaced with stomach growls that eventually drive us out of the hotel room and back into the present. Under normal circumstances, I would want to part with Tom and digest the events of the day in private, but neither of us has anything to eat and the hunger pains are ruthless. Besides, it's safer to have company when looking for food after sunset in a strange city. We decide to keep it simple, taking the elevator to the famous rotating restaurant on the top floor of the Ritz. The place has an elegance that's past its prime, with a stale smell of food and old-fashioned furnishings. The headwaiter is apologetic when he tells us that the kitchen closed at ten, a few minutes before, but offers to make us a reservation for lunch the following day. We look at each other and nod. Tomorrow is Easter Sunday, and celebrating it with a priceless view over Cape Town isn't a bad idea. In return, we get the name of a nearby restaurant that should still be open at this hour.

'I don't have to regret reading that poem to you, do I?' I ask when we're sitting at a bistro around the corner.

'No, not at all,' he says, taking a swig from his pint. 'Why do you ask?'

'The purpose of our trip was to put out fires. Not so that I could hand you a brand new box of matches.'

He smiles. 'You have the best metaphors. And I promise, nothing that'll be said this week will be used to light new fires.'

We could use an effortless conversation, I think, glancing at Tom. Truth be told, we both look like we've been to hell and back.

'Do you know the game Never Have I Ever?' I ask him over the edge of my glass. When he doesn't answer, I continue: 'The way I learned it, you're supposed to state something with the words 'never have I ever' and if one of the players *has* done it, they take a sip from their drink. The only downside to this game is that it often morphs into an excuse to trade sex stories, but it's much more fun if people keep their minds out of the gutter.'

'Yeah, I think I've played this game,' he says. 'Go ahead.'

'Alright. Never have I ever …' — my thoughts go to the little boy who is always on top of my mind — '… loved someone so deeply, it made me want to become a better person.'

I take a sip. Tom thinks about it and seems about to take a sip but is torn. 'I'm not sure,' he says, lowering his glass.

'Alright. Your turn.'

'Let's see … Never have I ever performed a song I wrote in front of a big audience.'

'I haven't,' I say, pushing my glass away only to gasp: 'Wait a minute! I sang a song I wrote in front of fifty thousand people when I was a speaker at the Women's Strike demonstration! Ha ha!' I take a giddy sip, but Tom doesn't. 'OK buddy, here's one for you to wet your lips. Never have I ever gotten a tattoo.'

He takes a large sip, and so do I. He looks surprised. 'What, you have a tattoo?'

'Don't you remember? My best friend and I had them done in the summer of 2000 as a birthday present to one another.'

He squints. 'Where is it?'

My mind goes to the tattoo on my lower back and I'm convinced that he's bluffing. 'Wouldn't you like to know?'

'Oh. So it's in your ... nether regions?'

'No. You really don't remember?' I ask him, baffled.

In all honesty, Tom's forgetfulness about my tattoo shouldn't come as a surprise. The only time he could've seen it was when he returned to Iceland in the summer of 2000 and I pushed him up against the wall in the laundry room. I wasn't going for sex; I was going for power in a calculated, emotionally detached manner. My goal was to reclaim the control he'd stolen from me four years prior.

Recalling the bitterness that drove my actions makes me uneasy, and I shove it aside out of old habit, sinking the fork casually into my grilled sandwich. 'No wonder you've forgotten about it. I guess you never saw me naked that summer. We were half clothed when we ... you know, in the laundry room,' I say, gesturing with my knife so I won't have to finish the uncomfortable sentence.

'Sure I did, when we had sex in the shower. And in the upstairs bed. And in the car,' he replies calmly, and continues to eat, unaware that my jaw has dropped to the floor.

I can feel my cheeks turn blood red. *Can it be true?* I only have one patchy memory from the laundry room, which I'd written off as a rash, vengeful attempt to reclaim my physical autonomy. Apart from that, and the loss of my virginity, I have absolutely no memories of undressing in front of — not to mention having had sex with — the man sitting across the table from me. And yet, I don't doubt that it's true.

In panic, my mind starts to rummage through old experiences, tearing open cabinets, shaking drawers upside down, and throwing memories all around. Coming up with nothing, all I'm left with is humiliation. Having sex only to forget about it radically contradicts my self-image. *Unless — of course — I didn't see it as sex.* My mind locates an old feeling and dusts it off. In the next second, it comes crashing down on me with overwhelming force and familiarity: Wanting to hurt Tom.

The discovery hits me like a tsunami.

That's why I believe him, that's why I accept every last forgotten time. Because I know, *I can feel* how I wanted to hurt Tom as deeply as he hurt me. And I knew what would cut the deepest. He taught me himself.

'Are you OK?' he wonders. I realize I've sat motionless without touching my food.

'I seduced you that summer because I wanted to break your heart,' I hear myself say.

He stops chewing, staring at me for a moment like he's never seen me before. 'Well, if that was your intention then yes, you succeeded.'

I look at him across the table, across the roles we've played, across the perpetrator/survivor distinctions, across the years and miles we had to travel for this very discovery to take place: *I took the power back.* That's why tension ran so high in the Westman Islands that everything boiled over. My mind locates the pedestal I built for myself, holding a burning torch to it. I wasn't above revenge.

My self-deception goes up in flames. *I wasn't above revenge.*

My last inkling of doubt about forgiving Tom goes up in smoke. Revenge healed no wounds and left nothing behind. Nothing but a broken memory I've evidently shied away from for half of my life.

After years of therapy and studying the consequences of rape, I know full well how post-traumatic stress can warp one's memory. Yet the blanks I'm drawing about the summer of 2000 are nothing short of alarming. My mind, which is normally like a proud manager in a giant, chaotic library, is reeling from the shock of having misplaced the memories from those weeks. Beneath the shock is something else: a knowledge that *it did happen, nonetheless.* My body confirms it with sporadic flashes of fingers, skin, and salt. I comfort myself with the notion that some things are forgotten for a very good reason. *And some things are better kept in other people's memories.*

'Tom?'

We're sitting on the patio of the bar around the corner from the Ritz, completely worn out. It's almost midnight and yet we've avoided breaking our connection, seeking strength in each other's company to deal with the vulnerability that comes with having our chests cracked open. He looks up from a burning cigarette and straight into my eyes. 'Yes?'

'Tell me about the summer of 2000.'

He hesitates. 'You want me to?'

'Yes. I remember working in a clothing store downtown. It smelled of leather. Mom and Dad had just renovated the sunroom. I remember many things from that summer. But I have very little memory of what happened between you and me, apart from the Westman Islands, of course. After which you went straight back to Australia.'

'I thought about it earlier, whether or not I should tell you more since you seem to have such a limited recollection of those weeks,' he says. 'But I decided not to. I don't want to bring up anything that I could ... use against you, somehow.'

Our eyes meet and this time, I'm the one to say: 'I don't want you to spare me.'

He nods. 'Alright. I started preparing the trip to Iceland months before ...'

By the sound of it, the story is going to be long and rich with detail. I listen intently, eager to recover this lost information, but my focus is shattered when the aftershocks start hitting me, one by one. Words from our conversation in the hotel room flash through my head. *I wish I could tell you why I did it ... I raped you ...*

When the first aftershock hits me, Tom is describing how he saved up for the plane ticket to come to Iceland in 2000. I concentrate on his lips, forcing myself to focus on his mouth while the words *I took what I wanted* ring relentlessly in my head. When he describes how he boarded the plane to Iceland, another spasm shoots through my body. His story wafts away from me like the smoke from the cigarette between his fingers. Already dizzy, I sense the impending dissociation. Desperate to fight it off, I grab his cigarette and take an impulsive drag. The taste is disgusting, but the shock of sucking smoke into my lungs has the desired effect, landing me unmistakably in the present. Tom stares at me, perplexed.

'I'm sorry, Tom,' I cough, handing him back the cigarette. 'Asking you to embark on this story tonight was a mistake. Mind if we do it tomorrow instead?'

'Not at all,' he answers. 'It's been a long day.'

I nod and get up on wobbly feet, leaving a full glass of wine on the table. Right now, I've had more than my fill of everything.

Tom walks me home, and we say our goodbyes under a lamppost in front of the Ritz lobby. Riding the elevator up to my room, I feel like I've been hit by a truck. An emotional eighteen-wheeler.

It's almost one o'clock when I pull the cool linens over me. My phone beeps with a text from Vidir.

You've got mail. Sleep tight, my love.

His love spins me a silky cocoon. I'm a truly lucky girl. An exhausted, loved, and lucky girl who withstood the storm, and now falls asleep in the soft debris.

From Tom's diary

Saturday

I didn't know the name of the classical piece that was playing when we sat down, but I'm familiar with its grandeur and I know it's lifted me before.

She was sitting a couple of feet away and I glanced at her. Her shoulders were loosely slumped, and she looked really relaxed. My gaze continued on an arc past her, and I reconnected to the song as my eyes moved up towards a beautiful stained-glass window above her and then over to the pinnacle of organ pipes. I acknowledged the polished pillars as my gaze drifted past and then sank immediately ahead of me, resting on the darkened timber of the altar.

I issued myself a gentle request to let go and focus not on the sights surrounding me but on resting there. My fingers were splayed out and I was stroking the colored fibers of the pew. All the mental wanderings stopped and time just melted. I joined the uprising of my breath, filled my chest, and then attempted to control a slow and even release of air. By the time the tapered breath was over, I felt as if I had arrived. I remember thinking *I am housed.*

Safe. It was so very safe in there.

The strings had settled into a deep familiar chorus, and I was floating amongst the paradox of being earthed in that very second but alive to the history that brought us there.

Listening to the song, I was thinking about her life, as it is now, with her partner and her son, her work and investment in her projects, her activism. She's healthy and from what I had learnt, she seemed to be on sure ground. She laughs a lot. I know she is loved. Despite years of emails, I still hadn't known the true state of her soul after what I did …

My God, she is okay.

Thank you.

I looked up again and felt the faint weight of tears behind my eyelids as the song built into a slow, pulsing plateau. It was all so grand and overwhelming that I wondered if there was something divine at work in there. Prayer and reverence have normally shifted me in my seat, but right then and there it was as if I had been put exactly where I should be.

I walked out of there feeling — it sounds clichéd — *cleansed.* A bit lighter, and a bit braver, I think. Resigned, maybe, that all was in its place. And I'm glad that was the feeling, because tonight our life stories reached the night of the Christmas Ball. 17th of December, 1996.

It was initially so horribly awkward, walking into her room. After I sat down, I started to prepare myself a bit. I was staring out over the shrouded pool and streetlights below. I could hear the kettle slowly heating up, but the bubbling was barely audible against the sound of the wind doing its best to bend the windows. It was wild out there … angered weather, and it roared at the thin film holding it back. I was thankful for the glass, and became aware of how dry, contained, and safeguarded we were, separated from the harshness but still able to hear it.

Now I was waiting to hear and appreciate her anger.

She asked me if I wanted to see it today, on the bus.

I was bracing myself for it. Sitting there it felt like it was now time to be raw.

In the past we'd always had our practiced precautions, and had been so very careful not to step on emotions.

I'd wanted her anger for my own purposes. I'd been consciously and unconsciously trying to lure her into judging me. I'd wanted her hatred and anger quite desperately. It would have been some additional weight to add to the tails of my whip, and lucky for me she's known this.

This week has increasingly felt like it's about overturning stones and searching for everything that has been left unsaid. Tonight it was about saying it *all*. Not for me to receive some overdue penance, but because I hadn't been back there with her yet.

She's been restrained with me about that night, and the outcome. I've known she has held things back in our correspondence. So have I.

But now it was time for the padding and filters to be dropped. Where we can be for once angry and brave and free.

I was sitting there pushing down with my hands and straightening my arms to try and stretch out the knot in my stomach. I looked over and she was standing by the dresser, unwrapping two tea bags and dropping them into cups. I could see that she was deep within her thoughts and was moving almost automatically when she poured the hot water.

I wondered to myself if she was fearful, but then figured fear was not part of her mind space. We'd been moving towards that moment for years, and I had no doubt that she was completely prepared for what we were about to walk through. She didn't seem to have any tension in her stance, and her calmness gave me cause to relax a bit more. Despite the wind it became strangely tranquil in there, and seemed mutually agreed upon. As were the small ceremonies we were both carrying out. Any remaining fears joined the swirling winds outside and dissipated.

I knew we were about to time travel. I didn't doubt that those seconds and minutes were the last ones before we became younger, before we became our 16- and 18-year-old selves. I prepared to walk with her into that dark cave, knowing she would light up demons hiding in the corners of my self.

I wanted those demons to speak. I wanted the dark corners to have explanations. The questions of 'how' and 'why' have echoed down to the depths of that cave and no answer has returned, no matter how loud I've screamed. Right then, I wanted there to be revelations and new understanding. I wanted the darkness to talk.

No hiding. No softening or omissions.

I thought about the questions she was going to ask as I thanked her for the warm cup of tea.

I then let go of any mental pushing and pulling. I remember thinking perhaps it wasn't about the answers.

Perhaps all I needed to do was to just listen.

Recall all I could.

Own my violence in all its ugly entirety.

Perhaps it wasn't about what came out of the darkness, but more about seeing it for what it is. It's mine ... and I will find no peace in there if I'm screaming out questions.

She explained to me the horrors. I remembered flashes and feelings. I remembered being on top of her. I remembered her room. All the black pieces fit. Even how I broke up with her days afterwards.

We went there.

Now ... it feels like there's more simplicity.

I took what I wanted. I took what I wanted and I wasn't caring about what I left behind.

She told me tonight what I left behind. It was in her poem.

I could hear it in her voice when she read it.

There was your answer, Tom. In the anger she spoke to and in those bleeding words.

Now I know what I did ... and the why matters less.

Day Five

31 March 2013 (Easter Sunday)

The face of my grandmother, whose name I bear, dissolves as I regain consciousness. As I ponder the meaning of the dream, Tom's words echo in my head: *'You only do it in your own name.'*

I sit up in bed and search my soul for signs of a hangover from last night's vulnerability binge. Everything seems to be unscathed, thank God. I look to where Tom was huddled on the floor. I wonder if he has a bad case of vulnerability hangover this morning? Or on the contrary — does he feel like a weight has been lifted off his shoulders?

Thoughts surface of the lost puzzle that fell into place last night. *My retaliation.* The reason I'm certain of it is that despite my memories being clouded by shame and trauma, I clearly remember the *feeling*. I ponder whether this discovery gives me reason to second-guess my entire memory bank, but come to the conclusion that Tom is the only person in my life whom I deliberately tried to hurt back in this way. Owing to our youth and the novelty of our relationship, we introduced one another to a whole array of emotions and experiences, ranging from delightful to absolutely detestable. Come to think of it, everything that has happened between Tom and me has been a deviation from the norm in one way or another.

After a quick shower, I put on a tank top and pair of capris, noting with excitement that the palm trees outside are standing up straight in the calm sun. A long line of people snakes through the dining room, eating up the half-hour I intended to use to write and reflect. *Damn it.* The past few days' discoveries and experiences are way too valuable not to be documented before my memory distorts them, misplacing their detail. With a mouthful of half-chewed fruit, I run to the sofa overlooking the lobby and hammer away at my laptop until Tom arrives, looking rested. There's an air of fragile relief between us after last night's discussions. In a sense, we have managed to walk through fire without major burns, although there's still a way to go.

Relieved that the sun is finally out, we decide to check out the popular Camps Bay beach that's two miles down the road. We would've preferred to walk, but our table reservation puts us on a tighter schedule, and so we settle for the polite Roy, who pulls up to the Ritz and opens his taxi doors to us. Wearing a white short-sleeved shirt, he's professionalism in the flesh. Tom and I get into the backseat, where we admire the coastline as we drive along it.

'I woke up to the singing paperboy again,' Tom tells me, chuckling. 'What a talent.'

All of a sudden I realize that I have a knot in my stomach and, for the first time since I got here, it has nothing to do with the past.

'I'm nervous about wearing swimwear in front of you,' I blurt out. 'No use in pretending I'm not, bullshit like that never works. The only thing that works when you're nervous about something is to say it out loud, poke fun at it, and go on with your life.'

He stares at me, baffled. 'Can't say you're lacking in the honesty department, Thordis. But since you brought it up, then yes: I'm nervous too.'

Roy the Professional pretends that he doesn't hear the unusual confessions taking place in the backseat. I smile appreciatively at him in the rearview mirror.

'So what do we do now?' Tom asks. 'Do we skip the beach?'

'Hell no, just the opposite. Fear, almost without exception, shrinks when you've put it into words. Now we poke fun at it and go on with our lives.'

He nods, a smile touching the corners of his mouth.

A moment later, we find ourselves in front of the lively beach bars and cafés of Camps Bay. The atmosphere is a stark contrast to everything I've experienced in Cape Town so far. Most of the people around us seem to be young British tourists, based on their accents. And overflowing with hormones, judging by the tacky flirting going on.

We hurry across the street and straight into the light sand. To my frustration, the sun has gone behind thick clouds that render the sky colorless. Shuddering, I pull my cardigan out of the backpack in which I'd gleefully packed it when the sun was shining. 'What the hell, man? Is it impossible to get some sun around here?'

'Remarkable. It seems to have only been above your hotel,' he says with a wry smile. 'In other words, you just paid someone to drive you out of it.'

'I came to South Africa straight out of six months of dark, freezing Icelandic winter,' I mutter. 'And what do I get? A storm and overcast beaches.'

Nevertheless, we kick off our shoes on the shore. My feet celebrate their emancipation from sandals that have been filing the skin off my heels. The water is freezing cold, which explains why nobody is swimming except for a ten-year-old daredevil in a pink bathing suit. Tom takes off his backpack with a gleam in his eyes. 'I'm going in.'

The moment when he takes off his clothes is just as awkward as I'd predicted. Turning away, I look to the mountains with stiff shoulders. Having made it a habit to hide behind my phone in awkward situations, I fumble for it, deciding to familiarize myself with the panorama settings on the camera. *Just look busy.*

Snapping away, I understand why the mountain range is sometimes called the Twelve Apostles, in light of its many peaks. The bustle on the beach is also worth photographing. A few well-dressed, middle-aged couples enjoy their Sunday paper on orange tanning chairs, each with a respectful distance between them. Muscular guys with bare feet play beach tennis nearby. A young woman in black holds hands with an old, white-haired lady wearing a sunhat, walking slowly along the shore. I take a deep breath, steeling myself. *C'mon, be an adult.* I turn to face the ocean.

Tom's footprints form a straight line pointing to the sea. His back is turned to me. His tanned, toned body stands out from the bottle-green water and gray skies. Swiftly, I turn away again, unsure of why I'm so uncomfortable. Perhaps due to the past we share, perhaps out of respect for Vidir, perhaps because Tom is unaware of me watching him.

He doesn't last long in the frosty water and a little while later, we're both on dry land and fully clothed. Walking along the beach, we stop to marvel at massive rocks. The largest ones are as big as trucks, sculpted by the sea and winds. Their coarse surfaces bear huge slabs covered in saffron-colored lichen. Propped up like a mammoth game of cards, the rocks balance hundreds of tons on ridiculously small surface points. Walking in between them, I gaze up at a rock pile that looks like it could come crashing down on me any minute. Yet I'm sure that this elephantine stack of boulders is safer than any man-made structure I've ever entered.

Eyes resting on the colossal rocks, Tom asks: 'Isn't it your turn to tell your life story?'

'Okay. Can you take my picture first?'

When he nods yes, I hand him my phone. Not wanting to pose, I start to climb these fossilized dinosaur eggs, shy of his stare through the lens and conscious that the picture will capture me in a moment that will forever be from his point of view.

A moment later, we clamber over a sunbaked rock, giving us a good view of the ocean. The teal sea and the Twelve Apostles, who watch over the curved coast, provide a stunning view.

'At the age of eighteen, after two years in the school where you and I met, I gave up,' I say, hugging my knees. 'The memories were too painful. I transferred to a different college where I enjoyed my studies and met interesting people out on smoke breaks. But all the unresolved stuff kept dragging me down, and I was still in a self-destructive spiral.'

Picking up a random rock, I weigh it in my hand before throwing it off the cliff.

'Little by little, I became convinced that I was a freak who didn't fit in anywhere. So I started to seek out other freaks. Guys who were misfits for various reasons — addicted to drugs or mentally unstable — hoping that their company would make me feel like I belonged somewhere. That I was somewhat "normal". Sometimes, it worked. My eating disorder and self-harm seemed innocent next to the drug habits and suicide attempts of the guys I hung out with. It was comforting, somehow. Who would've thought normalcy could feel so good?'

Tom confirms the feeling with a knowing sound.

'One day, Mom caught a glimpse of one of my friends,' I continue.

'Afterwards, she told me she didn't want me to "consort with the likes of him". I had to bite my tongue not to hiss at her that she had no right to judge my friends by their appearances "because I was raped by a model student and you sure as hell didn't mind him at your dinner table".'

I look at the model student sitting next to me. 'No offense.'

'None taken.' He rests his eyes on the horizon and for a moment, neither of us says a word.

'I have once spoken about a particular side to me, Thordis. I'm sure you remember? It's that irritable and selfish "flash". The point I've been scared of when I'm either tired or flat or impatient ... the one that I'm deeply fearful of because it can undo any calmness or steady rationale. It's only self-directed, and the frustration is only ever with myself or circumstances I've become impatient with. Pretty natural emotion, I guess. But nonetheless, I hate feeling so self-involved in those moments. They scare me, because ... I really want to stay grounded and mindful of others around me. If I'm going to be somebody's life partner someday, I'd want to be on top of that stuff.'

Knowing how Tom has spent nearly half of his life regretting and reflecting on a bad decision, I trust him to have more self-knowledge than most. Yet I understand his questioning. After years of self-hatred and pushing loved ones away, it is hard to allow oneself to care and be cared for. We both learned that the hard way. Lost in thought and cradled by the ocean and mountain range, it feels as if we are suspended in time. If it weren't for our restaurant reservation, I'd gladly surrender to that timelessness and spend the rest of the day floating from one existential reflection to another. Reluctantly, I look at my watch and break the silence. 'Time to go. Food awaits.'

'Speaking of ...' Much to my delight, he pulls two boxes of chocolate out of his bag, handing one of them to me. 'It's Easter, after all.'

We climb down from the boulder, slip into our shoes, and slide into the backseat of a metered taxi.

'Should I put on a dress?' I think out loud, watching clothing stores and restaurants flash by. 'I mean, because it's Easter?'

'Ah, no, I'd say that's unnecessary, don't you think? I only brought this,' he says, looking down at his plaid cotton shirt and shorts.

'Yeah, and it'd be too date-like, wouldn't it?'

'There's that too …'

'Well, I'm glad we had this conversation, then,' I tell him. 'Just say it out loud, poke fun at it, and go on with your life.'

'Quote of the day,' he says in an amused voice.

When seen from the rotating restaurant on the twenty-first floor of the Ritz, the massive trees below look like sticks of broccoli. Dramatic clouds hover over the steel-gray sea, and a cargo ship lurks a few miles off the coast. Tomorrow's destination, Robben Island, rises proudly out of the water.

Once we've been seated and the waiter has taken our order, Tom chooses his words carefully. 'Can I suggest something?'

'Sure, what?'

'It's inspired by your suggestion that we tell each other our life stories. How do you feel about searching your soul and asking me anything?'

'Anything?'

'Even if you've asked it before. After all, posing a question in writing is very different from asking it face to face. This week is about tying up as many loose ends as possible, isn't it?'

'It is.' A question instantly springs to my mind and yet I find myself hesitating. 'My question is: Why did you stay silent … if you realized what you'd done to me, how come you didn't acknowledge it before I confronted you all those years later?'

He inhales deeply. 'I think … I didn't face what I'd done. I don't remember feeling shocked or remorseful the next day. I have a recollection of a hollow feeling. I can only believe that I didn't realize the damage I had done to you, how I had taken your trust and used it to undress you, how I'd … forced myself into you. I know I was naive as to the sensitivities and workings of a woman's body, but it is a mystery to me how I could have been thinking that me having my way with you would not be causing immense damage and pain.'

That makes sense, as you didn't concern yourself with my feelings that night, I think, but feel no need to state it out loud.

'I remember breaking up with you,' he continues. 'Sitting in your room that night, I didn't feel guilty for abusing you and was convinced that I should end our relationship. Hence, until you told me in 2000 of what I had done, I didn't apologize. I didn't cry. I didn't think myself capable of doing that to you. Even when I broke up with you, it was because I had created doubts about my feelings towards you, but I don't think fear and guilt drove me. That's how perfect my denial was.'

He looks away. 'But when you confronted me, that triggered something. The ignorance didn't work any more … I was there that night too. This was not news to me. I had buried it with shovel-loads of disbelief that Tom Stranger, with his balanced and nurturing upbringing, could have done something so odious.'

Denial. I know it all too well myself.

He continues. 'But when the disbelief cracked, it became about more than just protecting me — it meant that I had to recognize that I'd deeply hurt you. This came with an acknowledgement, and I guess it was prizing my eyes open to see something that I was maybe blind to, or *wanted* to stay blind to. Whether it was conscious or unconscious, I still didn't want to use the frame that shook things up.

Pity didn't work with that frame, and my choices and the results for you took precedence over feeling sorry for myself. And plus, I had strong feelings for you during that summer ... so a part of it just did not compute in my mind. How could I have done that, to you? So again, I didn't want to explode things and I shoved it away.'

I contemplate his answer for a few seconds before adding: 'This goes both ways, you know. You, too, can ask me anything.'

'Fair enough.' He gives it some thought. 'I've often wondered why you didn't press charges against me. Why you still talked to me.'

I'm surprised at how pressing this question still is for me, even after all these years and the thought we've given to it in our earlier communication. 'Well, I was a 16-year-old kid with a head full of misconceptions about rape. It was something that happened at knifepoint in dark alleys, committed by strange lunatics. It didn't happen in your own bedroom, and it certainly wasn't carried out by your own boyfriend. Over the next few years, when my eyes started to open to the fact that I had indeed been raped, I tried my best to outrun the truth, much like you. I didn't want to believe that the first time I gave my heart away, this is what happened. I wanted to be able to trust people. I wanted to be able to have healthy relationships, to be present in moments of intimacy, not detached or disconnected. I wanted to be able to make love, as opposed to just fucking someone.' Grimacing in frustration, I add: 'Besides, everybody knew I was crazy about you. I lost my virginity to you. I'd even introduced you to my parents. I wore a short dress that night. I'd had a lot to drink. All you would've needed to do was to say that you didn't do it.'

He nods quietly. 'In the past, when I saw on the TV news incidences of women being raped and men being charged, most of the time not convicted ... my invisible arm shot out and claimed "I'm different from you!". I wanted to put space between me and any predatory violence, and it was a well-developed response over the years. I refuse to relate to that level of inhumanity. It's me claiming some naivety and innocence, like I was wrongly sentenced.'

Before I have a chance to respond, he quickly adds: 'But I would never dare deny or shirk my responsibility and my owning of my choices. That is another crime, another theft.'

'To be honest, pressing charges was never a possibility I took to heart. You were ten thousand miles away by the time I could identify what happened as rape, and my physical injuries had faded into scars. Besides … the justice system is notorious for letting victims of sexual assault down, especially in cases where time has passed since the assault. I wanted to take matters into my own hands, to ensure that justice would be served on my terms.'

The waiter returns with our drinks and we sit in silence as he fills our glasses with water from a glass pitcher. I feel myself shifting in my seat as the question I dread most burns my lips. 'Tom?'

'Yes?'

'Have you ever feared that it might happen again?'

Although I know the answer from our correspondence, I still feel how everything within me comes to a standstill. Our entire communication has rested on the principle that what Tom did to me was a one-off.

'All I know is that I am still coming to terms with the one night of my life where I did something that I never thought I was capable of,' he tells me. 'And the need to have power over somebody like that is an entirely alien emotion to me. I have never contemplated nor come remotely close to harboring thoughts of abusing another like I did you.'

His answer leaves me with mixed emotions. The overarching feeling is relief, but I can't help the cynical part of me raising her ugly head and hissing: *And that's supposed to make me feel special?*

'Can I ask you something?' he wonders.

'Go ahead.'

'I am still lost as to how you spoke to me when I returned to Iceland in 2000. How come you didn't grab me by the throat and scream "why!"?'

'Having lived with what happened for years, I wasn't in a rush to confront you. On the contrary, I'd surrendered to the thought that I'd never see you again. I'd done my best to move on and heal my wounds. Ripping them open again was a daunting thought, and yet I felt a strong urge to make you aware of the pain and confusion you'd caused me. So I kept you close that summer, hoping that the opportunity to uncover the past would present itself. When I realized I had the chance to get even, I must've seized it. I must've felt it was easier to hurt you back than to slice open my scars, dragging myself through the torment again. But no matter what action I took, the unspoken words were right there, throbbing just beneath the scab. The fury I felt for you in the Westman Islands only propelled them to the surface.'

Our food arrives and while we eat, another question brews in my mind. 'What was it like to grow up with what you did? I mean, how did it shape you?'

He rests his eyes on the landscape out the window while gathering his thoughts. 'In developing my identity, I took from the cleaner "materials" and not my impurities. What my parents and friends think of me, my political beliefs, the love of the outdoors, surfing. Because I couldn't speak to anybody about my past, it seemed futile to hold on to it and absorb it as part of my self-image. Obviously, it is entirely incongruent with the person I had hoped to become, and it's an intimidating image to face in the mirror. Hence, I had "it" trailing behind me somewhere. Sometimes, I pulled on the chain and tried to reason with it. Tried to divorce myself from that naive 18-year-old who knew better. Maybe that's why I didn't give counseling a proper chance. Because I was happy with that long chain and didn't want it shortened.'

All the while my *chain was so short, it kept me from leaving the scene of the crime*, I think.

After settling the bill and deciding to meet up with Tom later, I'm sitting in an internet café around the corner from the Ritz. My anticipation peaks at the familiar ring sound. My parents appear on the screen. They gesture for Vidir to come to the computer, bringing Julia and Haflidi with him. My heart beats faster as my beloved little ones step into the frame.

Haflidi holds up a colorful plush-toy turtle that I haven't seen before. 'Look at the turtle, Mommy! It's a turtle-mommy!'

'Her name is Silja,' Julia adds in a grownup tone.

'Is it true that you're being blown off your feet down there in Africa, dear?' my mother asks.

'Actually, it's a bit less windy today—'

'Happy Easter!' my sister says, suddenly appearing on the screen.

'Happy Easter to you too! Wow, is the entire family there?'

'Yeah, haven't you seen your grandmothers? Grandma!' my sister hoots.

'Have you eaten anything?' my mother wonders.

'Yes, I just finished a proper Easter feast. Cajun-grilled fish.'

'Did you have company?' my father asks. There's sharpness in his voice.

'Is that you, Thordis?' my maternal grandmother asks, peering at the screen.

'Oh hi, Grandma! Happy Easter!'

'Happy Easter, dear. How's the weather?'

'It's windy—'

My paternal grandmother sticks her head into the frame. 'Hello, dear. Happy holidays.'

'Hi, Grandma! Wait a minute, I had a dream about you—'

Haflidi cuts me off. 'CAN I COME WITH YOU ON THE PLANE, MOMMY?'

I drink in the wonderful family cacophony and diligently describe the hotel, the food, and the weather to whichever family members happen to be in front of the webcam. Finally, they all turn to other things, leaving only Vidir. He closes the door to the room, lowers his voice, and asks: 'How are things going with you and Tom?'

'Yesterday was hard. But we're doing well.'

'Are you sure you're alright? I had the worst dream,' he says anxiously.

'About what?'

'Didn't you read the email I sent you?'

'No,' I admit with a pang of guilt. 'I'm sorry, love, I haven't been able to access the internet because they were out of Wi-Fi codes at the hotel and then you were in the summer house with bad reception and—'

He cuts my string of apologies short. 'It's OK. It was just a nightmare anyway.' In spite of his attempt to shrug it off, I sense his disappointment and it cuts me like a knife.

'I went looking for wedding rings,' I say in an encouraging voice. 'Considering the good price and the wide selection, I'm hopeful I'll find something. If I do, I'll send you a picture, of course.'

The timer on the screen tells me we have less than two minutes left.

'Can we talk on Skype tomorrow night? I'll be at home,' Vidir says. 'I miss you, honey.'

'Of course we can. I miss you too.'

Moments later, I walk out of the internet café, lost in troubled thoughts. My grandmothers didn't know I was traveling to Africa. Yet they didn't ask. I wonder how my trip was explained to them? And that unread email from Vidir. I need to respond to it asap when I get back to the hotel.

I arrive at the café where Tom and I decided to meet up. Soft reggae music plays on the sound system, and a pungent smell clings to the furniture. Tom sits inside, reading the papers. He looks up when I enter and gestures for me to come quickly. 'Look!' he says, pointing at the horoscope for the Aries sign.

I read out loud. 'You're busy facing your past and settling old disputes. Forgiveness will play a key role.' We look at each other, flabbergasted. 'Are you kidding me!?'

'Yep, that's a joke,' he says, excited. 'One hundred per cent.' He tears the prediction out of the paper for a keepsake, fishing a ragged mobile phone out of his pocket and smiling like he'd just heard a good joke. 'I got a text from my mother. She has auto-correct on her phone and it messed up her message. She probably meant to write "Love you, Mum", but instead, she sent me this.' He hands me the phone.

I read:

Lo ego you. Mum.

'It may not be too far from the truth, actually,' he says with a laugh. 'My ego has taken quite a beating in the past few days.'

We walk across the Promenade and sit down on the soft grass next to it, munching on the chocolate Tom had bought. Teenagers on rollerblades dare each other to go faster, giggling and shrieking. Mothers push fashionable strollers past us, deep in conversation.

Eager dogs in all shapes and sizes drag their owners along the beach.

'Your turn,' Tom says.

I try to remember where I left off in my life story. 'I'm aware that I've made my teens sound like a period of prolonged suffering. That isn't true. I have good memories too. I got elected to the student council and wrote in the school paper as well as working shifts at a local fast food restaurant to be able to afford some traveling of my own. I did some acting and made some really colorful friends along the way. And I didn't only date assholes. As a matter of fact, I had a wonderful boyfriend when I was eighteen, a great guy I'll always care about. But I was running hard from my past, living life at two hundred miles per hour. Having ideas like drinking a six-pack of beer on the roof of a high-rise with my feet dangling off the edge. Somehow it was always … all or nothing.'

Tom nods eagerly. 'I can relate to that. I've been so dangerously reckless, it's a miracle I'm even alive. Once, a couple of friends and I got the idea of soaking a tennis ball in petrol, lighting it on fire, and playing "fire golf" for an entire night. When you hit the ball, there was a blue explosion and it left a streak of fire in the night sky,' he tells me with a gleam in his eye. He describes how he lay on the roof of a car, inebriated as hell, holding onto the rusty roof-rack while his friend drove ninety miles per hour, all the while screaming with laughter and urging the driver to go faster.

These ridiculously dangerous ideas make perfect sense to me. I remember exactly what living too fast felt like. It takes a certain carelessness, a lack of respect for your own life …

Idly, I pluck up a strand of grass. 'Speaking of recklessness … Intimacy was, of course, a problem throughout my teens and twenties. Sex was—'

Suddenly, Tom scoots away. 'I have to move away from you,' he interrupts, fumbling for words. 'It's ... my taste hasn't changed,' he says, rocking back and forth with unease.

Baffled, I shake my head.

'I just don't want to fuck this up. But my taste hasn't changed, Thordis ... it's an aesthetic attraction.' The words seem to surprise him and he gasps in shock. 'Oh God ... I mean, you look the same. Shit. I just needed to say it because please trust me when I say I would never make a move towards you ... but in the same breath I don't want to hurt you by moving back and creating a distance between us. Not when a connection is important for what we're here to do. I wouldn't dream of ... that would be the lowest thing I could imagine.'

Before I can utter a word, he hides his face in his hands, cowering in the grass.

I sit and stare at the human armadillo next to me. Why is he hiding? Is he crying? *What am I supposed to do?*

Tentatively, I hold my hand over his back before patting him lightly. 'Look at me.'

He doesn't move.

'Look at me, Tom.'

Finally, he reluctantly looks up, shamefaced. His hair is a mess and his cheeks are flushed.

Locking eyes with him, I ask: 'Don't you think I feel it as well?'

Suddenly, the lawn where we're kneeling opposite each other feels like an island, separating us from the vibrant flow of people on the Promenade. 'We used to be a couple, Tom. It's only normal for there to be attraction between us. But it doesn't mean anything and as a result, it doesn't matter. I'm glad it's been acknowledged though, to get the awkwardness out of it.'

He nods slowly.

'... and so we can make fun of it and move on,' I add with a grin.

'Quote of the day, right?'

He lets out a nervous laugh as his clenched body starts to relax. 'Jesus, that was frightening. Such a relief to hear you say that.'

'Good,' I say, smiling back.

'So good to have that extreme honesty with you! Whoa ... that needs to be celebrated. Handstand ...'

To my surprise, this isn't a figure of speech, and he actually does a handstand. I'm weirded out when he starts to stumble around the lawn on his hands. It's almost six o'clock and an apricot line rests on the horizon, like a shimmering filling between the gray skies and the sea. I pull out my phone and step aside, pretending to take sunset pictures, but the truth is that I'm a bit unsettled by the emotional gymnastics taking place. The questions pile up in my head. *Is he simply relieved after airing his fear of unwelcome feelings threatening our mission, or is this some kind of ego flip as a result of me acknowledging that the attraction is mutual? Or is he masking other feelings altogether with this spontaneous romp?*

I slip the phone back into my bag while also slipping back into my cool. 'I don't know about you, Stranger, but in my world, it's happy hour.'

'Sounds perfect,' he says with a broad smile.

We sit down in a nearby restaurant that offers free Wi-Fi. The email from Vidir sits at the top of my inbox and I read it when Tom disappears to the bathroom.

Hello love,

 I'm sitting here in my parent's summerhouse, thinking of you and missing you dearly.

 I had a terrible dream last night and I haven't been able to get it out of my head. I was a music teacher, taking a student of mine on a walk down to the harbor. My student was a young woman. We decided to go sailing. She boarded the boat ahead of me but when I was going to board, the owners of the boat wouldn't let me. They pushed me away, untied the boat and sailed off, kidnapping my student. I made it aboard another boat and figured out where they'd gone. Then, I realized that they'd locked my student up in a building along with other girls, where they were being raped repeatedly. By the time I managed to rescue her, she was broken and scarred by her ordeal. I felt awful for having invited her on an innocent walk to the harbor.

I don't know what it means, but in my dream, you were the student and I was the teacher. It's probably a result of my fear that you're alone out there in Africa and the fact that we haven't been able to talk much since you got there. Added to my awareness of what you're working on with Tom, of course.

I hope you're making progress. It's got to be a strange feeling to meet up somewhere far from home to discuss an incident that took place when you were just teenagers.

Dearest Thordis, know that I love you endlessly and support you 100% on your journey. I hope something beautiful will result of it. Forgive me if I've been odd about this trip lately, I think I avoided admitting to myself that you were leaving. As the journey moved closer, the more I suppressed my feelings. I'll say it again, to remove all doubt, that I understand, respect, and admire what you're doing — although I sometimes feel a bit left out of it.

Hopefully we can talk on Skype tomorrow. But most of all, I'd like to kiss your soft lips.

If you see this before you go to bed tonight, text me.

xxx

Vidir.

After reading the email, I want to stretch my arms across the Atlantic and wrap them around his neck. I don't take his contribution lightly. Taking on a big task is one thing, but being forced to let go and trust that everything will work out is an even bigger task. Tom and I may be treading some difficult waters, but the true hero in this story is Vidir. And now he's having nightmares because of me. My heart beats faster as I reply, telling him that I'm being very careful and can't wait to hug him in a few days.

Just as I look up from my phone, Tom resumes his seat across the table from me. He is high on adrenaline, ordering wine-baked Camembert and cracking jokes with the waiter.

'Are you feeling OK?' I wonder, still suspicious of his drastic change in mood.

'I'm great, thanks. I'm so relieved after the talk we had out on the grass. Just to have it expressed and it feels somewhat … safer now,' he answers, gleefully raising his glass.

I raise my glass as well, although my mind is working overtime trying to dodge the questions. *What was he so afraid of? That I'd want to rekindle old feelings? If so, was he worried that his guilt would've made it impossible for him to reject me — knowing full well how much I'd stand to lose when it comes to the family I've built with Vidir? Was he worried that by the end of this week in Cape Town, he'd once again have ruined my happiness?*

He interrupts my thoughts when he shakes his head and says: 'Funny, how fear can lock you up. A psychologist I once saw told me that fear blended with guilt confines you to a point where it can stunt emotional growth. I think there's truth in that.' Lowering his voice, he adds: 'To be honest, I think I'm living proof of it in that my reactions and emotional landscape seem like they are, or have been, bogged down in a certain time and state. With some things, I'm still in my teens.'

'Like what?'

'My reactions and "balance" in certain situations seem ... like my self-awareness is short of my age. Strange example, but I never outgrew my insecurity over my hairy back. I eventually had laser treatments to remove it, two years ago.'

I react to his confession with a raised eyebrow.

'I have friends with hairy backs too, and I saw how they managed to make peace with their bodies as they grew older. I didn't. I clung to my fear. It didn't help that I had my share of inconsiderate comments. I've made out with girls who've asked me to put my shirt back on. Petty really, but such things can unhinge my self-confidence.'

'Ouch. That's not just inconsiderate, it's plain rude.'

'I started to panic if I had to take my shirt off. Or in intimate situations. Sex became ... complicated.' Suddenly, he's deflated and exposed, sitting across the table from me. His vulnerability creates an imbalance between us. I decide to even the score — and, while I'm at it, to lighten things up a little.

'I can relate to that. Giving birth messed me up pretty good. Everything tore down there and when it healed, it was all crooked. Not a pretty sight.'

Tom gawks at me, unsure of how to react to what I just said.

'Vidir and I agreed it looked a bit like this,' I say, sticking out my chin and contorting my face.

Tom realizes he's allowed to laugh. Which he does, loudly and heartily.

'Vidir does a better impression of it than I do, though,' I say modestly. 'And yes, sex was complicated for some time. But we decided to make fun of it. Everything becomes more bearable when you're able to laugh at it.'

He's wiping his eyes when I add in a more serious tone: 'Sometimes,

I become aware of how easy it would be for me to shame you back into our familiar pattern — you wallowing in self-pity and contempt as the big bad rapist, and me in the role of good-Samaritan free-therapist. But I'm really tired of that, Tom. I'm over it. And here's the thing: I'm not that different from you.'

He looks at me in confusion.

'After looking long and hard at what it is that makes people wrong others, I've traced it back to a few catalysts, the first being Anger. For example: "I'm fucking you up because you pissed me off". Then there's Fear — for example: "I'm fucking you up because you're a threat to me"; Ignorance: "fucking you up is going to cure me of my ills"; Greed: "I'm fucking you up because you have something I want"; Emergency: "I have to fuck you up or I'll be screwed myself"; and last is Mental Illness and Addiction: "the voices in my head told me to fuck you up". I don't know what your reasons were for raping me that night, Tom. I'm guessing you were greedy and ignorant. You wanted something and you took it, regardless of how it'd affect me. Well, I have done that too. I've been greedy and put my own needs first. I may not have raped another person, but I surely know what it's like to be self-centered and egotistical and take from others. What you took was of great value to me and, in my subsequent anger, I tried my best to break the most valuable thing in your possession: your heart. Don't get me wrong, I'm not claiming that our actions carried the same weight, nor am I saying that I've rid myself of all negative emotions towards what happened. But I think I'm closer than ever to understanding it.'

Before he gets a chance to respond, I add: 'A few years ago, we hit a rough spot in our correspondence when we disagreed on the purpose of it. You said it was understanding, I said it was forgiveness. But now, I think we were both right. In the end, perhaps they're the same thing.'

'I'm sure you know I don't want any power, Thordis,' he says emphatically. 'I think I've been trying to surrender it to you because of my stealing from you in the past. Three of the catalysts you named were right. Ignorant. Yes. Greedy. Yes. Anger doesn't entirely fit, but its ugly cousin frustration does … perhaps like the "flash" I spoke of before. But you hit the nail on the head. You have been the therapist, and I the forlorn victim. I've been trying to pour out my apologies, hurt, regret, and sorrow and it's like … the dog that bit someone sheepishly rolling over in surrender. I wanted to be kicked. Not a nice metaphor, but it feels apt.'

I know what he means and I'm aware of how, when the opportunity arose, I did in fact kick him as hard as I could. 'Which is why I want us to level with one another, Tom. If you talk about your fears or make yourself vulnerable this week, I do the same. No upper hand any more, OK? Equal, that's what I want.'

'Agreed.'

Easter Sunday is coming to an end, and the city is slowly recovering from yesterday's storm. Leaving the restaurant, we walk past a bellboy sweeping the verandah of a nearby hotel and a bartender struggling with a handful of sunshades into a tavern. All around us, restoration is taking place on the very day that's dedicated to resurrection. Four trees were uprooted and scaffolding blew off buildings, but nobody was hurt in the storm. And in the midst of it all, vaporous words were whispered and scattered by the wind, ensuring that they'll never again form the same stinging sentences.

'I want to show you something,' Tom tells me.

'What?'

'Stuff I brought with me from home. Memories and keepsakes from years ago, all from my time in Iceland.'

I know he's referring to his torture tools — the things he's used to torment himself and feed his guilt. He's often mentioned this box of memorabilia in our correspondence and how he's forced himself to go through it regularly, hoping to reach a state of mind that will help him understand his actions that fateful night.

I agree to the idea, and we start walking towards Tom's guesthouse. *Our work isn't done yet*, I think as I stick my hand into my bag and squeeze the rock.

His bedroom is considerably smaller than my room at the Ritz. It's almost too intimate to be alone together in this space, and it would've been unthinkable a few days ago. It only has one chair, which I sit down in while Tom digs around in a bag on the floor. A ludicrously large round lampshade made of paper hangs down from the ceiling.

'Here it is,' he says in a hoarse voice, pulling out a stuffed plastic sleeve. He empties it on the bed, and the memories are sprinkled over the white sheets. It's a surprising mix of ticket stubs to dances and concerts, programs, flyers, and photographs.

Astonished, I pick up a purple entrance ticket. 'Club Tetriz!' I exclaim. 'I'd totally forgotten that place! Of course! In Fischersund Street, now I remember! And the Apple Ball, how could I forget?' I'm rambling excitedly, oblivious to the fact I'm essentially rummaging through Tom's thumbscrews, his whips and chains.

'This is my black box and some of the keys I've tried to use to unlock my memories,' he tells me. 'It's not much. I've tried to use these little triggers to rewind time. This stuff petrifies me though. I don't like to look at it unless I'm in the right headspace … it feels like evidence.'

I dig a photograph out of the pile, catching my breath at the sight of myself at the Westman Islands festival in 2000, sporting black hair, a tight jacket, platform shoes, and a dangerous gleam in my eye. The picture was taken only hours before the moment of truth that permanently changed our lives …

'And then there's this,' he says, handing me a stack of papers. It turns out to be a collection of poems I wrote and gave to him when I was sixteen. I scan the pages and recognize poetry that is definitely juvenile but not as bad as I'd expected. Just as I look up from the pages, Tom pulls a ticket out of the pile and hands it to me. 'For years, I thought that was the ticket to … you know, the Christmas dance.'

I take the ticket and study it, instantly noticing that the date is wrong.

'Look at the picture,' he says, pointing at the corner of the ticket. It has a drawing of the Grinch who stole Christmas with red, devilish eyes. 'Creepy, don't you think?' he asks, his voice barely a whisper. 'It all felt very fitting, somehow. That there would be an evil-looking creature on the ticket to the ball. I only recently discovered that it's the wrong ticket. I don't even have the right one.'

I look, but the only thing I see is a tacky drawing on an old piece of paper and a broken man holding it. 'Is there more?'

He shakes his head, pale faced. 'No, this is all of it.'

My eyes wander from him to the pile on the bed, and back to him. 'But this is just paper.' Leaning forward, I pick up a handful of snippets. 'It's just paper, Tom.'

He makes a strange, pinched sound; a mixture of a moan and exclamation.

'This …' I point to the bed, 'can't hurt you.'

The turmoil inside him is palpable.

'I hope it lost its power over you when you showed it to me,' I add quietly.

He nods. 'There's one more thing, a letter from my parents. I want to read it to you.'

Tom told me in an email a few months back that he'd admitted the violence he perpetrated against me to his parents. It moved me deeply, and I catch myself holding my breath as he pulls out the folded paper I recognize from the bus yesterday, when he decided it wasn't the right time to share it. Now, he clears his throat and reads it out loud. It's written by his mother and father, alternately. With love and care, they describe their concern for their son and the depression, shame, and guilt they feel he is consumed with, which is keeping him from finding happiness. Tears well up in my eyes as Tom's mother describes, with great tact, her thoughts on whether her anxiety during the pregnancy affected Tom's temperament. *It was just so worrisome with the IUD and all*, she discloses.

His father speaks of the future and Tom's proposed meeting with me in Cape Town. He wishes his son good luck, advises him to trust his instincts, and sends his best regards to me. The letter is complete with reading recommendations and a reminder of how much they love and care for him.

Tom looks up from the pages.

'You're very fortunate.'

'Believe me,' he replies, 'I know.'

'Thank you for sharing.' I gesture towards the bed. 'All of it.'

The room is a quivering mass. In the center is a skinned man, surrounded by his fear and guilt, and the witness he let into the tenacious core of his shame. He couldn't be more stripped even if he took off all his clothes.

It's peaceful and quiet in the kitchen as Tom makes us coffee. The other guests of the villa are either out discovering the city or already tucked in. Tom's movements seem quicker and lighter after the 'memorial service', so to speak. We take our coffee out on the roofed part of the patio, where he lights a cigarette. I sit down opposite him to avoid the smoke. Suddenly, I feel like closing the circle. 'I need to tell you something.'

'Sure. I'm listening,' he says, taking an unsuspecting puff on his cigarette.

Taking a deep breath, I feel my shoulders tensing up at the thought of what I'm about to say. 'You broke something in me, something that was intact before I met you. I spent the following years in a fumbling search for the right glue to put the pieces back together. Sometimes, I searched the bottom of empty bottles in parties that went on for days. Sometimes, I searched my physical limits. But most of the time, I searched for the glue in other people. As you know, I didn't feel like I fit in with "normal" people because I had a big, ugly secret. Which is why I identified with individuals who, like me, had something to hide. And most of the time, they were ugly secrets too.'

Our eyes meet through the pale-blue smoke.

'You're not the only one to have been violent with me.'

His eyes widen and he sits up straight. Even the smoke from his cigarette seems to await my next word.

'You were, however, the first, clearing the road for those who came behind you. Who bent me until I broke. Scarring me inside and out.'

His mouth opens in silent shock.

'Don't get me wrong, I'm not making you responsible for violence that other people carried out against me. The perpetrator is always the one responsible in every case. But to answer the question of how you affected my life, the answer is that you caused a chain reaction, Tom. After you spilled my blood, I discovered how many sharks there were in the water.'

He pulls his legs up, hugging his knees. He looks so miserable that I almost feel bad for him. Instead, I whisper: 'You wanted to know what I am really forgiving you for. Now you know. Now you know the context.'

He nods slightly. There's something shattered in his eyes. At last, he says: 'Sorry how drained I am after what you've told me … It's you who should be spent, not me.'

'I didn't want to write about this in our correspondence. I wanted to do it face to face and have the words … dissolve, in the moment.'

'It's best you've told me now … but oh God, Thordis …' he says as his head sinks forward. 'The thought that what I did that night could cause you more, and more, and more hurt … I don't know what … to say.'

Of course he doesn't. Words escape me too, when it comes to the knowledge stored in my muscles and tissues; the things my body knows. It knows the raging screams that escape the throat when being pinned down, it knows the sound that pantyhose make when they rip. It knows what it's like to fight back with primal wrath that leaves a bloody taste in the mouth; it knows how to numb itself when losing the fight; it knows the burns, the bruises, the breakage. It knows how to armor up with cigarettes and leather and sarcasm and carry on. It knows that it will always keep fighting back even if it kills me because I'd rather die than lie defenseless on my back like the 16-year-old I've spent my whole adult life contrasting.

Our eyes meet. We are emotionally depleted and exposed after having peeled back so many layers of ourselves tonight. I wonder if the consequences show as obviously on me as they do on him. His blonde hair is messed up, his complexion is a sickly ash-gray, and both of us are shaking from head to toe.

'Here,' he says, handing me his duvet as we step back into his room. 'This might help with the shivers.' To cure his own trembling, he puts on a bathrobe over his clothes.

I wrap the thick duvet around me, standing like a white cone under the giant paper ball hanging from the ceiling. The combination makes me look weirdly like a snowman.

'Surreal,' I exclaim.

'In so many ways, Thordis,' he says, shaking his head. 'So many ways.'

From Tom's diary

Sunday

There were so many stars out tonight. Familiar stars too. I made out what I believe to be the distinctive red binary star Antares, sitting low in the night sky. I visualized the world from a distance, and imagined myself walking on another land mass of the Southern hemisphere, far away from my native Australia but still on the lower portion of the earth and facing the same stars. It is truly strange to be here.

I walked back to my villa after accompanying Thordis to the Ritz. It'd become a familiar route so I didn't need to give much thought to the lefts and rights. Instead I just lazily tracked down the middle of the back alleyways and listened to the gentle slapping of my flip-flops on the tarmac.

The sharing of my 'black box' went relatively well. Not pleasant but deeply necessary. I was glad to bring those things with me, and showing her the photos and ticket stubs felt like maybe the last time I will have any use for them. It was good to voice how they've weighed on me, but it now feels like those keepsakes from my year in Iceland are inessential. I've stared at those things too many times, trying hard to re-inhabit the body of my 18-year-old self. Now that we're actually in each other's presence, and able to discuss the events of '96, that small packet of prickly memories seems to have lost some of its intimidating force.

Albeit I did feel a sense of being misunderstood. She seemed to dismiss my collected traces of that year as merely 'just paper', and the utility and power of all their embedded, dark connections seemed to be somewhat lost on her. At one point, I felt kind of silly explaining them. Little does she know though, those pieces of paper conjured such fear that they've been reserved for when I've felt calm and strong enough to try to uncover my memories. Even just the word 'Iceland' can fire me back into history when I hear it in the news, but those thin little pieces of paper can do worse. They connect me to it.

But maybe she didn't see that? Maybe she and I work differently? Maybe the work that she has done in dealing with the traumas connected to that night did not need to be aided by photos and old passes to nightclubs?

Perhaps her memory isn't as foggy and unclear as mine.

Actually, I know it is not.

I know she doesn't have to try to remember like I do.

On many occasions she's remembered words and moments with crystalline clarity. More than once I've been astounded by her ability to recount the small and not-so-small details. In all truth, the quality of her memory has helped us both.

And yet, I learnt the other day that, like me, she's also suffered from the suppression of memories. For once, the tables were turned and it was me helping her recall something.

It's one of the things I *do* remember well, that bizarre and erratic relationship we had in 2000. It was right there in some of those photos we looked at tonight. When we were dressed up and out partying together but still sitting meters apart. I remember clearly how there was a conditional distance and how the intimacy was like some kind of broken but still hopeful light bulb. *On*. Off. *On*. Off.

But, memories or no, I'm beginning to comprehend why certain things are rendered forgotten. It makes sense to me that the mind 'misplaces' things that the body takes no pride in.

I'm fighting a memory right now. On the walk home I was trying my best to avoid revisiting what she said to me on the patio. But when I walked through the exact space in which she voiced them, her words were already echoing around my head.

'You're not the only one to have been violent with me.'

'… you caused a chain reaction.'

I've been sitting here for ten minutes trying to fight the momentum of their meaning.

She's been raped by other men.

How?

Why?

There's a thick sadness trying to take root. She said she looked for 'glue' in others. She spoke of seeking out broken others. I knew she'd been through a hugely traumatic breakup and has hinted at other troubles in her relationships … but never this.

I'm picking up fragments of the recent and distant past and trying to make a picture of her … but where do I put these pieces? Are any of them mine?

One question keeps swinging around my head with growing intensity: Is it all my fault?

I know I scarred her ability to trust, but should I own the violence of others as well?

What a whirlpool; all these questions ... I can feel myself being sucked in.

Stand up, Tom.

Don't do this now. She told you so that you can understand the full meaning of her forgiveness. Don't start new fires ... not tonight.

Go brush your teeth. Go to bed. This will find its place.

Day Six

1 April 2013

It's 9am when room service awakens me. Last night's exposé lingers in my thoughts. *Tom now knows about the detrimental domino effect that tore through my late teens and early twenties.* It makes him in no way accountable for my choices nor anybody else's who crossed my path, but it tells him how the harm caused by violence is by no means confined to the deed itself. Another piece of the puzzle has found its place in the complex mosaic that is our story.

Pulling back the curtains, I'm met with a gloomy sky. A downpour could happen any minute. I'm starting to regret having packed my shorts, mocking me from inside the closet. *Whaddya say, those pale Icelandic legs could use some fresh air, eh?*

After a hot shower and a bowl of fresh pineapple, a text arrives from Tom.

Getting up for breakfast now. Meet you for a coffee?

At 10:30am, an hour and a half before the boat leaves for Robben Island, Tom and I start walking along rainy streets towards the Waterfront. Bundled up in my woolen jacket, I can't help but stare in disbelief at Tom's bare legs.

'Won't you be cold?' I wonder.

'Not my legs, no,' he replies, as if his legs in no way belong to the rest of his body.

I bury my hands deep in the pockets of my jacket.

'You don't have to answer if you don't want to, but how was the treatment you had for post-traumatic stress? I mean, if you can explain it to me, I'd like to know what you have been taken through?'

'Well, it was exposure therapy,' I tell him.

'Of what kind?'

'Exposing the client to the feared object or context. I had to write down accounts of the violence I've been subjected to, recalling every sound, smell, and feeling down to the smallest detail. Then, I had to read it out loud, over and over again. The goal is to grow a callus over the hurt, so eventually it doesn't sting as much, isn't as tender. But to begin with, it feels like being punched in an open wound. Over and over again.'

'When do you ... reach the therapeutic endpoint?'

I envision the white plastic door-handle in my mind's eye while answering: 'When you can step into the core of your fear without falling to pieces.'

'Geez.' He whistles.

'When I started exposure therapy in January 2007, I couldn't even say the word "rape" out loud when referring to my own experience. Luckily, my therapist is a smart woman who allowed me to do things at a pace that I could handle. Two and a half years later, I'd gone public with my story in my book and also in the press interviews that followed.'

'That's beyond amazing, Thordis.'

'Thank you; I'd like to think of it as my graduation,' I say with a genuine smile.

All of a sudden, a car coming out of a side street a little further down the road brakes with a loud screech. This is followed by a string of curse words, and a man crawls to his feet. On the street next to him lies a scooter on its side. He rubs his hip, fussing and swearing but seemingly unharmed. 'You could've killed me!' he screams at a sheepish woman sitting behind the wheel of the car. She's too far away for me to make out her words, but whatever she's saying, the man doesn't like it one bit. He thunders: 'Forgive you? THIS IS UNFORGIVABLE!'

Unforgivable. The word rings in my ears. I'm going to a prison where innocent people's rights were violated in the most gruesome ways. I'm going there with a man who raped me. And on my way, I cross paths with a man who thinks it's unforgivable that another motorist nudged his scooter.

Squeezing the rock in my pocket, I wonder if Robben Island will be the right place to hand it over to Tom? Wouldn't it be symbolic to leave the rock in prison, where it can shoulder the blame for centuries to come, allowing us to carry on with our lives free from the burdens of the past? Pushing these speculations to the back of my mind, I tell myself that when the right time comes, I'll know it.

Despite the gloomy weather, the Waterfront is lively as ever with its street musicians and eager shoppers. We're admiring a great jazz quartet made up of four old men in matching baseball caps when my phone beeps. It's a text from Dad.

Many days to go, still. Careful, precious, careful. Dad.

'The more I learn about sexual violence, the better I understand that it doesn't just affect the survivor,' I think out loud.

'Yes, I've thought a lot about that too,' Tom says. 'Your loved ones ... the people surrounding you. Which brings up the question — how do you feel about me writing a letter to Vidir and your parents?'

The question comes as a surprise. 'I'm not sure, it's been nine years since I told my mother about what you did to me ... and well, she doesn't want to shoot you any more. Perhaps she could handle getting a letter from you at this point. But Dad ...' I shake my head. 'I really don't think I would recommend that.'

'I understand,' he says with a nod. 'If I were your father, I wouldn't want to hear the mention of my name. I'd be scared of what I'd do, honestly.'

'Out of the three of them, Vidir is most likely to appreciate a letter from you. But to be sure, maybe it'd be best if I read it over first?'

'Absolutely.'

We pass an arts-and-crafts store selling sculptures in all shapes and sizes. Dozens of them adorn the street in front of the store, forming an open-air museum of sorts. The largest sculpture is that of a life-size buffalo made of hundreds of thousands of black beads. Surprisingly, many statues are of women, especially mothers with small children, reminding me that Cape Town is called the 'Mother City' by South Africans. These plump mothers are carved out of solid black rock, with chubby children peeking from behind their skirts and baskets bursting with fruit on their heads. In other words: Abundance embodied.

Ahead lies our destination: The Nelson Mandela Gateway to Robben Island. Long, colorful banners adorn the building, hanging from columns that frame the entrance. I read the words 'freedom' and 'humanity' from the banners as Tom announces that he's going to get us coffee from a nearby shop.

The first thing to catch my eye as I step inside is a picture of Mandela and the number '27', referring to the years he spent behind bars for his political beliefs. The atmosphere is elevated and solemn. On the right is a blood-red wall with a silver inscription:

While we will not forget
the brutality of apartheid
we will not want
Robben Island
to be a monument
of our hardship
and suffering

We would want it
to be a triumph
of the human spirit
against the forces of evil
a triumph of wisdom
and largeness of spirit
against small minds
and pettiness
a triumph of courage
and determination
over human frailty
and weakness

Ahmed Kathrada, 1993

My eyes well up with tears, my skin breaking out in goosebumps. Standing at the entrance to a landmark in world history is nothing short of overwhelming. It's overwhelming to be in a country with such a mangled past, accompanied by a man many would expect me to despise. At that very moment, he appears with two coffees, upbeat and unsuspecting. *Revenge gave me nothing*, I think as I accept the cup from his hand, *only darkness and stagnation*. Being here, in a country where hatred was defeated after generations of its cruel reign, gives me hope that suffering isn't pointless pain but provides an opportunity to learn.

We wander into a souvenir shop where the shelves are bursting with books about heroes who fought against apartheid. I miss seeing women's faces on the covers, knowing that they contributed greatly to the resistance movement and were imprisoned and killed alongside their male counterparts. Just as I'm having these thoughts, I notice a t-shirt that says: 'History depends on who wrote it.' *Ha! My sentiments exactly.*

After a security screening and X-ray (*hatred must still have powerful allies*), we board the boat. 'I've got butterflies in my stomach,' I say as Tom takes the seat next to me.

'So do I. It'll be a memorable day, that's for sure.'

The windows are foggy as the boat takes off, bobbing on the waves. On a flat-screen in the center of the room, a video about Robben Island and its role during apartheid starts to play. I recognize a young Mandela and listen carefully to the part about how he co-founded the ANC's Youth League. When we're halfway to Robben Island, women's contribution to the resistance is first mentioned in the video: 'As a general rule, male political prisoners were kept on Robben Island, but the female prisoners were kept in the Kroonstad prison.' To my disappointment, that's the only mention of women's involvement in the fight against apartheid that I hear.

When we set foot on Robben Island, the bleak weather turns out to be the perfect backdrop. The island is barren, the earth parched. Scraggly bushes tuft out of the cracked soil. A few crooked trees in the distance add to the air of desolation. The prison buildings ahead of us are made of solid rock, enclosed by a wall with barbed wire winding on top of it like a fanged snake. A surveillance tower in the middle of the premises reminds me of photographs of the Nazi death camps. I shudder and it has nothing to do with the weather.

The group is divided in two. Tom and I start off on a walking tour around the prison with about sixty other tourists. The coldest wind I've felt in South Africa yet ruffles my hair as we walk through an opening in the wire-mesh fence and enter one of the buildings with pale fluorescent lighting. Preoccupied with the surroundings, I don't catch the name of the former prisoner who introduces himself to the group as our guide. I'd heard and read about former prisoners of Robben Island working as guides here, but I still can't help but stare at the man as the group gathers around him. He's probably over seventy years old and bald, wearing brown pants and a blue V-neck sweater. As his story unfolds, we learn how he was arrested in 1982 when he was a member of the military wing of the ANC. 'They tortured me. I was naked, chained, and strung up by my hands and feet, like this,' he says, stretching his hands up. 'I confessed to everything. I showed them where we kept our weapons. I was found guilty and convicted to seven years' imprisonment on Robben Island.' He tells his story in a calm, almost neutral voice. Pointing at his glasses, which are tinted despite the gloomy weather and poor lighting, he tells us: 'Many of us suffered eye damage when working in the limestone quarries. The sun projection was so strong it burned our corneas, ruining our vision. When we asked for sunglasses, we were denied. They told us it wasn't part of our prison uniform. Many prisoners' tear ducts were also damaged. They stopped producing tears, rendering them unable to cry. Respiratory diseases were also common, due to the amount of dust we had to breathe in while working in the quarries.' He produces a small straw mat. 'We slept here on the concrete floor, on this. The floor was very cold, especially in the wintertime,' he adds, looking at us over the rim of his glasses. 'We were divided into different ethnic groups; coloreds, Indians, and blacks who were called Bantu. Our ethnic group was a deciding factor in how we were treated. Blacks got less food than the other groups. Coloreds and Indians got long pants and long-sleeved shirts, but blacks only got shorts and t-shirts. There was also a subdivision into groups A, B, C, and D. Prisoners in group A had certain privileges, they were allowed more visits and letters — heavily censored, of course — more food, and even cigarettes. We racked our brains trying to figure out how the system worked, why some prisoners were immediately put in group A while other prisoners had to work their way up there. Some had to endure years of group D, no matter what. Eventually, we realized that the system was arbitrary and its sole purpose was to create inequality and division amongst us, to weaken our spirit. But we found a way around that,' he says with a sparkle in his eye. 'We decided that group A prisoners had to share their privileges with other prisoners, making everybody equal. We had to live by our vision.'

He gestures for us to follow him and the group gets moving. I'm lost in thought about grand victories that revolve around cigarettes and baked beans. The notion that the prisoners were robbed of their freedom is tragic enough, but the thought that they were also robbed of the ability to shed tears over their circumstances is devastating.

Our next destination is the courtyard, enclosed by a four-meter tall concrete wall. 'Here, we were allowed to play sports,' our guide tells us, resting one hand on his hip. 'But only certain sports, approved by the government. Like tennis.' Again, his eyes light up. 'We cut holes in the tennis balls, stuffing notes with handwritten messages inside them. Then, we shot them over the wall to message our allies in other divisions of the prison. That way, we coordinated ourselves.'

Via correspondence, I think, automatically looking at Tom.

'Would you like to see Mandela's cell?' the guide asks, and the group murmurs eagerly. We enter another building and walk along a narrow corridor with cells on both sides. The group forms a line, stopping to peek into the cell where Mandela served most of his long sentence. When it's my turn to look, I'm taken aback. Between white iron bars I see a space that's no bigger than a broom closet. The small straw mat on the floor extends from wall to wall. The only other items in the room are a steel cup, a stool, and an iron bucket that must've served as a chamber pot. The walls are painted in an ugly green color that reminds me of an operating room. Six thick bars secure the only window in this small space. *To corrupt authorities, free thinking is the most dangerous thing in the world*, I silently conclude. If you get an idea that ruffles the feathers of tyrants, you might have to spend the rest of your life in a cell like this.

The group's cheerful chatter has given way to silence as we enter another courtyard. When we stop, the sea breeze slides its cold fingers down my neck. Far above our heads, the steel-gray sky is laced with barbed wire.

'So here we are,' I whisper to Tom, aware of the people near us. 'In prison, after all these years.'

'Seems fitting,' he mutters.

I hesitate. 'If you'd been found guilty of violating me, your sentence would've been less than a year, Tom. Having sex with someone unable to fight back wasn't even considered rape in Iceland at the time.' The truth leaves a bad taste in my mouth.

For a second, he just stares at me in shock. 'That's so ... mild.

It's ... just unfair.'

All I can do is shrug.

'I reminded myself a few times through the years what my sense of a jail cell would be and how soul-destroying such a sentence would be. I've asked myself if I think I deserved that, to be locked away. A part of me still thinks that is what I deserve, and it might gain me a bit of redemption in my own eyes and in that of society.' After a moment's hesitation, he asks: 'Would it gain me anything in your eyes?'

My eyes go to the thick-walled prison behind us as I contemplate my answer.

'A prison cell is a place of punishment. Figuratively speaking, you can walk around with a maximum-security prison cell in your head for years without ever actually setting foot in one. The punishment you gave yourself was far more effective than any punitive justice the outside world has to offer, I believe. So, yes. The time you spent in your private prison gained you something in my eyes. It was a form of resurrection for me, as it allowed me to swap places with you. For the first few years, I was the one behind bars, so to speak. I blamed myself. I didn't see a point in respecting or loving myself when other people could treat me like trash, even the ones who claimed to love me. When you shouldered the blame, you let me out and took my place. That was a necessary step along the way. But the time of punishment is over. It's time to heal. Which is why I wanted us to meet up in person so we could finally close the cell and throw away the key.' I squeeze the rock in my pocket and add in a hopeful voice: 'Together.'

Could this be the right moment?

He fails to meet my eye and the moment passes. We both know this pattern very well from our correspondence. Whenever I bring up the question of him forgiving himself, he closes up. He's given a handful of excuses through the years; he isn't ready to forgive himself;

his sense of justice doesn't allow him to; even that it's impossible until he reaches a better knowledge of self. I want to grab him by the throat, shake him, and scream: 'How DARE you not forgive yourself IF I'M WILLING TO? YOUR GUILTY CONSCIENCE ISN'T HELPING ME ONE BIT!'

Instead, I look at his somber profile, overwhelmed by the irony of it all because a person who is plagued by guilt and suppresses his emotions is one step closer to becoming a person who blows his top one day and does something he'll regret. *Don't you see that, Stranger?*

'This way,' our guide says. The prison tour is over and we're being ushered onto a bus where another guide will take us on a ride around the island. The group forms a single line to thank the former prisoner for taking us through the history of the prison, intertwining it with his own life in a way that left nobody untouched. My heart beats faster as the line grows shorter and by the time it's my turn to shake his hand, it's pounding so loudly he's bound to hear it.

His handshake is firm, his palm leathery.

'I've got a question.'

'What's that?' he asks. Brown spots dot the whites of his sharp eyes.

'Is it possible to forgive what they did to you?'

For a moment, he looks at me as if the question is completely absurd. Then his mouth opens to let out the most heartfelt, genuine laughter that comes cascading from his core and hits me like a tidal wave. 'Of course,' he answers with a beaming smile. 'We've forgiven all of it. It's the only way forward.'

This simple yet powerful truth lights up my face as I walk out of the prison towards Tom.

'You look like you just won the lottery,' he says.

'Forgiveness is the only way forward, Tom. He told me.'

'He's an incredible human being,' he says with deep respect as the bus takes off and an energetic young guide with a microphone begins the tour. 'Imagine surviving the times he's been through, the things he has seen, and then retelling your history for a job …'

I nod in agreement. I wonder if any women who served time for their political convictions make a living retelling their stories? The rights of black women were even more curtailed than black men's during apartheid. Was incarceration a different experience for them? Were they raped in prison? What about pregnant women? Were they allowed to have their children or were they taken away from them? Did any children grow up behind prison walls?

'It's hard to comprehend how an entire society can unite in an institutionalized discrimination against one group of people,' Tom says.

'But that's not how it happened. "Society" didn't invent apartheid — a small group of white men did. They made up the rules and made sure nobody else could threaten their power. Yes, apartheid may have favored white women over black in vast and systemic ways, but it certainly didn't favor women as a gender. They were expected to stay at home and rear children, as in all fascist ideology. In Nazi Germany, laws were passed that kept women from enrolling in universities. This widespread and systematic trend to keep women from politics and power is probably part of the reason why today, women own only one per cent of the world's wealth.'

'Um, you don't need to preach to me, Thordis,' he says, laughing awkwardly.

For a second, all I can do is stare. 'What do you mean?'

Looking flustered, he says: 'I just … feel like you're being patronizing.'

I'm at a loss for words. 'Patronizing?'

The chirpy tour guide tells the group to look to the right. 'Here, you can see the graveyard where they buried lepers,' he says.

Patronizing? 'Lepers were banished to Robben Island well into the twentieth century,' he adds. *Patronizing?*

I clench my fists, outraged that Tom is comfortable with being guided through hours of a decidedly male history of discrimination but can't stand to hear me talk about discrimination against women that still takes place and even erases their contribution from major world events. A discrimination that's so widespread it exists in every country on the face of the earth and manifests itself financially, politically, and, last but not least, in violence against women. And that cuts too close to the bone. That I can't condone coming from Tom.

His words shut me up like a slap on the cheek that's forceful enough to turn my head to the window. I fix my stare, cheeks burning, listening absent-mindedly to the story of Robert Sobukwe and other great heroes of the resistance who were imprisoned on the island. The magnificent bird life outside the window doesn't budge my heavy heart, not even the penguin that waddles wide-eyed past the bus, having been separated from its flock. *Does he even realize how patronizing it is of him to shut me up just because he finds the truth uncomfortable?*

The silence isn't broken until we're on the undulating boat-trip back, when Tom asks: 'Are you OK? You're very quiet.'

'I'm fine. I'm just disappointed.'

'Why?'

'With your reaction earlier. I'm disappointed that you get uncomfortable when I speak of inequality. After all, that's what we're here to discuss.'

I turn to face him.

'Rape is one of the most brutal manifestations of gender inequality. An overwhelming majority of those who rape are men and the vast majority of rape victims are women. Rape is an everyday occurrence across the planet, even in situations where women are supposedly safe, with men who ought to be worthy of their trust. Rejecting the different realities of men and women, thinking that it has nothing to do with the past we share, means you don't get it. If I'd been a boy, you wouldn't have raped me.'

He shakes his head.

'But you raped me because I'm a girl, a girl you felt entitled to. Something gave you the idea that your pleasure mattered more than my consent, even if I was too sick to consent to anything. I don't know why, Tom. But I believe it has something to do with the fact that men have more power and influence on all levels of society and that's how it's been for centuries. Perhaps this archaic tradition has caused people to adapt to the notion that men are simply more important than women. Perhaps that's why you felt that you and your lust mattered more than me, that night. From what I know, you're what most people would call a "normal guy", which is why I believe this incident to be part of a much bigger picture where women have less value than men. I can't allow you to filter that out just because it makes you uncomfortable.'

'I didn't mean to filter anything out, nor silence anything, I just felt patronized ... like I was the "other",' he says in a quiet voice.

I lose my patience and half-scream: 'I was sharing historical facts! You've been listening to a history of discrimination all day, but when it comes from me, suddenly it's patronizing!?'

'Can we discuss this when we get back?' he suggests. The atmosphere between us is arctic. The warm connection of the last few days is gone and thereby the basis for the interaction we came here to have. The result is a terrifying free fall.

A little while later, we're sitting by a white-clothed table in an empty restaurant on the Waterfront. Tom rubs his hands together and clears his throat nervously. He speaks of having studied social science at university and having a basic understanding of gender-based violence and forms of patriarchy, but then stalls and stutters. I point out a discrepancy in his argument that he claims isn't a discrepancy but a misunderstanding on my part. His explanation makes no sense to me, and I can't even trace myself back to the point in the conversation where I stopped following him. Suddenly, it's as if we're speaking different languages. Although we've lived worlds apart for most of our lives, I've never felt as far removed from him as I do now.

'I don't know how to continue,' I say, looking him straight in the eye. 'I don't understand how we're supposed to make sense of the violence you subjected me to if you're not willing to discuss the context it belongs to. Violence isn't bred in a vacuum. It has societal causes and consequences that must be part of our conversation. Silencing is part of the problem.'

All of a sudden, his eyes well up with tears. 'I don't know why I ... I feel like I'm on the wrong team.' Jumping to his feet, he adds in a breaking voice: 'I just want you to like me.' He darts out for a smoke, but I suspect that the real reason is that he doesn't want to cry in front of me.

Bewildered, I'm left by myself, unsure of how to react. *I just want you to like me* is not an argument, but it is bravely sincere. Not only do I respect Tom for it, but I also want to find my way into the same kind of candor. I could continue to debate gender inequality and bombard him with statistics and facts I know all too well, but it wouldn't help us out of the rut we're stuck in. When he returns, smelling of cigarette smoke and visibly unsettled, I'm ready with a proposal.

'How about we make a deal?' I say, studying his face. 'You try not to get defensive when I talk about gender inequality and I try not be patronizing when I do.'

He smiles and stretches his hand out. 'Deal.' We shake hands. 'I've got to tell you also, I was out there standing in the rain smoking, all dramatic on the edge of the harbor, and it was your trick that flipped things on its head. I thought to myself "go back in there, Stranger, and even though it's tough, find a way to laugh about it".'

Smiling back, I say: 'Good plan.'

A motherly waitress arrives with our food. Although the argument is behind us, the trust between us is severely damaged and our conversation suffers. The smile on my face feels strained, and I'm afraid that anything we say could be misconstrued, fueling further misunderstandings. Desperate for a moment to recuperate, I suggest to Tom that we separate and attend to private matters. A part of me feels rejected and frightened when he immediately agrees. The new distrust in our relationship is like an elephant that doesn't settle for just being in the room — it forces itself between us, snorting and swinging its trunk.

As soon as I exit the restaurant and hit the rainy streets of the Waterfront, my nagging doubts take over. Was I too optimistic to think that I could make sense out of the violence Tom subjected me to — and forgive him for it — if he can't even hold a conversation about the system it belongs to without getting defensive? Is his remorse based on an understanding of himself as part of a bigger picture, or is it an egotistical analysis that ultimately feeds his self-pity and not much else? Gulping for air, a toxic thought invades my mind: *Is our entire mission in danger?* My stomach turns at the thought and I slump against a wall. Desperate for something to calm my nerves, I longingly eye a group of teenagers seeking shelter from the rain under a marquee. *Fuck. Why did I quit smoking?*

An hour later, I've nervously treaded nearby souvenir shops, buying beaded merchandise and other South African artifacts for my family, all the while trying to soothe the voices in my head and steady my quivering core. As before, I try to find a turtle for Haflidi Freyr but without success. The thought of him is accompanied by a wave of angst-ridden guilt. How can I face my son and stepdaughters after having missed out on Easter with them to chase what seems to be a lost cause? And Vidir ... How can I possibly return home and tell him that the worried conversations and energy I cost him were all in vain, that mutual understanding turned out to be an impossible goal for Tom and me to achieve?

When Tom appears, also with souvenirs in a bag, I'm momentarily relieved to see him, but the fear flares up when the elephant comes trotting behind him. Every word we utter is like edging further out on a sheet of ice that could break any second. I can't think of anything safe to say. Except: 'I need a drink.'

'Agreed,' he mutters.

We sit down by the bar in a restaurant that smells of old fried fish. Above us is a statue of a sailor in a yellow rain-suit holding a fishing net. It reminds me of a horror film I saw once, where the murderer gutted his victims with a steel hook. The air between us feels similarly hollowed and lifeless.

'Cheers,' Tom says cautiously, stretching out his bottle of beer.

'Cheers,' I reply, and touch his bottle with mine.

Neither of us knows what to say next. What's unbearable is the fact that without trust, we'll accomplish nothing. Without trust, this whole trip is an overpriced farce and a massive inconvenience — for nothing.

Tom looks no less shaken than I am, with darkened eyes and a closed expression. Much like me, he seems to be racked with doubt about the prospects of the work we came here to do. The atmosphere is spiked with dread. Before I know it, the words come tumbling out of my mouth. 'We're so vulnerable.'

'I know,' he says, twisting the damp bottleneck between his fingers. 'There's still a fragility, even after all our years of email.'

After all those emotions, all those letters, all that goddamn counseling, all the pain and here we are, I silently conclude. *Utterly fucking lost.*

With nothing left to say, I clutch at my last straw when muttering: 'I just wanted something good to come out of this. That's what I've always hoped for.'

'Perhaps we can share what we've learned, sometime.'

For a moment, I'm at a loss for words. Then I stammer: 'Really? You want that?'

Memories surface of how he's insinuated once or twice in our correspondence that the lessons we've learned are worth sharing with others, but deep down I thought those were just empty words: something he thought I wanted to hear given how passionate I am about the cause of preventing sexual violence. *Is he serious now?* Is this the same man I sat out in a tropical storm with a few nights ago, who confessed to me that his greatest fear is being discovered? Is this a result of my words about coming clean with our story as opposed to living life in fear of it?

'I think so,' he says with a nod. 'I have no idea how, but I feel too much hard work has been put into this for it to not be used, somehow. We've moved through so much.'

My heart beats faster just thinking about it. If men like Tom — who belong to a social group that often escapes analysis and scrutiny because they conform to what is seen as the 'norm', who come from stable backgrounds, and enjoy various privileges — would confess to having raped and to regretting it, it might provide the foundation for a long-awaited conversation about the root causes of sexual violence. In order for people to better understand this type of abuse, they need a three-dimensional view of those who perpetrate it, not two-dimensional stereotypes that either vilify the perpetrators as 'monsters' or glorify them to the point where their crimes become unthinkable. The ripple effect could be enormous, the possibilities endless. The big picture, indeed.

'It goes without saying I'm scared of the reaction I'd get,' he says, resting his elbows on the bar. 'Of the flow-on effects for my loved ones. Of the public condemnation.'

'Would you condemn someone in your shoes if you heard our story, with all the healing wonders we've experienced?'

Now it's Tom's turn to be speechless. 'We? As in both of us, together? Seriously?'

'Of course together! How else to go about it?'

'So you'd be willing to tell our story — with me?' he asks hopefully.

I'm confused. 'What do you mean? It's the only thing that makes sense. We're much stronger together.'

'Without a doubt,' he says with relief. 'That changes everything.'

We smile at one another and this time, the moment is reinforced with mutual trust. *We did it!* The load that's off my shoulders practically lifts me out of my seat. Within the realm of trust, there's no limit to what we can accomplish.

Tom is visibly relieved. 'So, what would be our format?' he wonders, smiling into his beer. 'Film? I know a great filmmaker ...'

'Too glamorous,' I say, shaking my head. 'And besides, they'd edit out my skillful post-partum vagina impression from yesterday,' I add, sticking out my chin and contorting my face.

'Yeah, truth,' he says with a laugh. The smile on his face fades and he starts to fiddle with the label on his beer bottle. 'I can't help but imagine the response if I were to announce to my circles that I once raped my girlfriend. Thinking of individuals around me, taking a rough stab at their values, and postulating who would shun me and who would think of me as being more than my choices. I also wonder if anyone I know would come out of the dark and admit that they too have abused loved ones. Purely by the statistics, I'm certain I know men who have been sexually violent, although nobody comes to mind as the kind of person who would be abusive. But then again, I know the vast majority of people who know me would be in utter shock and disbelief to learn of what I've done.'

'I did that too, for years,' I admit. 'Asking myself how life would be different if it were public knowledge that I'd been raped. I dated men who confirmed my fears and men who weren't fazed in the least. Some of them used it against me. If I didn't want to have sex with them, they'd say I was frigid because I'd been raped. Wanting to prove them wrong sometimes led to me having sex against my will. The emotional manipulation was worse, though. If I disagreed or questioned their behavior, they'd say my feelings couldn't be trusted because the rape had left me unstable and irrational. It was obviously a load of crap and a form of abuse, in itself. So I know what it is like to be defined by a single incident.'

'Sounds awful,' he says.

'But that's also why it's important to set an example. To show the world that people who've been both ends of this scale, whether they're receivers or perpetrators of sexual violence, aren't soulless monsters or damaged goods. They're people; imperfect, fallible, unmistakably human beings like you and me with all kinds of thoughts, jobs, backgrounds, life-styles, and beliefs. People who pay their taxes and love their families and make mistakes and live right next door. Who collect trash on the beach,' I say, and poke him in the shoulder. Checking the time on my phone, I add: 'Sorry, but I've got to go. I have a Skype date in five minutes.'

Across the hall is an internet café, where I put on a pair of worn headphones and log onto a desktop computer.

Vidir answers straight away. 'Hi, honey,' he says, his eyes glowing with tenderness. He adjusts the webcam to reveal Haflidi, who is sitting in his lap. Despite my best efforts to have a conversation with my three-year-old son, he's less than enthused about this digital version of his mother. He tries repeatedly to climb out of his father's lap to see what his half-sister Julia is doing, who's at least there in the flesh one room over.

When Haflidi is gone, Vidir closes the door behind him.

'How are you?' I ask, trying to sound upbeat.

He sighs and shrugs.

'How are the kids?'

'They're watching TV. Haflidi finished his chocolate Easter egg in ten minutes yesterday.'

'Well done! Was he foaming at the mouth and swinging from the chandelier?'

Vidir smiles faintly. 'Something like that, yes ...'

I smile a little too broadly, nodding my head a little too eagerly before Vidir states the obvious. 'This is so weird, Thordis.'

'I know,' I whisper, lowering the mask.

'Do you know how weird it is that you're in South Africa? With a man I've never met? That you ... share that past with? It's only dawning on me now. How ... ridiculous it feels.'

'I would've regretted it for the rest of my life if I hadn't—'

He cuts me off. 'You don't have to explain anything; you know I support you. I just had to express how weirded out I am that you're there, that you guys are there together.'

'If it's any consolation, this won't happen again.'

He looks away and doesn't answer.

Instinctively, I lean closer to the screen. 'I don't have any other unfinished business that calls for a trip across the planet, Vidir.'

Finally, he looks into the camera with a boyish smile that makes me catch my breath. 'Well, that's a relief …'

And just like that, my heart melts.

It's almost 9pm. The wet streets of the Waterfront glisten under the streetlamps, and the rain drips from nearby roof gutters as a hungry Tom and I wander into a restaurant. After we fought and made up, the atmosphere is different. It's almost chummy, for lack of a better word.

'Your turn, Stranger,' I say as I sit down on a bolstered bench with red leather upholstery.

'Wait, let me see. I was up to twenty, right?' he says, frowning. 'At twenty, I was at the University of Newcastle up the coast from Sydney with some twenty thousand other students, studying social science. I lived close to the campus and would sometimes go to class in bare feet. Long hair, no shoes, quite the look I was going for. I didn't do so well in my final high school exams, mostly because they were two months after I got back from Iceland, and I was a bit of a disjointed wreck after trying to settle back into life at home. This meant that my university entrance score was pretty low and my options were kind of limited. I didn't pick the hardest degree, and I managed to fit in a fair amount of partying and surfing — most of the time they went hand in hand. In my first year, I failed two subjects just on bloody attendance.'

I can't help but think about all the troubled youngsters he's supported through his youth work, after making what he describes as a haphazard decision about his studies. 'Do you believe in fate, Tom?'

'I'd like to, but no. I think the idea of fate undermines the power of choice and agency. And rids people of responsibility for their actions.'

'Do you think life could be a mix, somehow? You know, that some things are consequences of the choices we make, but other things are simply meant to happen?'

'Possibly, but it ... doesn't make complete sense to me,' he says, wrinkling his forehead.

I lean back into the bolstered leather. Perhaps it's the wine, perhaps it's the new level of trust that came from working our way through a disagreement, but the question is on my lips before I know it.

'Tom?'

'Yes?'

'That night all those years ago ... was there any part of you that thought that what you were doing was pleasurable for me?'

'No,' he replies without hesitation. His frankness feels like a kick to the stomach. Yet there's something comforting about his answer. We've come too far to sugarcoat things.

'Was there any part of you that thought that what you were doing was painful for me?' I ask, unsure whether I crave the answer or dread it.

'I don't think I was thinking about you, Thordis,' he says. His face is expressionless; his voice matter of fact.

Relieved, I straighten my back. No justifications, no bullshit. His actions were driven by selfishness all those years ago, and somehow it's comforting to hear it said out loud.

'Carry on with your story,' I say, looking him in the eye. 'You decided to come back to Iceland in 2000 ...'

He puts down his utensils and resumes his story. 'Right. During my second year of university in Newcastle, in which I was faring OK, for one of our subjects we went "camping" in an eco-tourism resort in a national park on the coast. A couple of us were offered jobs at the resort for the summer and I ended up getting the position of Head Guide. It wasn't just guiding. For more than six months I cleaned foul toilets, ran the kids' club, mowed lawns, did the garbage runs, managed the restaurant, surfed and drank way too much, and left only twice to visit friends and family. Hard work, but I saved money quickly, and decided to defer university and return to Iceland with my A$6000. The ticket cost me over A$4000, but that was no issue. I wanted to see my Icelandic family, and, as I acknowledged, I also wanted to see you.'

He pauses momentarily.

'The drive and motivation to see you is ... clouded. I remember calling you, and for some reason I can remember fumbling for coins when standing on the timber decking where the public phone was, nervously dialing your number.'

'I remember that phone call,' I say in a quiet voice.

'Like I've said, I was on an island of denial, disconnected completely from the fact that I had raped you four years earlier. The memory was sunk so deep, in such a dark place. I remember a feeling of being very unsettled, entirely unfulfilled, and wanting to always be moving. And when I returned to Iceland ... this strange relationship developed between you and me.'

He hesitates, as if he's trying to pick out the right words. After a fraught moment, I realize I'm holding my breath.

'We first met up in that place downtown, Café Paris. The "hello" was awkward and it was a pretty rigid first meeting, being that we essentially just spoke about superficial things. Your manner was different — more confident and almost intimidating. And you seemed older with your black hair and cigarette in hand ... there was an intensity, I remember. We caught up a few more times and I eventually met some of your friends. I wouldn't define it as a friendship, as it wasn't that simple or reliable. After a drive downtown one night, you dropped me home. The farewell kiss on the cheek shifted into something more. We moved into the laundry room and you surprised me with how pushy you were. Afterwards, you didn't talk to me, which confused me entirely. The next time we were alone again, you wasted no time. Ordered me around. I didn't even have the imagination for some of the things you had me do. Some of it was ... well, humiliating. Took me way out of my comfort zone. And it felt at times uncomfortably cold and impersonal. Mechanical, almost. Or ... rough. Like you were trying to shock me.'

I correct him: 'Rob you of control.'

'And in between, you were rarely in touch. We didn't hang out much and when we did, it was usually on your terms.'

'That was the whole point, Tom,' I say, tiredly rubbing my forehead. 'When the opportunity arose to make you feel like a piece of meat, I seized it. The alternative would've been to lower my defenses, bare my wounds, and confront you with what you'd done, at the risk that you'd deny it. Which would've driven me over the edge. I wasn't strong enough to give you that kind of control over me, again. So I chose the option that allowed me to take back some of the power you'd robbed me of, all the while hiding how scarred and vulnerable I really was. When I didn't have the strength to confront you, attempting revenge was another way to channel my hurt.'

'If that was revenge, it all makes sense, finally. It was a confusing time ... sometimes feeling close but never being let in. Hearing you explain it though, it helps untangle things a bit. It felt like I was chasing after you at times, which of course fits.'

'Is the food to your liking?' a smiling waiter asks, suddenly appearing next to our table. I glance down involuntarily at the piece of meat on my plate.

'Very good,' we answer in unison, and the waiter leaves.

I look out the window at the street lamps on the harbor, evenly spaced and rising proudly out of the concrete. Each one of them becomes a milestone in the past Tom and I share. His betrayal when he raped me in 1996. Our mutual escape from the truth. My misguided attempts in 2000 to take back the power he robbed me of. The tension and chaos that brewed during the summer, boiling over in the Westman Islands. The years of silence that ensued. The letter about wanting to find forgiveness in 2005. Eight years of correspondence and confrontations now reaching a peak in a strange city halfway between Reykjavík and Sydney in 2013. The milestones form a glittering chain in the dark and the context lights up my mind.

'I'm not proud of my behavior that summer, which is probably part of the reason why it's been so neatly erased from my memory,' I tell Tom. 'But I believe you. I understand the reasons behind it and I assume responsibility for my actions.'

I want to add something, something that acknowledges the confusion I caused him. The words 'I didn't mean to hurt you' are on the tip of my tongue, but I quickly swallow them. *Hurting him was my intention exactly.*

'After the fiasco in the Westman Islands, I started running again, thick and heavy with brand-new guilt. I remember a confusing last meeting at my host-family's house, a walk to the bus stop with you, and a dramatic, tearful farewell. I jumped on the first flight to Australia. It had many detours and stopovers, but I didn't care. I thought it was worth sleeping in five different airports and spending days without a shower or a bed just to get the hell away from Iceland. And you.'

'Can I offer you dessert or coffee?' asks the waiter, again appearing without warning. Tom and I look at one another and shake our heads, rising to our feet simultaneously.

When we step out into the dark night, the Ferris wheel towers over us like a phosphorescent circle. Music pulsates through the air, echoing from a place called Mitchell's Waterfront Brewery. The outside tables are empty beneath wet, heavy sunshades, but the pub itself is crawling with people. 'Scottish and Irish pubs,' I say with a grin. 'You can always count on them to be buzzing.'

'Like most of the people in there,' Tom says, glancing inside with apparent interest. 'What do you say we have a drink here? It may not be live music, but at least it's good.'

'Let's do it.'

On all sides of the bar, people are happily chatting amongst themselves. Tom turns to me with a question in his eyes.

I shrug. 'Whatever you're having.'

He nods and turns back to the bartender. I catch myself staring at his hands on the table. Golden hairs are sprinkled across the tanned skin. It's strange to think that I've held those hands ... but also dug my nails into them and bitten the fingers ...

'Here you go.' I snap out of it as he hands me a draught beer. We exchange a few jokes, which is like scratching something that's been itchy for days. It's nice — no, straight up *necessary* — to talk about something for a moment that isn't directly linked to our most painful secrets. Leftover tension from the argument and accumulated fatigue results in a silliness that we only seem to encourage in one another.

'Some soul searching we've done these past few days,' I say, shaking my head in disbelief.

'You can say that again,' he says, leaning an elbow on the table. 'It's not every day that you tell your life story to someone.'

I hesitate. 'I have an idea of how my relationships were affected by our past. How it affected intimacy, sex. But I've not dared to ask how you were affected.'

He stares at me in surprise.

'Well, until now.'

He realizes that I'm serious, raising his brow. 'How sex …?'

'How the past we share shaped that part of your life, yes. I'm not going to pretend that sexual health doesn't affect one's overall wellbeing. Love. Happiness. Intimacy. The whole shebang.'

'I see.' He buys himself time by sipping on his beer before shaking his head. 'I wouldn't know how to answer that …' he says awkwardly.

'Oh come on, Stranger. We've traveled all the way to South Africa to confront an incident that profoundly shaped our lives. And because this incident was of a sexual nature, it's only natural that it would affect us in that area. I'm not trying to pry about your sex life. I'm just trying to locate the damage.'

Looking unsure, he twists his glass between his hands. 'A few years ago, my brother and I were out at a bar and we were approached by a girl wearing glasses. She sat on the stool next to me and then fell off. "I've just fallen for you." We ended up going to another pub and dancing together. After some enthusiastic kissing, she and I ended up in an alleyway behind the bar. All of a sudden, she leaned across the hood of the nearest car and pulled her skirt down. I was instantly uncomfortable and felt … sorry for her. As if I would be taking advantage of her if I went any further. I stumbled through an explanation of why I couldn't do anything more. She seemed initially embarrassed, but we went back inside, to my relief.'

She may just have wanted a quickie, I reason, but the reasons could also have been darker. 'Did you know that people who act out sexually are more likely to have been abused or raped?'

Tom looks down at his hands, flushed. 'Yeah, I'd learned about that in my work. Which is why my alarm bell was ringing. I can't stand the notion of exploiting someone's vulnerability like that. I have to take it slow and be very careful. Sometimes, I get very anxious and start to sweat. Get panic attacks, honestly. There have been times where I had to stop in the middle of things, incapable of explaining my way out. My partner has to take the lead so there's no question about what she wants.'

So you'll never again be responsible for crossing another person's boundaries, I silently conclude.

Tom exhales. 'Again, this week's honesty is pretty extraordinary,' he exclaims with an awkward smile.

'For me, the biggest challenge has been to identify what's a result of the violence I've experienced and what's simply part of my nature,' I tell him. 'There have been times where I needed to give up all control in intimate situations. Maybe I needed to see if I could handle giving over power, or maybe I just liked the freedom that comes with leaving the decisions to someone else. I don't know which is what, in the light of everything I've experienced. But I try to stay connected to my emotions as opposed to disconnecting like I did for so many years.'

Loud laughter cuts through the air, coming from a couple of girls who look about twenty, smoking cigarettes under the overhang. Tom takes a look around and smiles faintly. 'Christ, Thordis. I can't believe we're discussing this.'

'To brave conversations,' I say with a smile, raising my glass. 'After all, healing is giving up all hope of a better past, isn't it?' I down the rest of my glass and slam it on the table. 'But no more juice for me tonight.'

'Why? Feeling tipsy?'

'Worse, sentimental. Let's go find a taxi.'

We say our goodbyes in front of the Ritz after having decided to sleep in. When Tom texts me that he's home safe, I'm standing by the hotel window. I reach for the light switch and turn it off. The city lights stretch out below me like a shimmering blanket, and I connect the dots with my finger on the cool glass. The memories may have been erased from my mind, but my skin is aglow with secrets. My reflection in the window takes on the face of revenge: the cruel creature who wanted to bring my tormentor to his knees. Growling softly, she stretches lazily before meeting my eye. *I licked your wounds*, she purrs while flashing her claws. *You think you have the right to judge me now?*

I turn away from the apparition, seeking solace in how far I've come through understanding and patience. Revenge grabs hold of my chin with bony fingers and forces me to face her. *Admit it*, she hisses. *You enjoyed making him squirm.*

You're wrong, I hiss back. *It healed nothing*.

Snarling, she retreats into the shadows. Her presence lingers, its remnants pulsating through my body until sleep finally pushes me off the edge and into the subconscious of the African night.

From Tom's diary

I interpreted her passionate words on the Robben Island tour bus as a dividing line, a statement of limits, a condemnation of men, of which I am one. I felt like I should have been nodding, but internally I was shaking my head. I knew full well that our shared history and my deeds took place within a bigger social context. I know something of the realities, and I know that we are part of these horrible statistics. I've studied and read and thought intensely about issues of inequality.

I questioned her internally. *Does she think I'm ignorant? Doesn't she know how I feel?*

For a moment it felt like I was being lectured, and that's where a real discomfort set in. Something changed on that tour bus and it shattered what I had presumed to be a possibility. It was a thought born from a crazy hope: that during this week I could regain some respect in her eyes. Forgiveness was beyond my wildest dreams, and always enough, but I can't deny I hoped I could somehow redeem myself. Crawl out of that pit and show myself to Thordis as somebody trustworthy, considerate, well raised, and balanced.

On the ferry and in the restaurant I wanted to spill out all that I understood, felt, and was sickened by. I wanted to tell her I agreed and felt as she did when walking amongst the hard, gray injustices of Robben Island. Instead, there was a bottomless gulf that had cracked open between us, and the miles grew between our two chairs.

I felt male, white, and clothed in stupidity.

I was the colonizer of bodies, the thing that sickens me the most.

I was shocked back into the position of rapist, and I think I had somewhat misplaced that truth in the time and conversations we've shared so far. I was back on the wrong side.

When I couldn't explain myself, I began to crack. I stood up and announced I was going for a cigarette as the first tears appeared. Taking my jacket, I walked slowly out into the pouring rain, although inside I was bloody sprinting.

I was panicking and searching for words. Any ways to explain myself that wouldn't insult Thordis and jeopardize the whole week. Just as I finished my cigarette, her words came to me: *find a way to laugh about it*. That's exactly what needed to happen. I was running, there was a hugely difficult space to work through, but I needed to get back in there and find a way to laugh about it. It felt ... educational, and I knew she deserved my composure. I wasn't sure we'd close the gap, but it couldn't be allowed to widen.

Luckily, we somehow came through it. I don't know if I expressed myself properly, but she worded out a truce that seemed to bring some peace.

I know the dynamic between us has historically been skewed. She's been the driver of proceedings at most turns, further along on her journey, and I've been the agreeable one, nodding my head. On some level I understand this as a natural history, given that Thordis has been the instigator, and I've been wanting to apologize and surrender control. I also admitted to myself a long time ago that I've found her intimidating. But will I ever feel confident in challenging her if I disagree? Thordis is very intelligent — do I have a personal problem with that? No, that's not it. It's the pattern whereby she's the assigned leader and I'm the meek, under-confident follower. I look forward to when we can both speak to each other outside of our roles and without fear of failure or insult.

When we were having a drink later she also said that she only wants something good to come out of this. It's what she's always wanted.

After all the twists and turns, here we are. In South Africa of all places, doing our best to mend and transmute the past pains and choices.

Yes, something good has to be born from this, for both of us.

Despite our at times lopsided dynamic, our correspondence has still been a safe haven of self-exploration for me. Thordis has asked about and listened to the hardest of it. That's where the work has been done, in those cringing, tense, and searching emails we exchanged.

Then there were also the lighter and more promising ones.

I remember when she signed off 'take care, Tom' for the first time in an email. It felt significant, as if there was something achieved ... something being built out of the ruins. Something that not everyone who has been on either side of a traumatic experience gets a chance at.

I remember a simplified, epiphanic statement I wrote to Thordis once:

'Understand your choice as much as you can, if possible make amends in any way you can, learn from it, help others to learn from it, never do it again, and move on.'

I must have written it when I was confident and decided, arrogant even. From here, I know I don't have a right to presume others need or want help, nor do I have the right to believe I am some kind of trustworthy, valid voice.

And yet, I do think if I start talking about my experience of being male, my privilege, and the culture of men ... I'll be ostracized or meet some serious judgment. I think if I paint myself as in any way representative of men as a whole, I'll rightfully be shot down. But don't I want to ask questions, of myself and of others, about our ways of being men? About our relations with women? Don't I want to contribute to the acknowledgement of a problem? In one ear I hear the word 'hypocrite', and in the other I hear the word 'complicit'.

All I know is that this seems to have morphed from the two of us redressing our bleak past into something that feels bigger. If we walk off lighter but scared to talk about it, it's just giving in to the fear that we have been working so hard to find our way out of. Confronting fears has been a theme, and I want that theme to continue. I want to keep talking, let the circle expand. It's the talking that has led us here.

The purpose that brought me here also feels like it could stretch past just me and her. Coming to Cape Town to meet Thordis initially busied my head with trepidation, around what it would achieve, how I'd have to look her in the eye when speaking, and also the fact that I'd have to explain the reason for meeting Thordis to my then girlfriend. But with some thought and time it became obvious that we both needed this, even though she had initially proposed it. I needed the repair that would only come with voicing past damages — letting go was essential to secure me a healthy and open future. Nothing else would get me there. Even though we'd been emailing, the claims to our past were still unsigned. Ownership hadn't been established. And I feel this is a very human thing that we share with many others. Sometimes, the responsibility gets shoved around, or placed on a dusty shelf, or even strapped to those who don't own it. If I've learnt anything, it's that denial leads to decay … and the opposite is also true.

Maybe the sharing of our history might just act as a circuit breaker, and allow for an open and alternative conversation. If so, then I think it might be a greater fear worth facing.

Jesus. Grand (and almost wantonly noble) aspirations, Tom. Just get through this week and see how you feel. Maybe even lighten up a bit!

I was glad for the 'easier' dinner conversation tonight. After that rocky day, it felt good to have a less serious occasion. I found myself pondering less serious matters, and after the constant analysis I think it's wise to just let the conversation be less directed.

We chatted about wine, and I thought about how healthy she looked. Just well and clear-eyed, like somebody who has found that elusive life balance. I reflected on the Thordis I used to know, also noticing a couple of quick comparisons. There's no more excessive smoking. Her hair is a natural color, as opposed to the jet-black I recall from 2000. The style of her dress is completely different now, as is the way she wears it. The tight, dark, and risqué outfits have become a simple long red jacket that matched the bench she was sitting on. The vodka I remember her ordering at bars is instead a tall glass of red wine. She's barely had mascara on, whereas I recall thick eyeliner and varying shades of lipstick. She's worn comfortable sandals this week that I don't think the old Thordis would have worn.

Her accord with herself has shifted completely along with her relationship to her body. Of course it has. I know very well how much work she has put into understanding herself, and I also know how we grow into our own skin.

Plus, she's a woman now and a mother ... and it's been almost thirteen years. I knew I was to meet the adult Thordis, but I was smiling at myself again for believing that I'd be meeting the same person.

Day Seven

2 April 2013

My mouth is a desert. I sit up in bed, only instantly to regret it. The hangover has my head in a vice. *Fuck. Me.* Didn't I only have two beers at the Scottish bar? Man, how uncool is it to be hung-over from two beers and a glass of red wine? I remember the days when I could show up at school fresh as a daisy after having won a tequila-shot contest the night before. *Girl, you've obviously lost your touch.*

As I stumble out of bed, thoughts flit through my foggy mind about how Tom and I managed to bridge the gap that our disagreement created yesterday. Frightening as it was, it served to reinforce our mission of not looking away even when we're scared of what we may find within each other. *And perhaps more importantly, within ourselves.*

In the shower, water flows across my scalp like liquid pain relief. *Breakfast can wait, though*, I think as I stagger back to bed, equipped with my phone, which beeps a few minutes later, piercing my throbbing head. The message is in broken Icelandic:

Hi, I'm upside and done eating, and look like filth, but still
am ... relieved and sort of ... smiling. I'm going in shower
and was thinking about walking to you soon.

I laugh out loud at the wonderful mistranslations. What a champ, though, to be able to make himself understandable in Icelandic half a lifetime later without even having an Icelandic keyboard on his phone. I text back:

Filth's the word. See you soon.

I check my email to see if I've gotten a reply from the Rape Crisis Cape Town Trust, the only destination I was determined to visit while in South Africa. It's a non-governmental organization for people who have been subjected to sexual violence. When I told Tom about it in an email shortly before the trip, he surprised me by saying he'd like to join me, as the visit could be useful to him in his work at the youth refuge. To be honest, I doubt that he's ready to come with me to a place where rape survivors go after their lives are ripped apart, but I respect him for even considering it. I wrote back saying he was welcome to join me, and it wasn't until after I'd hit the 'send' button that it dawned on me: *What a surreal full circle that'd be.*

But alas, still no reply from Rape Crisis. I reach for the landline and dial the number listed on the organization's website. Shy and self-conscious, I explain that I'm a published author of a book about gender-based violence in Iceland, who would find an opportunity to learn about the work of Rape Crisis most valuable. I'm advised to call back after twelve o'clock and ask for Shiralee, whose name I jot down on a piece of paper.

An hour later, I meet up with Tom in the lobby, where I carefully lower myself into the floral sofa next to him. 'Hi,' I grunt.

'How are you feeling?'

'Fresh like a damp rag sock. You?'

'I've been better,' he says with a grin.

Having grown fond of our habit of talking through our lives while traveling around Cape Town, we decide to have another go at Table Mountain. Nigel is sitting behind the desk in his little travel agency, as well-ironed and tidy as ever. He lights up when he sees me and rushes to his feet.

'I found your tree!' he says with a triumphant smile.

I have no idea what he's talking about, but Nigel continues eagerly. 'It's called the Upside Down Tree here in South Africa. That's why I didn't know what you were talking about when you asked me about the baobab. To me it's the Upside Down Tree!' He smiles enthusiastically, awaiting my response.

I stare at him, not understanding a word of what he just said. Judging by the look on Tom's face, he's just as dumbstruck as I am. 'My tree?'

'Yes, the baobab you were looking for,' Nigel replies, giddy with excitement. 'I called my friend who is a gardener and he told me. It's in the botanical gardens!'

I'm still in the dark. 'You must be mistaking me for someone else because I haven't asked you about any tree,' I tell him in a tentative voice. The pure joy radiating from his face has me wishing that I were, indeed, the right woman.

He studies our faces with an embarrassed smile, like we're making fun of him. 'Are you sure?'

'Yes, I'm sure I haven't asked you about a tree—'

'Was she wearing pajamas and doing this?' Tom asks, stretching his hands out like a sleepwalker. He bursts out laughing.

Nigel laughs politely at the joke before turning to me with a serious expression on his face. 'The tree is in Kirstenbosch, the botanical gardens. The blue bus will take you there.' He hands me the bus schedule.

My laughter dries up and my whole body tingles as I take the bus schedule from his hands. 'Thank you, Nigel.'

He does us the favor of calling Table Mountain to see if the cable car is running today, but tells us that the phone line is busy. We thank him for the help and he waves at us, happy to be of service. 'I hope you enjoy your tree,' he shouts out.

'Whoa. That was weird!' Tom says as we walk out into the sun. 'But at least you've found your tree!'

'Perhaps I'm meant to go there,' I say in a casual voice, despite meaning every word.

On our walk towards the bus stop where we're hoping to catch a ride to the top of Table Mountain, Tom turns to me and says: 'I wish I had my iPod with me. I'd be tempted to play you a song called "Stranded on Earth" when we get there.'

'Who's it by?'

'A group called The Herbaliser. I've had intense, almost spiritual experiences when listening to that song. I once listened to it on top of a mountain outside of Vancouver that I had climbed, while admiring this jaw-droppingly beautiful vista of snow-capped mountains with not one trace of humanity visible. So surreal and powerful — I remember the song building and rising up and giving me full-body tingles.' He gestures towards the beach. 'One second, I need to make a quick stop here.'

'Go for it,' I say, and take a seat in the sand while Tom wades in and splashes seawater in his face. Thank God my hangover is subsiding. The sun peers out from behind wispy clouds. For the first time since I arrived in South Africa, I can take off my cardigan and enjoy walking around in a tank top, much to the delight of the Icelander in me.

Suddenly, I feel like we're being watched. Looking sideways, I discover four men about fifty meters away, watching us carefully with silent, serious faces. 'Let's go,' I say, throwing the backpack across my shoulder. Tom nods and we quicken our step. When we're back on the street again, Green Point Lighthouse greets us with its brightly painted lines.

'Speaking of Vancouver, you know how I wrote to you from internet cafés in Canada?' Tom asks me. 'Well, I was there for three years, from 2007 to 2010. Three pretty mobile but amazing years. Initially, I was with my brother, living a snowboarder's dream in the mountains for one winter. Then we worked various trade jobs while basically living out of a van and friends' houses. When one year stretched into two, I gravitated towards Vancouver and ended up being approved to use my youth-work qualification. It was a job I got at a multi-modal school that solidified it for me — that I enjoy working with kids and young people. I was new to working with kids with more complex needs, some of whom were non-verbal with autism spectrum disorders. But you were working one on one, so it was very intensive, and the relationships that were built were amazing. I remember it as being up there with my most challenging jobs, but without a doubt it's the one I value the most.'

We stand by the bus stop and he takes off his backpack, resting it on the ground. 'Speaking of my job, I took a short training course in case management last year and found it brilliant. It was just so practical and dealt a lot with real-life professional situations. But at this training they asked for a male volunteer. Now, I have a policy to fire my hand up if a volunteer is ever requested. More often than not it has helped my confidence in front of groups, but sometimes it's ended up in me having to do something decidedly stupid.'

'Oh. I can imagine where this story is going.'

Tom shakes his head. 'Wait for it. This time, I role-played a character who made me sick to the core of my bones. I had to play Neil. A man who beat his wife. A man who believed violence against his wife was justified because she pushed his buttons, caused him "to lose it" and "lash out at her".'

I cringe at the notion.

'Anyway, I was handed the script and then played the character for about fifteen minutes to an audience of around thirty. I played Neil well. I scared myself with how well I slipped into his shoes. Numerous people said I was "believable" and that I "should act". I was upset by these remarks. I could feel myself playing the ignorant, selfish, angry Australian male bigot that I know so well, and then right in the middle I panicked because I thought I might be revealing a believably violent and vicious side of myself. I heard myself reading the lines and justifying my violence, getting defensive, and denying any responsibility for my violence because it was out of my control, because my wife was the one who enraged me. It was her fault. Which is obviously such a bullshit childish notion, to claim that one has no control over one's emotions, or that another person "made me do it"!'

'What a mind-fuck,' I blurt out.

'Right? I was a bit of a mess afterwards.'

'But you can rest assured that everyone has a place within where violence sleeps, Tom. I can imagine situations where I'd pull the trigger. The fact that you played that character well doesn't make you worse than anybody else, it just means that you're able to make a clear distinction between the violent part of you and the rest of you. Which, I'd say, is a good thing.'

'This exercise brought up some questions in me. Did I feel anger towards you that night? Because I chose to look after you in the bathrooms, did I feel like I was … powerless? Like I had no choice but to be responsible for you? It gives me a sick feeling in the pit of my stomach to pose such questions. Have I shifted to a selfish point before, where I lost all considerations of others and lashed out like Neil? I've spoken of entitlement before … but did I have some kind of unwarranted blame towards you that night? Disgusting to consider, but I want to be transparent.' His willingness to bare it all is evidenced by the open sincerity written across his face. *Heartening*, I note, *but unnecessary*.

'It doesn't make a difference to me, Tom. I know we've talked about how understanding can be vital to forgiveness, or even one with it. But I've understood enough. For me, it's time to start letting go.'

A bus with the words 'Red Line' across it comes whooshing around the corner, pulling up to the curb. We climb onboard and get a seat on the upper deck.

'Thank you … for the level of trust last night,' I tell him.

'Likewise.'

'Well, I didn't share a lot about … the topic at hand,' I say, lowering my voice as I realize that the young couple in front of us are not wearing their headphones. 'Intimacy used to be a minefield for me. I spent many years being emotionally detached during sex. Twisting it, turning it into something it's not. For a while, I even had allergic reactions to sexual stimuli and had all kinds of medical tests done. The health-care professionals who treated me seemed ill-equipped with knowledge about sexual violence and its impact on survivors, and as a result I don't know what's cause and what's effect, what's physical and what's emotional.' Looking away, I add: 'What I'm trying to say is that I'll never know how sex would've developed for me had you not … been my first.'

He nods solemnly. I see my reflection in his sunglasses and contemplate how detaching myself from my body was the only way for me to stay sane during the 7,200 seconds of violence he subjected me to, and how this survival strategy later prevented me from being present in my body when receiving physical affection. The thoughts are tender, and I'm grateful that he's listening in silence. The film over this part of my life is too thin to bear the weight of his words.

Suddenly, he looks to Table Mountain and frowns. 'I think the cable car is closed.'

I squint my eyes but I can't make it out. 'How do you know?'

'It isn't moving.' He blocks the sun with his hand, peering for a long time at the mountain. 'Yeah, it looks closed to me.'

I recover quickly. 'It's OK, though. I have a date with a tree, anyway.'

'Too true,' he says, smiling widely. 'That's on the 'Blue Line'. Come on. We need to hop off at the next stop and change buses.'

The next stop turns out to be in the buzzing city center, a stark contrast to the ghost town we experienced on Good Friday. The air is practically vibrating with energy. Men in suits with briefcases hurrying to important places sidestep tourists with their cameras aloft. Laughter pours out of a KFC restaurant and the sound of jackhammers echoes through the dug-up streets. Cape Town smells much like a fast-food drive-thru, where the aroma of deep-fried meat is indistinguishable from car emissions.

'This feels more like a city now,' Tom says excitedly. Then he looks around wildly. 'Hear that!? Someone's singing!'

I close my eyes, drinking in the urban cacophony. *So here you are, Cape Town. Nice to finally meet you.*

Tom studies the map for a short time before reading nearby street signs, trying to find out where the nearest bus stop for the Blue Line is. 'This way,' he says. We stop at a crossing on a busy, sunlit street.

'Tom?'

'Yes?'

'Ten o'clock.' I gesture discreetly with my head towards a van that is waiting on a red light. Tom sizes up the driver, a tall, skinny man with a cap who has rolled down his window and glued his eyes to me.

'You mean that guy who's checking you out?' Tom asks.

'I think so. If that's what that is.'

'Oh. That's blatant.'

'So it feels.'

'Amazing. He doesn't even try to hide it.'

'Nope.'

'And taking his time too.'

'Is he still looking?' I ask, locking my eyes on a nearby palm tree.

'Yep.'

'How about now?'

'Yep.'

'Still?'

'Yep.'

'Wow.'

At last, the light turns green, and we cross the street in a big herd of pedestrians. The van driver takes off, burning rubber. I'm as good as naked after his lewd stare, feeling exposed. I glance at Tom, strolling next to me with no worries in the world. The likelihood of a woman staring him down in a threatening sexual manner is close to none — and in the unlikely event that it happens, the odds of him feeling threatened are negligible. This basic difference in perspective will always separate us, down to the smallest stitches in life's fabric.

He stops opposite a shiny tower with polished windows and gilded columns. 'We should turn here,' he says, gazing into a small side street.

'But first I need to take a look inside,' I reply, pointing at a jewelry store on the corner. After smiling politely to the security cameras, we're buzzed in through two robust gates with steel bars and electric locks. A petite woman in a hijab welcomes us to this fortress. 'Can I help you?' she asks. Her face is fair, almost childlike. I explain that I'm looking for a wedding ring. She opens one cabinet after another with a jangling key chain, pulling out a tray with rings and placing them in front of me. Her presence is timid; her slender fingers fluttering from one ring to the other like the winged fairies I saw in a cartoon when I was little.

'This one,' I say, pointing to a men's ring with a snakeskin pattern. Framing the silvery snakeskin is a thin gold loop at the top and bottom. The overall look is sophisticated and stylish. Vidir would love it. We decided long ago that our wedding rings didn't have to be a pair or even come from the same store — what matters most is that we like them enough to wear them for the rest of our lives.

She chuckles softly. 'Good choice, miss.'

'Mind if I take a picture of it?'

'Go ahead,' she says, handing me the ring. I slip it on my thumb, pull out my phone and take a picture, sending it to Vidir.

'When are you getting married?' she asks, smiling at Tom, who's standing by a glass cabinet admiring rings.

'What?' he asks, confused. 'We?'

Damn it, how could I not foresee this?!

'We're not getting married,' I quickly answer. 'To each other, I mean. Not to each other.'

'I'm not tying the knot anytime soon,' Tom answers with a good-natured grin. 'There's the small matter of finding a girlfriend first.'

'Thank you for letting us take a look,' I hurriedly tell the assistant. 'We might come back later.'

When we step out on the street again, I turn to him. 'Sorry. I should've known what that looked like, you and I ring shopping together.'

'No worries.'

I spot a coffee sign half a block down the street. 'Come on, Stranger. It's time for coffee.'

To our surprise, it isn't a café but a tourist information center. Behind the big streamlined service desk is a white wall with the word 'Welcome' in eight languages. Touch-screens adorn every surface. It's all so modern and white and user-friendly that I feel like I'm in an Apple store.

Looking at the clock, I realize it's time to call Shiralee at Rape Crisis and am delighted to discover pay phones towards the back of the tourist center. She turns out to have a youthful, composed voice when apologizing for the lack of reply to my email inquiries. 'But you're welcome to pay us a visit tomorrow morning. How does 9:30 sound?'

'Very well,' I say, bouncing with excitement. 'I'm traveling with someone who works in a shelter for homeless youth in Australia and is very interested in the work you're doing, just like I am. Can he come along?'

'Absolutely,' Shiralee replies, and I admire her warm South African accent before hanging up. The confrontational work with Tom has demanded so much of my attention in the past few days, I didn't realize how much this errand mattered to me as well.

Looking around, I spot Tom with a pair of large headphones on, listening to CDs in the center's souvenir shop.

'You can come with me to see Shiralee at Rape Crisis tomorrow,' I tell him once he removes his headphones. To be honest, I still have my doubts that he will actually come, but I'm willing to play along.

'Cool. What did you, ah, tell her about me?'

'You know.' I shrug. 'The truth.'

'What?'

'You know, that you work in a youth shelter and that you'd find it very valuable to get an insight into the work they do at Rape Crisis.'

He exhales loudly, deeply relieved. 'Whoa, I almost had a heart attack there, when you said you'd told her the truth.'

I suddenly realize what he's referring to. 'Oh, THAT truth? No, no I didn't tell her that.'

'That's a relief,' he says with a sigh. I burst out laughing at the misunderstanding, even though it's freakishly odd to laugh at his fear that I'd tell a woman whose job it is to assist survivors of rape that he raped me. Yet there's something strangely satisfying about it, like the laughter somehow dulls the edge. So many tears have been spent on this.

A moment later, we exit the tourist center and cross the street to the bus stop. The red behemoth pulls up to the curb seconds later. My phone beeps as we sit down on the upper deck.

Beautiful ring. Let's buy it. Love you. Vidir

I feel like climbing the skyscraper reflected in Tom's sunglasses and shouting from the rooftop that I've found a wedding ring for the man I love and that I'm on my way to visit my tree in company that's proving to be healing, regardless of the past. I'd predicted a lot of emotions on this trip, but stupid happy was certainly not one of them.

'Can I ...?' Tom asks, taking the sunglasses off my nose. He polishes them with his sleeve before handing them back to me. The gesture is effortless and mundane and yet so intimate that it renders me speechless.

'As much as I like glasses, I can't stand it when they're smudged,' he explains. 'A past girlfriend wore glasses. She was lovely, calm, and so very generous. I think she was one of the first women I shed some layers with and opened up to. Our relationship was patchy, and I think she was aware that I was guarding some bones in my closet, but she still persisted with me. I just remember her being patient and *real*. At one point, when we were intimate, I was getting panicky and sweating, but she just grabbed hold of me and got me to breathe through it. She was really giving and understanding of me, but unfortunately I made various excuses and "wandered" off from that safe relationship to go and work a ski season. Reflecting on it, I think she also had some well-founded reservations about me. I was pretty reckless at that point and wasn't exactly stable. I was smoking some grass and I was dedicated to escapism, which meant I had a fairly mobile, itinerant lifestyle for a while.'

My mind goes to my own wanderings: from being a magazine columnist to a playwright, a librarian, a translator, an actress, a copywriter, a television reporter, a government official, a producer, a public speaker, a director, and a full-time writer. And that doesn't even include my time as a bartender, a car salesman, and a gogo-dancer.

The look on Tom's face is pensive. 'It's very clear to me that I can no longer harbor or hide this weight,' he continues after a brief pause. 'I thought there was enough love of myself there to be in a relationship, but I've just recently admitted to myself that I'm not there yet. I've got one hand out while having the other dragging a heavy memory behind me. I need to release my grip on it and let it go. I've been thinking that with some strength and resilience, and your forgiveness and understanding, I could battle it out, and that on some level I deserved the battle as a sort of ongoing penitence. But I'm wasting a wonderful life holding on to a big stick, ready to beat myself with it every time I make a mistake. No more excuses.'

'That goes for me too,' I admit. 'Standing still felt dangerous, it invited too much self-reflection. I too wandered off from stable and nurturing situations and to this day, I've never lived more than five years in the same place. And my CV ... it looks like someone played Twister with the Yellow Pages.'

He nods with a faint smile. 'Aren't we a pair of vagabonds? Perhaps that's why I've liked cars that I can sleep in the back of. I've owned a couple that have allowed me to "camp" in back, loving the freedom to pitch up where I wanted. One memorable night, I slept under a few cardboard boxes behind a dumpster in Edmonton in minus-seven degrees. Due to some shitty budgeting after a stint on the Alberta oilrigs, I came back to town without a cent to my name. I remember chuckling to myself though, wearing all the clothes I had and trying to sleep in the snow. Kind of symbolic, as I've never been too interested in money and I've never learned the art of saving. It's only been a short while since I faced the fact that I'm not a nine-to-five, mortgage, family, routine type of guy. With all due respect to those who are.'

As I listen, I wonder just how much of our self-image was shaped by the violence he perpetrated against me when we were teenagers. Would we each have led a more conventional life if it hadn't happened, with less foolhardiness and wanderlust? I also ponder the freedom and fearlessness that color Tom's stories and I can't help but attribute that in part to his gender. I don't know many women who would chuckle at the thought of spending a night behind a dumpster, as they would be fearful of being attacked or raped in such a situation. Again, the odds that Tom and I face will always be differently stacked, no matter how willing I am to face my fears. *Now that's a worthy challenge,* I think, smiling to myself, *changing the odds altogether. What's to say that being a woman has to mean being afraid?*

The bus meanders through streets we've never seen before. We hit the highway, framed by sky-high trees. It takes us to the other side of Table Mountain, the 'backside' not visible from the city. The beauty of the mountain is fierce, with precipitous wooded cliffs, and clouds resting on the top like whipped cream.

The bus stops in a tidy parking lot in front of a ticket booth with a straw roof. Walking through turnstiles, we enter Kirstenbosch: Cape Town's botanical gardens. Beneath our feet is a paved road that winds through the gardens. The air is thick with bird song and whispering canopies.

'Amazing ...' I mumble at the sight of a majestic cactus plant that looks like a lion's mane.

The path swerves to the right, and I catch my breath in awe as the garden unfolds before us in all its glory. A creek flows past a bright, lush lawn. Barefooted children wade in the creek, splashing and laughing. Plants, barely upright under the weight of their enormous flowers, fill sprawling flowerbeds. Soft xylophone music wafts through the air as birds strut around in the grass. A lake surrounded by tall weeds reflects the breathtaking mountain brooding over the garden. An occasional ray of sunlight penetrates the clouds and cascades down the wooded mountainside. The beauty is simply hypnotizing.

'The scent ...' I exhale after a speechless moment.

'Yes,' Tom says, stunned. 'So rich ...'

'... so fertile.'

He takes off his shoes and walks barefoot onto the lawn, where the grass is soft and swelling, like moss. The color is so green and juicy one can practically drink it. I come to a halt. In front of me is a sight I'll never forget. At the outskirts of the lawn is an oak tree. Stretching its branches fifteen meters into the air, the canopy draws its dark outline in the clouds. It proudly presides over the lower plants surrounding it. The mist in the slopes of Table Mountain adds to the prehistoric beauty in the background.

'This is paradise,' I whisper.

Tom also comes to a halt. Awestruck, we marvel at the oak and its kingdom, stretching as far as the eye can see.

'Tom?'

'Yes?'

'Have you ever eaten from the tree of knowledge?' I hear myself ask.

He looks away. When our eyes meet again, his soul is open so wide it startles me.

'Yes. I took a bite once,' he says in a quiet voice.

I know what he's referring to. *I was there too.*

Suddenly, the sun breaks through the clouds over the mountain, bathing us in golden light. My feet collapse as the tears start to trickle down my cheeks. My heart is like a helium balloon bursting out of my rib cage.

He takes a seat in the grass next to me, his eyes worried and inquisitive.

'Safe,' I whisper through the lump in my throat. 'I haven't felt safe until now. This is a divine place. Like coming home.'

He nods in respectful silence. I allow the tears to flow freely until my heart settles back in my chest. And that's when I know it. *This is the place.*

I reach into my backpack. The rock is smooth and cool in my hand. 'I think it's time.'

He swallows. Our eyes are locked as I take his hand, placing the rock in it and closing his fingers around it. He inhales sharply and starts to weep. I place my hand on top of his closed fist; his other hand forms a seal on top of mine, enclosing the hard core of the past.

Within me, everything falls silent. It takes a moment to get used to the dark. Then I see a faint but familiar sight. The door. I hear the muffled moans seeping through the keyhole along with steady squeaking.

For the thousandth time

I press down the white plastic door handle

breathe in the stench of alcohol and vomit

barely making out the bed in a faint light from the streetlamp outside the window.

The young man hunched over the girl.

His blonde hair covering her face.

For the thousandth time

I stand by the bed

and watch as Tom rapes me.

His fists digging into the mattress on either side of me,

my hand dangling lifelessly from the edge of the bed.

Hear the fleshy sound when his weight slams repeatedly into my body

and the metallic banging of the bedpost against the wall.

For the thousandth time

I note the teen posters on the walls,

the stuffed animals that still adorn the bed

the all-encompassing childhood that starkly contrasts what's happening.

I look to my guardian angels who are standing by the footboard — the confidantes I've let in on the truth and into this room, one by one. Silent and loyal, they stand by the edge of the bed, giving me strength. I meet the eyes of a friend who had no words for me when I finished the story but hugged me instead with all her heart.

For the thousandth time

I turn towards the bed
and for the first time ever
I stop Tom.
For the first time ever
he rolls his weight off me and sits up.

With strong hands, I raise myself to a sitting position in the bed. Wipe the tears from my face, the blood from my thighs, and dress the girl I used to be in a clean nightgown. Lifting her chin, I make her a promise:

You'll never be counting seconds again.

Then I open the door.

First, the guardian angels exit, one by one. If I'm not mistaken, they're accompanied by a faint flap of wings.

Tom gets up. With big, firm steps, he exits the room without looking back.

At last, I'm alone.

Ready? I ask myself.

As soon as I exit the room in my mind's eye, I let go of Tom's hand. My fingers open slowly like a lotus flower, revealing his closed fist. When I open my eyes, his cheeks are streaked with tears.

I smile.

I smile because the South African sun is hot on my skin.

I smile because I know that this moment marks the beginning of a new chapter in my life. *I emptied the room. I did it!*

And then I smile from ear to ear because suddenly, as if by divine intervention, a big fat African turkey is standing next to me. His head is bright blue, a red pouch dangles from his beak, and dark and dotted feathers cover his robust body — which seems way too large for his tiny bald head. He blinks and scrutinizes us sternly. I look up to the playwright in the sky and nod approvingly. *Nice plot twist. Things were getting too melodramatic and we needed some comic relief. Cue turkey.* I couldn't have written it better myself.

Tom blinks, wiping the tears from his cheeks with the back of his hand while looking at the bird. 'It's just not fair that the feathers don't cover their heads too,' he mutters. The turkey gives him the evil eye and doesn't seem to feel the least bit sorry for himself. On the contrary, he tries to snatch the cigarette Tom just lit up.

'You had that coming for saying that about him,' I point out as Tom defends himself from the attacks. The bird pecks angrily at his thigh and makes another attempt at the cigarette. 'What's more, he doesn't want you polluting the air in paradise, see?'

I go through my backpack and find a bag of nuts. 'Are you hungry, buddy?' Wasting no time, the bird gobbles up the nuts I sprinkle in the grass next to me. I grin guiltily at Tom. 'This is probably against the rules, don't you think? Feeding the animals?'

'Hardly if it's in self-defense,' he says, grinning back.

Having wolfed down the nuts, our ungainly new friend looks contemptuously from me to Tom and back to me, as if making up his mind whether to spare our lives or not. After a short deliberation, he turns his majestic backside to us and wobbles away. The laughter spurred by this chance meeting is most welcome, before I turn back to Tom and select my words carefully.

'I'd planned to give you the rock on Robben Island. In my mind, there was something symbolic about leaving the rock on a prison island, allowing us to walk away free. Then things got a little … sour … between us there so I changed my mind. But that's not the only reason. It's because our story deserves a good ending. It shouldn't end in a place of suffering and injustice. It deserves to end here, in paradise.'

Visibly moved, he agrees with a nod. 'At the roots of the Upside

Down Tree,' he adds.

'Good idea. Now let's go find that tree.'

Before we can stroll further into nature, Tom has to answer its call so we walk down a narrow path to a restaurant with a straw roof. I chuckle quietly.

'What?'

'Nothing. I'm just happy. And lighter, somehow.'

'I know what you mean. It's like having a helium balloon inside your chest,' Tom says.

I stop dead in my tracks.

'What?' he wonders again.

'Nothing … It's just … I had that exact same thought a few minutes ago,' I mumble. *What are the odds?* I ask myself as he disappears into the bathroom. *Does the confrontational work we're doing call for such an intense meeting of minds that our thoughts basically merge too?*

Suddenly, a cheerful voice next to me says: 'You should have your face painted.' The voice belongs to an upbeat bald man in a beige shirt with the name of a restaurant embroidered on his chest. He points to a woman wearing a tunic and a headdress, standing next to the entrance to the building. In front of her, three children are impatiently waiting to have their faces turned into a work of art.

'Nah, that's OK,' I tell the man. Judging by the queue, face paint is cool as long as you're nine years old or younger.

The man acts like he didn't hear me. 'Do a nice one,' he tells the woman, eagerly pointing at me. Not wanting to turn down this display of local hospitality, I drag myself reluctantly to the back of the line.

When Tom comes back, white dots line my forehead leading down to my left cheek. Small symbols that resemble butterflies adorn the corners of my eyes.

'You too?' the lady asks Tom. I've started to suspect she had a few puffs of a reefer this morning.

Tom's face lights up. 'Sure — could you paint something related to water?'

She gives him a stoned smile and starts to paint lines around his right eye. When we're back on the path leading to the gardens, he asks with anticipation: 'What did she do? Does it remind you of water?'

'No.'

'Not even close?'

'Does a foot remind you of water?'

'She drew a foot?' he asks, surprised.

'Stop that, you're making your foot all wrinkly,' I say, pointing to his forehead.

'She did seem just a little bit … high, didn't she?'

'Like a kite, you mean?'

The beauty of the garden silences us as we walk across the grass towards the big oak. A tingling feeling in my stomach grows stronger with every step that brings us closer to the tree, though I know it can't possibly be the Upside Down Tree. As we reach it, I rest my hand on its robust trunk and climb with my eyes to the treetop. Meanwhile, Tom bends down and picks up an acorn.

'She has lots of little babies lying around here,' he says, gesturing towards the oak.

I take the acorn from his outstretched hand. 'The Mother tree.'

He concurs. 'The Mother tree.' Pointing to a man who is carefully smearing grout on the path ahead, he adds: 'Perhaps that guy knows where to direct us.'

'The Upside Down Tree?' he repeats after Tom, getting up and wiping beads of sweat off his forehead. 'Ah yes, it's down there. In the glasshouse. You can't miss it.'

My instinct is to follow his directions and go straight down the path to find the glasshouse. Whatever that is.

'Do you mind if we wander up and take a look at that tree there first?' Tom asks me, pointing up the path in the direction of an impressive canopy that triumphs over the other foliage on the mountainside ahead. 'I've got to see the tree that all that belongs to.'

It's more than optimistic to think we'll find the tree that this particular canopy belongs to in the middle of the forest, but since our entire trip is the result of a giant leap of faith, I walk with Tom up the path without a word.

'This way,' he says, pointing to a path that leads deep into the forest. The sight makes me feel like Alice in Wonderland. The path crosses a small pond. A bridge made of carved wood is reflected in its green surface. A bench is overlooking the pond. Branches and reeds are wedged between its boards. Sun seeps through the foliage, collecting in pools of light on the occasional branch. A slanted tree forms a crooked frame around the picture. Beneath my feet, the earth is breathing.

We drink in the environment for a moment. Without a word, I start walking across the bridge. Our weight makes the wood creak.

The path twists between the trees and suddenly, Tom stops. He looks up and squints his eyes against the sun. 'It's not a single tree, Thordis,' he says, agape.

I look up. High above our heads, the branches interlace like fingers in a prayer.

'It's a community of trees,' he whispers.

The majestic canopy is the result of a collaboration. To add to my amazement, the trees are not deciduous but evergreens stretching twenty meters into the sky.

'Look, they've been trimmed back repeatedly and always grown in a different direction. Amazing,' he mutters.

I study the work of art above me and am reminded of my own words about sexual violence not only affecting survivors but the people who love them as well. To overcome it, an entire community has to grow in the same direction, trim off the misconceptions, and join their efforts.

Neither of us says a word. The wind stirs the branches in a quiet song, and my senses are open wide. Little by little, the forest intoxicates me, making my limbs heavy with nature. Tom seems just as hypnotized as I am. He sits down and leans against a tree trunk. I take a seat on the other side. For a long while, I'm part of a millipede's journey, clambering across the colorful bark and cutting across my foot. Like a fingerprint, the tree's coarse skin is patterned with winding curves in brown, orange, gray, and white.

I have no idea how long we've been sitting there when we simultaneously get up. In silence, we walk back across the bridge and down the path to where the Upside Down Tree awaits us. My mind is tranquil and calm, filled with the single notion that everything is in the right place, somehow. Even the foot on Tom's forehead is exactly where it's supposed to be.

Our walk through the garden is a wordless adventure. An Egyptian goose and her three chicks swim between water lilies on the lake, sheltered by tall reeds. Purple flowers extend on the right, tropical ferns on the left. Graceful statues rise out of the vegetation. One of them is of a mother cradling her baby. Her long body is curved around the infant, a braided necklace around her neck and a smile upon her lips. Suddenly, a ray of light breaks through the thick canopy and lights up the statue as if she were an actress on stage.

It was impressive enough already, I tell the playwright above. *Now you're just showing off.*

'This way,' Tom says. We're standing in front of a building with a stately glass roof. As I walk through the door behind him, my heart is pounding.

My first observation is that the space forms a spiral. Flowerbeds with thousands of plants form a prayer circle of sorts around a massive tree, rising like a totem pole out of the middle. The tree is about ten meters tall, almost reaching the glass ceiling. The rest of the vegetation is comprised of short plants, cacti, and shrubs, so there's no doubt who the star of the scene is. *Dare I ask if this is ...?*

The space is circular, and one can go either to the left or the right. Tom goes to the right, but I automatically go to the left. Thousands of little plastic signs stick out of the ground with the name of each plant in Latin. For a second I'm overwhelmed. How on earth am I supposed to find the Upside Down Tree in all this flora? I don't even know what it looks like.

'Thordis, come here!' Tom shouts suddenly.

'You found it?' I hurry over to him.

He's standing by a large sign made of glass. Stopping next to him, I read: THE UPSIDE DOWN TREE.

'Is it ...?' I ask, but the sentence dies on my lips.

'Yes,' he replies, and gestures with his head towards the massive tree in the heart of the spiral. 'This is it.'

Leaning my head back, I study the tree I've happily accepted as mine, thanks to a strange twist of fate. Dark-green leaves grow out of branches that seem petite compared to the sturdy trunk.

'It's called the Upside Down Tree because according to African folklore, the Great Spirit gave each of the animals a tree. The hyena received the last tree, a baobab, and was so upset that he planted it upside down,' Tom reads from the sign. 'And look, here's a map.'

The map shows the tree's journey. Baobab is the largest succulent in the world, growing only in dry areas. This seven-ton, century-old tree was hauled from the diamond mines of Limpopo in the north of the country. From there, it traveled across South Africa to end up here, in the botanical gardens of Cape Town, making it the southern-most baobab in all of Africa.

A traveler, I can't help but think. *Just like us.*

Without second thought, I step into the flowerbed. Carefully, I creep up to the baobab, making sure I don't step on any other plants. Tom follows cautiously behind me. Luckily, we're alone in the glasshouse, and I use the opportunity to kneel at the foot of the tree. He kneels next to me. The trunk reminds me of an elephant leg, grayish and studded with knots and lumps. I place one hand on it and gasp in surprise.

'What?' he whispers, also placing a hand on the tree.

'It's hard like stone,' I whisper back, baffled. 'Feel that?' I dig my fingernail as deeply into the bark as I can, but it doesn't even leave a mark.

This time it's Tom who whispers: 'I think it's time.' He takes the rock that carried the weight of our story for the past sixteen years out of his pocket and places it inside one of the knots in the bark; an almond-shaped fissure that looks like an eye, which in turn makes the rock seem like a hazel iris. It barely fits, protruding a little from the rounded edge but remarkably steady nonetheless. The outcome is like the last piece of a puzzle that finally found its place. I lean back and smile. *Thank you for seeing us. Thank you for letting our story end here, this way*. It's a silent prayer, like many others I've said today.

After having patted my tree goodbye, I sneak out of the flowerbed. Tom lingers a while longer. The sight of him kneeling by the bulging eye of the baobab, surrounded by fanged cacti and drooping branches, is forever etched into my memory.

I circle the tree, studying it from all sides. There's also a glass sign on the other side. The first tears fall from my eyes as Tom stands beside me.

'THE BAOBAB — A TREE OF LIFE,' he reads from the sign.

I lean on his shoulder and cry as we read about how the baobab is literally the tree of life, where every part of it has value to either man or animal. It's sometimes the only source of water for people and animals in a large area, casting vital shade in the deadly heat. Its leaves, seeds, and fruits are eaten by humans and animals alike, while the roots are used to dye clothes. The bark is used to make ropes, fishing nets, and medicine, while empty seed shells become food bowls and hollow trees become home to entire families. The tree of life lives up to its name, and I cry at its feet. I cry over the heavy burden of secrecy that often threatened to break me, but will from now on be carried by one of the greatest living things on earth. I cry because I finally eye the finishing line on a journey that brought me halfway across the planet and half a lifetime into the past.

'There's a sign by the entrance that says Succulent Survivors,' I realize, looking at Tom. 'We're in the house of survivors.'

His eyes are open wide as they meet mine. 'Remarkable,' he mumbles. 'Just ... remarkable.'

It truly is my tree. And for some reason, Nigel knew it.

When we exit Kirstenbosch and board the tourist bus, nippy winds blow through our hair as it's almost six o'clock. I'm satiated after an amazing day when Tom turns to me with a thoughtful expression.

'Thordis?'

'Yes?'

'Where did you keep the rock all those years?'

'In a pen jar on my desk. It's quite remarkable that I still have it, to be honest. Since you gave it to me, I've moved six times. It's gone with me from Iceland to the States and back, to Australia with stopovers in Singapore, London, Norway, and Turkey.'

'And this is where it ends up. Here, in South Africa.'

'For good.' The discovery hits me and I can't help but shake my head. 'The pen jar. It's a storage for writing materials.'

'Yes, I think we've definitely found our format,' Tom says, and the face paint around his eyes crinkles as he smiles. 'Writing has to be it.'

Suddenly, a shantytown appears on our left. A sign that points to the township reads: WASTE DROP-OFF. Fragile sheds of corrugated iron cling to the mountainside. Clotheslines cut through the settlement with colorful shirts fluttering in the wind. The name IMIZAMO YETHU is hand-painted on a container. On the street, an old lady is resting her weary bones on a plastic crate. In front of her is a small table with goods for sale. I spot two signs that say REAL SHOP, prompting the question of what an unreal shop might be. The evening sun shines brightly on the people sitting out on their steps or gathering around parked cars at the outskirts of the township. An armed police officer with a cap stands by a rusty police car, watching the people.

'From what I've read about Cape Town, township tours are one of the biggest tourist activities here,' I tell Tom. 'They may have their positive sides, but I can't stand the thought of going on an organized trip to gawk at people like they're on parade.'

'Yeah, poverty as a tourist attraction,' he says with a shudder.

Imizamo Yethu disappears but my thoughts linger with its residents. I wonder how many of the township's women are survivors of rape like me, but will never have their pain acknowledged the way I have? Who, due to their background, will not have the same chance to be heard and seen as I do? Whose daily battles leave them with no time to dwell on the past? It strikes me how even the most traumatizing event of my life is still a testament to my privilege. I've been able to publicly discuss my status as a rape survivor, without being ostracized from my community. I've been able to criticize men's violence against women, without being stoned. I've been supported by my family, not murdered to 'restore their honor'. I've received respect and recognition for something that my fellow survivors around the world are whipped, shamed, and killed for speaking up about. And here I am, having a voluntary meeting with my perpetrator, whom I wasn't forced to marry as a result of his violence towards me.

I shudder and note how chilly shadows have started to creep up the sides of the Lion's Head. Tom puts on a scarf and I pull an old shawl out of my backpack, spreading it over my legs.

'Oh my God, is that …?' he asks, staring at the shawl, which is bright-orange and decorated with stenciled pictures of lobsters.

I look down at my lap. 'Yes, I've had this since I was a teenager. Do you remember it?'

'You had that wrapped around you like a skirt one night when I met you downtown, in 1997. You were wearing a red jacket.' He's talking fast, fascinated like he just met an old friend.

I spread the shawl so it covers his legs as well. 'Well, this sure is a trusted, old companion,' I say, pleased. 'It's traveled with me across the globe and has been used as a skirt, a scarf, a towel, and a tablecloth. Imagine that — and never once have I washed it.'

Tom's face goes pale. 'Never?' he asks, looking with disgust at the shawl across his legs.

I burst into laughter. 'Gotcha!'

He starts to laugh too, relieved that he doesn't have twenty years' worth of bacteria in his lap. We climb off the bus at the Waterfront, lighter than we were before. Our ways part when Tom goes to find chocolates for Nigel as a token of our appreciation for suggesting Kirstenbosch to us.

The mall named after Queen Victoria has shops on both sides and stalls in the middle of the walkway. The stalls in Icelandic malls usually sell cheap merchandise like t-shirts or hair products. But not in South Africa. Here, they have diamond kiosks with gems in piles like candy. To think, I always believed Iceland to be a country of extremes with its erupting volcanoes and frosty glaciers, pitch-black winters, and summers where the sun never sets — but South Africa takes the prize with its lavish natural resources and wildlife next to gut-wrenching poverty and systematic violence. The extremes are spelled out on a sign in a jewelry store that says 50% OFF ALL DIAMONDS THIS MONTH! A diamond sale. *Now I've seen it all.*

It's waiting for me inside the store: the ring. It's delicate, with ethically mined diamonds that are cut vertically instead of the typical brilliant cut. As a result, they look like glass splinters that let the light through as opposed to a crystal that reflects it in different directions. There's something fascinating about the transparency. As a symbol of loyalty, I find it very fitting, representing the transparency in a marriage where neither person has anything to hide. And what's more beautiful than letting light through, helping it spill forward? There's something simply cool about a diamond that doesn't need to capture the light to prove that it's a diamond. *It's all about knowing yourself*, I think as I try the ring on. As soon as it slips into place on my finger, we make a pact: *People can think whatever they want but we both know you're a real gem, baby.*

I study the ring I intend to bear for decades to come as a symbol of my devotion to my wonderful man. Adele's voice echoes from the store's speaker system: *'Just take it all, with my love.'*

'I'll take it,' I tell the assistant. *With my love.*

Tom bumps into me as soon as I exit the jewelry store with the ring in a bag and a goofy smile on my face. Suddenly, I explode with hysterical giggling and have to lean forward to catch my breath.

'That was a massive step,' he says in an understanding voice. 'You just bought yourself a wedding ring!'

'As if this day wasn't epic enough already,' I mumble. *From now on I'll never forget April 2nd.*

'Can you help me out with something?' he asks.

'What's that?'

'Picking out a card for Vidir?'

A moment later, we're frowning in front of a completely useless selection of cards in a bookstore. Given that Vidir is not a lovesick zebra, a birthday boy, nor a father-to-be, there's no card that's even close to appropriate. I hold up a soppy card of two giraffes kissing.

Tom gives me the evil eye. 'Ha ha. Very funny.'

Soon, we walk past the souvenir shop with the towering beaded Mandela. 'Perhaps they sell cards?' Tom says, casting a hopeful glance inside. 'I'm having a look.'

'Can you do one thing for me, first?' I ask, handing him my phone before taking a stand next to the beaded giant.

'Serious?' Behind his inquisitive look is a broad grin.

'Dead serious,' I reply, determined. 'I'm not above this any more.'

The truth is that the trust that we've built between us in the past few days has given me the courage to be silly around Tom. My ego no longer crumbles under jokes at my expense. When he takes the shot, it's hard to tell who's smiling wider — the statue or me.

Shortly thereafter, we're comfortably seated on a bolstered bench in a nearby restaurant. The menu arrives in the shape of two large chalkboards perched up on chairs next to our table by a thin waiter wearing glasses. I realize to my horror that it's the only copy of the menu.

'What do the other dinner guests do while we're making up our minds?' I ask, fraught with choice anxiety.

'They wait,' the waiter replies with a smile.

'They wait,' I repeat, perplexed. In the western societies I've lived in, having to wait for food is unthinkable, as evidenced by fast-food chains where minimal time is spent on this underestimated primary need: eating. Here, however, a packed restaurant kindly waits during peak hour while I decide whether I want the chicken paella or the pork belly. Amazing. *After all, life isn't going anywhere*, I conclude. *It's here and now.*

I swallow a delicious mouthful of pork while Tom gets to work on his chickpea curry. The pork skin is salty, crunchy, and fat. He looks at it, curious.

'Help yourself,' I tell him.

'You know I'm vegetarian.'

'You're also dying to try it. I can spot it from a mile away.'

'I always did like the crackling, as we call it. But no,' he says with reluctance. 'Not a chance.'

'Why not?'

'Just 'cause. Meat has not passed through these lips for years.'

'I hadn't smoked for years until I took a puff from your cigarette the other day.'

'This is different.'

'Is not.'

'Is too.'

'I dare you.'

He rolls his eyes. 'What are we, twelve?'

'No, we're adults on a trip so crazy, we've hardly told a soul the truth about it. In order to come here, we had to do the impossible: to trust each other. And now, after all that, you're telling me a bite of pork skin is unthinkable?'

Without further ado, Tom pops the pork in his mouth. He grimaces. 'Way too salty,' he moans. 'What a disappointment.'

'Congratulations,' I say as I raise my glass with a wink. 'You just did the unthinkable. Twice in the same week, even.'

He shudders and gulps down a glass of water. Then he pulls a pretty brown box of chocolates out of his backpack and places it on the table between us. 'What do you say we write a note to Nigel, to accompany the chocolates?'

'Great idea.' I tear an empty sheet of paper out of the notebook in my bag.

'Let's write on either side of it, OK?' he suggests.

I nod, folding the paper.

Dear Nigel,

Visiting the Upside Down Tree — the tree of life — was an unforgettable and meaningful experience. If you ever visit Iceland, drop me a line. Take care of yourself and thank you dearly for your valuable help, my friend.

With warm regards,
—Thordis Elva

I shove the pen and paper across the table.

'I'm not going to read yours until I'm done writing mine,' Tom says, and turns the paper over. He jots down a few lines before shoving it back across the table to me.

'Funny,' I exclaim after reading it. 'We say the exact same things except you use the word "baobab" while I say "the Upside Down Tree".'

Soon, we're sitting at our local pub around the corner from the Ritz. The wonders of the day sparkle in my mind, bright like supernovas. Gazing at the night sky, I'm sure that gravity has a lesser pull on me than before.

'I'll never forget this day,' Tom says, staring into the darkness.

I watch the smoke from his cigarette coil in the air like a blue snake. 'Strange.'

'What is?'

'All this emotional intimacy, after so many distant, analytical years.'

'Yeah, it is strange.'

Only never to meet again, I conclude in my mind. Not too long ago, it would've felt like a feasible endpoint, but now the thought is accompanied by a sharp, unexpected sting.

I'm exhausted but happy when I stick the key in the lock of my hotel room and let myself into the moldy smell I've grown almost fond of. When emptying my pockets on the nightstand, I make a note of the missing rock. *Unburdened*. I feel so light that the sheet hardly crumples beneath me when I sneak into bed. As I close my eyes, the empty teenage room in my head is being refurnished with Paradise's birds, sheer diamonds, and a white butterfly trail surrounding the tree of life.

From Tom's diary

Tuesday

It was lovely to just stop. I shuffled around a bit on the brittle bark to find a flat spot so I could lean back on the base of a large tree. Looking up at the canopy, I smiled at how something that looked from a distance to be a singular rich green tree was actually a collection of trees. A tight-knit family sharing the sun.

I closed my eyes, inhaled deeply, and then let my shoulders hang loosely and my spine mould into the base of the tree. I 'checked in' with myself, just like I've practised at The Treehouse, my Wednesday-night meditation back home.

Everything felt so purposeful once we'd walked through the gates to that place, almost as if we were being carried by something greater than ourselves. There was a humming richness about those gardens that made the green look even greener. The earthen smells were so invigorating that I swear I could taste the dark soil below us.

Whatever the transcendental presence in that immense garden, it felt similarly 'touched', just like the calming space we found in the church the other day. Any intellect or logic I lean upon was defied by a gentle fatalistic feeling, and whatever was gracefully buzzing about had a divinity that I didn't so much need to label as to acknowledge and be comforted by. I felt light. I was simultaneously full and empty.

I registered the firmness of the tree against my back, the warm filtered sunlight on my skin, and the small, smooth rock against my thigh in my pocket. I allowed the sensation to grow into a thought and I reflected on what happened when we were sitting on the grass this morning.

I was glad she surprised me with the timing. The rock was as I remembered, smooth and elliptical, and cool when she put it in my palm.

I remembered the weighty significance of that small rock and what it had represented for Thordis. Initially an innocent thing plucked from a local rock pool, it had grown into an anchor. She'd told me that returning the rock to me meant forgiveness for her.

The small ceremony on the grass felt like an act of release, and with it a beginning and an end. I was happy to take it from her, wanting to feel the weight of meaning the rock had embodied.

I knew she also wanted for me to part with it, for it to be returned to where it came from. I saw myself throwing it as far as possible out into the ocean. But first I wanted to sit with it for a while. That rock had been in her room for years.

I know we're committed to leaving everything resolved and set free, so that meant the rock was soon to be placed by the Upside Down Tree. I felt a fleeting urge to hold onto that little familiar stone, but then I thought about how pissed Thordis would be if I kept a grip on it.

Allowing the rock to live momentarily in my pocket, I returned to focusing on the sounds around us. The wind rustling the branches above and the chirps of unfamiliar birds. Sitting there, I was enjoying some of the quietest inner space I'd found in years.

With each day passing this week, our time travel into the past seems to be easing a long-held disquiet about the future, and today was no different. Even in that moment, sitting amongst those trees, I felt like I was growing, too ... and it felt good.

The rock was given away shortly after that. We were both kneeling at the base of the Upside Down Tree, speaking quietly. I saw to my right a small rib-like opening in the bark. Its curves looked like a cross between an eye and a set of lips. I instinctively reached for Thordis's hand, my other hand holding the rock. There were no thoughts, no wondering if the rock would fit on that tiny ledge. There was no background noise, no second-guessing. Holding it in between two fingers, I placed the rock flat on the small smooth platform.

It balanced there perfectly, looking almost like it was going to be swallowed.

Looking at it resting there ... it was the most symbolic thing I had ever seen.

The effect of disarming that rock today feels clean and permanent, and nothing is left in our pockets. But this high and light feeling ... a part of me wants to tug on my bootlaces and remind myself that I'll be going home at some point. And when I do, I will also have to clean out my drawers and cupboards. I just need to remind myself that there might still be some work to do.

Perhaps some judgment will always be with me ... I don't know. I know there is more than that small rock anchoring me to my act. There's a chance I've viewed this as a simple equation that neatly balances itself out.

Maybe it's a case of doing what I can, just like the serenity prayer.

And then truly acknowledging what can't be done.

I'll never be able to change what I did to her. That's a simple truth. But somewhere in between the 'why' and my respect for myself, I don't doubt I'll find a solid place to carry what I need to.

Maybe look back at these pages two weeks after returning home. *How do you feel now, Tom?*

Move on and forgive yourself, if it feels right.

Day Eight

3 April 2013

As I sleepily open one eye on the morning of my last full day in South Africa, the amazement over my whereabouts has given way to worries about whether I've run out of toothpaste or not. That's life. In the end, the little things always win.

It's just past nine o'clock when I ask the receptionist in the Ritz lobby to call a taxi to take us to Rape Crisis. Tom is standing next to me, freshly showered and a lot less formal than me, wearing gray trousers and a red t-shirt. Nigel puts the phone down just as we step inside his shop. 'Good morning, dear friends,' he says in his usual warmhearted manner. 'What can I do you for?'

'We just wanted to thank you for tipping us off with the Upside Down Tree yesterday, and to give you a little token of our appreciation,' Tom says, handing him the box of chocolates.

For a moment, Nigel stares confused at the box. Then his well-groomed face lights up in a radiant smile.

'Was it good?' he asks, looking at me.

'It was unforgettable. I'm so glad you mistook me for someone else. It ensured a magical time,' I answer, aware of the disconnect between my calm voice and my pounding heart.

The smile on Nigel's lips is genuine as he cocks his head and asks me: 'You sure that wasn't you? I've got a good memory when it comes to people. Never forget a face.'

His words cause every hair on my body to stand on end, but Tom breaks into a good-natured laugh. 'I hope you enjoy them,' he says, pointing to the chocolates.

A little while later, Tom and I are sitting in a taxi on our way to the City Bowl, as it's called. The naming is no coincidence, as the center of Cape Town is shaped like a bowl, surrounded by Devil's Peak, Table Mountain, Lion's Head, and the butt of the lion, commonly called Signal Hill. The City Bowl is very unlike Sea Point, the yuppie hotel neighborhood I chose in my search for the safest part of the city. Here, we see mundane things like elementary schools, hospitals, and buses. It's good to finally feel grounded by graffiti and locals on their way to work, as opposed to whitewashed tourism. Having grown up in a middle-class family, I feel decidedly out of place in privileged neighborhoods with their private pools and uniformed personnel.

'Remember how I told you that they leave words of wisdom on my pillow every day at the guesthouse? I've got to show you what was waiting for me when I got back yesterday,' Tom says enthusiastically, handing me a small note.

'When you eat the beautiful fruit of great trees, remember to thank the wind,' I read out loud. 'No way!'

'Huge smiles when I saw that one. Couldn't wait to tell you.'

After finding our destination, Tom and I are buzzed in through a gate into a small courtyard in front of a terraced house. I stare at the doorknob of a brightly painted door, unsure of whether I should let myself in or wait for someone else to invite me inside. Standing behind me, Tom seems smaller than usual, somehow.

Seconds later, the door opens and we're eye to eye with a young woman.

'Good morning. We're here to see Shiralee,' I say in a nervous voice.

'Come in,' she says, and steps aside to let us in. 'I'll let her know.'

The lobby is bright, with a large window to the right. On the wall behind the receptionist's desk is a watercolor painting of a naked woman, reclining on a bed. The eroticism is obvious. *Odd choice of art for a survivors' center,* I can't help thinking. Though survivors react to rape in different ways, things of a sexual nature almost always take on a different meaning than they had before the violence occurred. For some survivors the slightest reminder of sex, such as this painting, can evoke a strong and difficult reaction.

I instinctively catch my breath when I meet Tom's eyes, wide and fraught with meaning. 'What?' I whisper.

Shaking his head, he points in amazement to a book sitting on a shelf on the left side of the desk. I cock my head and read the title: *Power of One*, by Bryce Courtenay.

'Incredible,' he mutters. 'What a coincidence.'

'We're way past coincidences,' I whisper back.

Shiralee turns out to be a softly spoken woman in her fifties. She's wearing a black shirt, long, fluttering pants, and flip-flops.

'Can I offer you some coffee?' she asks, and Tom and I accept in unison. We brief her about our professional backgrounds while she pours us a cup each. Out of the corner of my eye, I note that Tom's movements are unusually cautious, like he's walking on eggshells again. Listening with interest to our introductions, Shiralee shows us to an interview room. Steaming cups in hand, Shiralee and I automatically take a seat in two armchairs, while Tom settles into a fake-leather loveseat opposite us.

'Our vision is to support and empower rape survivors through the criminal justice system to reduce secondary trauma within the system, ultimately enabling more survivors to report rape,' Shiralee answers when I ask her about the vision of Rape Crisis. 'We have very few paid staff, but we have a large group of volunteers who get three months' mandatory training about the justice system, reactions to trauma, and support measures for survivors of sexual violence. We place great emphasis on the training program, to enable the volunteer to support the survivor through a very difficult process.'

'Are there any men amongst your volunteers?' Tom asks cautiously.

For a moment, Shiralee's lips are pressed into a thin line. 'All the male volunteers we've trained so far have disappeared quickly. It's a great loss, because we really need to get through to men, especially within the police. Police officers need to learn that it is unacceptable to tell a prostitute that she can't be raped or to tell a drunk woman to go home and sleep it off before pressing charges. It takes a lot of courage to walk into a police station and charge someone with rape,' she says empathetically. 'You don't tell someone who has mustered that kind of courage to go home and come back later.'

I agree wholeheartedly and tell her that in Iceland, seventy per cent of all rape charges are dismissed on average, a statistic that has been deemed unacceptable by the UN and many human-rights organizations. 'There are two people at the attorney's office who go through the evidence and decide whether the case goes to court or not. According to Icelandic law, the case has to be likely to result in a conviction or it's dismissed.'

'It's the same here,' Shiralee says. We shake our heads, equally outraged that judicial power has been transferred, it seems, from the judges to bureaucrats who now have the power to determine whether or not survivors get to see the inside of a court room. I've developed quite a fondness for this new, likeminded friend of mine.

'Can I ask, is it staffed twenty-four hours here?' Tom asks, reminding me of his presence.

'No, not any more. We used to be open 24/7, but now we close at 4.30. After that, we have a telephone hotline.' She explains the procedure for a typical phone call and how the first question is whether or not the survivor needs an ambulance. If not, he or she is urged to go to the hospital to get a rape kit done. 'We explain in detail why it's important that they get a medical and forensic examination. The fact is that to some survivors, it feels like another invasion altogether, to have their private parts examined by a stranger right afterwards,' Shiralee says. 'One of our survivors had been brought up in a very conservative way and had never spoken of sex before. She couldn't bring herself to tell the doctor that her attacker had raped her orally, not vaginally. The doctor assumed it was vaginal rape and only took samples from there, where nothing was found, of course.' She shakes her head.

'In the University Hospital of Reykjavík, we have an emergency clinic for survivors of rape and sexual assault where they do forensic examinations and offer medical assistance like you're describing. Unfortunately, they've suffered painful budget cutbacks and now they can no longer afford to do a screening for HIV or Hepatitis C,' I tell her.

Shiralee's jaw literally drops. 'But that's what survivors are most worried about!'

'I know! It's hard to comprehend how it's gotten to this.'

'Here, the next step after the examination is to prepare the survivor for the justice proceedings which typically take four to five years.'

Now it's my turn to gape in surprise. 'Why so long?'

'In most cases, capturing the offender takes a very long time. The sex-crime division of the police is understaffed and underfunded, dealing with an overwhelming number of accumulated cases.'

'I've read about South Africa being the rape capital of the world,' I say in a cautious voice, unsure of how Shiralee will react to the dubious title.

'Oh we are. Without a doubt,' she replies, so straightforward that it sends shivers down my spine.

'Why?'

'There's no simple answer to that question. This country is still healing the wounds caused by decades of apartheid. Apartheid is the most extreme form of patriarchy.' Shiralee puts her cup down. 'Sure, things have changed in the legislation. People say we've got this great constitution, but it doesn't speak to the law. There's still tremendous poverty. If you look at where people live, the lines are still there, dividing the neighborhoods. More black people have started moving into affluent neighborhoods, but that's it. Nothing else has changed, really. That's the problem of this country. It's full of people who feel utterly powerless after hundreds of years of oppression. Some people are desperate enough to snatch power in whatever way they can. That's what rape is about, it's about power and control. Skin color has nothing to do with it and perpetrators are black and white, just like the survivors.'

'What about infant rape?' I ask her. 'What drives people to do such a thing?'

'That's also about control, even if it's just over a little baby,' Shiralee answers. 'And then there's the widespread belief that having sex with a virgin cures HIV. Three-week-old babies have been raped around these parts. By adult men.'

Tom lets out a quiet moan that reflects my feelings perfectly: outrage and grief.

'We also have a big problem when it comes to underage offenders. Children imitate what they see around them. They see rape all around them. Then they simply copy that behavior.'

'In Iceland, we recently started a support measure where specialists offer treatment to children who show inappropriate sexual behavior. Including kids who molest other kids.'

'We could use something like that here,' she says, pensive.

'Your volunteers, are they survivors themselves?' Tom asks.

'Some are, but we screen them very carefully to make sure they're doing this job to help other survivors, not simply to heal their own wounds.'

Tom meets her eye. 'What about perpetrators, do you know of any services for them?' His voice sounds a little strained.

Shiralee wrinkles her forehead. 'Yes, I think so. But that's out of my territory so I frankly don't know much about it.'

'Where I come from, government institutions often fail to collaborate on the issue of combatting violence, which means that effort and money is sometimes unwisely invested and without proper oversight,' I tell Shiralee. 'Luckily, three ministries joined their efforts recently with the aim of preventing sexual violence and I was fortunate enough to work with them. This is the fruit of our collaboration and it's being taught in schools across the country.'

Curious, she accepts from me a DVD I pull out of my bag.

'It's a short film about the importance of getting consent for all sexual activity, to ensure that sex is a positive and mutual experience for those who have it,' I add. 'It's in Icelandic, but your copy has English subtitles.'

Shiralee thanks me and gives us a copy of Rape Crisis's Annual

Report in return. On the first page, the Chairperson of Rape Crisis confirms that South Africa has some of the highest reported rape statistics in the world and a province that is home to a city dubbed the Cape of Rape.

> *South African society, its culture and its institutions have been profoundly affected by the institutionalized dehumanization imposed by the apartheid system as well as the levels of force used, on the one hand to entrench these policies and, on the other hand, to resist them. In this way, the system traumatized an entire nation. Every person in South Africa has been affected by the violence, structural and physical, of apartheid in one form or another. At its worst, this continues to play out in a profound disrespect for human life and the integrity of individual human beings and an attitude of impunity where the consequences of violence are concerned, which in turn causes more violence.*

Because hate begets hate, I remind myself. Nelson Mandela's words cross my mind: 'Courageous people do not fear forgiving, for the sake of peace.'

We're standing next to a locked glass cabinet stuffed with different publications when Tom says: 'That belongs in there,' with strained cheeriness. He's pointing to a book whose spine reads in large letters: MAN.

'Yes, that's a good book,' Shiralee replies politely.

'Locked up, I mean,' Tom adds. The ensuing silence is thicker than tar, until he adds: 'Excuse me. I might wait outside for a taxi and grab some fresh air. Thank you so much for the time, Shiralee.' I watch him disappear, wondering just how challenging it was for him to breathe the air between these walls, battling the feeling that *Man should be locked up.* I decide not to go after him as I know there's nothing I can do. This is something he has to face on his own.

'What is the prevalence of men being raped here in South Africa?' I ask Shiralee as the door closes behind Tom.

'One in every five South African men is raped at some point in his lifetime.'

For a moment, I'm dumbstruck. 'One in five? I've never heard of such widespread sexual violence against men. They're raped by other men, then?'

'Yes, almost without exception,' Shiralee answers. 'And some are attacked more than once.'

'Yes, I've read studies that show that the odds of being raped again increase substantially once you've been victimized,' I respond.

'It makes sense,' Shiralee says. 'After being raped, the survivor's defense mechanisms are damaged, even destroyed in some cases.'

'And if perpetrators are hunting for easy prey, it'd make sense that they'd seek out people who've already been broken,' I add. My mind goes to those who were violent towards me, after Tom. *Did they spot my cracks?*

Shiralee's handshake is firm and warm as I thank her for the chat, which has exceeded two hours at this point. I'm lacking words to outline the importance of her work so I make do with thanking her for having been so generous with her time.

Tom is nowhere to be seen until I let myself out of the fence surrounding the house. He's sitting by an iron fence a little further down the street. I take a seat next to him and let out a deep breath.

He hesitates before gesturing with his head at Rape Crisis: 'How was that, for you?'

'Educational and informative, just like I'd hoped. How was it for you?'

'I'll give you an answer to that when we're sitting down somewhere with peace and quiet,' he answers in a hoarse voice.

'Was it that hard?'

'Yes, it was.'

We decide to walk to the nearest bus stop and climb aboard a bus with 'Cape Town City' on it. It is crowded with women with elaborate braids and solemn faces, sitting in silence. Next to me, Tom is also quiet and deflated, somehow.

'I'm almost done with my life story,' I tell him. 'Want to hear the rest?'

'For sure,' he says with a faint smile. 'We're not giving up now.'

I fast-forward through a tumultuous relationship I had in my twenties and the tough separation that resulted. I tell him about the humiliating period that ensued when I had to move in with my parents again, penniless and heartbroken, but also the freedom that came with having nothing left to lose. I quietly illustrate how hard it was to move back into the scene of the crime, my old teenage room. I was curled up on the floor in a sobbing heap when my mother grabbed my shoulders tightly and whispered: 'We need to find a way to bless this room, honey.' Then she waved her hands, humming softly like she did to soothe me when I was little and woke up from a bad dream. With her eyes closed and her arm sticking out in the air, the quiet chant flickered between the walls and filtered into me, somewhere between my ribs. Her sorcery was efficient, because two years later I'd written a 270-page book about sexual violence within those very walls. 'For the second time in my life, an event that took place in that same room transformed my existence, with the radical effect the book had on my career.'

'Sounds like you found your voice there.'

'And myself, somewhere amongst the ruins. That's when I met

Vidir. We had an amazing summer, full of love and sleepless nights. He was a patient listener to my rants about sexual violence during the writing process. After the publishing of my book, letters came pouring in from people who had experienced rape or abuse but were too ashamed, or too entrapped in silence, to face it. Their stories were jaw-dropping, and their resilience and strength remain my biggest inspiration.' My eyes fall upon a girl two seats over, with her hands in her lap and a serious expression on her face. I turn to Tom and add: 'I've come to believe that the toughest creature on earth is the teenage girl.'

'I remember when I read your email about your book and how it included the story of what I did to you, the computer screen started swaying from side to side,' he tells me. 'It was hard to focus, but I finished the email and quickly closed the window, paid at the internet café and left, feeling nauseous, uncoordinated, and heavy with self-loathing and disbelief. Shock, as you say. But shortly thereafter, I came to a turning point. I had realized that I did commit the crime, I *am* the person in your book, and you have every right to tell of that night however you see fit. And I must read it and re-live it and own it and be sorry for it and deal with whatever results from you talking about it. In coming to this point, there was a new feeling.' The expression on his face softens. 'It was one of ... relief. Relief that you had been able to express and talk of the hell I put you through. Relief that someone as strong as you can reveal themselves and their trials and offer other victims solace ... while helping people to understand how disgustingly brutal and soulless a crime rape is. Relief that it was out there, somewhere ... and that I was powerless in trying to bury it all. Relief that I had not been named as your perpetrator. And yet also relief that maybe I wouldn't remain anonymous. As you said, being scared for years is not healthy.'

The bus stops close to Greenmarket Square, and we get off. In the middle of the plaza is a large stage. Loud music starts to blare as we sit down at an Italian restaurant by the square, and I gesture for Tom to move his chair closer to mine, so we can hear each other. A waitress in a laced shirt tells us that it's a sound-check for tonight. 'For the Cape Town International Jazz festival,' she shouts, and takes our order for oven-baked vegetarian pizzas.

'Sounds good,' Tom says. His tanned skin seems even darker in the sunlight and he pulls out his sunglasses just as the drinks arrive at our table.

'So, there's no peace or quiet here but at least we're sitting down now,' I say, speaking loudly into his ear to compensate for the jazz singer. 'Want to share what Rape Crisis felt like for you?'

'At first, it felt like this,' he says, lifting one arm to reveal a huge sweat stain. 'For the first few minutes, I was looking at myself from the outside. It was like a full-blown panic attack, heart pounding and sweat pouring out while I sat there questioning myself and what the hell gave me the right to be even sitting there, under that roof, in that space ... that safe space.' He takes a sip of his water and thinks for a moment. 'Hypocrite, liar, rapist: such labels were bouncing around my mind. It took a while, but I managed to slow down and stop judging myself. When I was calm, that's when I could start contributing to the conversation. It was certainly something to witness, you and Shiralee discussing everything and questioning one another. I guess I just haven't seen you in your professional shoes, discussing policies, forensic testing, education.' He looks into his glass while formulating his words. 'I want to be a part of this, Thordis. I want to be comfortable in this space, not feeling part of the problem but a part of the solution.'

His words lit up the deserted teenage room in my mind that is rapidly becoming a sanctuary.

'I made many discoveries when I'd calmed down enough to think rationally,' he continues. 'If we're going to go public with our story, then I feel I truly want to know more about what survivors go through … I need to know more. Bloody terrifying, but I learnt something … about the "other side" of sexual violence. It's crucial that places like that exist. Just like telling your story out loud is incredibly important, talking through the chain of events and filling in what actually happened. Like you did, in the email you sent me some time ago.'

I know exactly to which email he's referring. I wrote it after Tom claimed that there hadn't been any 'cognitive thought process' on his end when he decided to rape me. Not convinced, I replied by putting forth a detailed description of the events of that night to underline just how many decisions he had to make to complete the deed. Everything from undressing me when I was gravely ill to protecting himself with a condom. 'You didn't react well to that email, though.'

He frowns. 'No? How did I react?'

The words still sting. 'You accused me of putting you on the stand for a crime you'd long ago confessed to.'

He flinches a little. 'Yes, I did, didn't I? What a selfish reaction.'

I shrug. 'You were scared.'

'Forgive me, Thordis, it wasn't right to say such things to you.'

'I already have, Tom.'

In more ways than you know.

After lunch, we go back to the jewelry store, where I purchase the ring that will seal my marriage to my soul mate. 'Congratulations,' Tom says when we step out of the store, heading for the bus stop across the street. 'Now there's nothing stopping you from marrying that incredible man of yours.' He whips off his backpack and fishes the map out of it. 'And now for our next destination …'

My ears are still ringing from the sound-check we'd just endured on the plaza and all of a sudden, I know exactly what I want to do. 'You know, Tom, I'm really not up for more wind, with all due respect to Table Mountain. To be honest, I'd like to go to the beach, where we can chill out and have a conversation without having to shout at one another.'

He looks up from the map, surprised and happy. 'I'm so glad you said that. I was thinking the exact same thing.'

'Pretty soon we won't even have to talk, any more. All we'll need to do is look at each other and nod.'

He folds the map up and puts it in his backpack. 'This may sound silly, Thordis, but I've been wanting to have our picture taken, together.' Blushing, he quickly adds: 'I think deep down, I wanted proof that this really happened, you know?' He shrugs. 'Anyway, I'm ridding myself of that idea. I've got plenty of pictures from this week in my head.'

I understand him perfectly. Neither the purpose of this trip nor the connection between us can be captured in a photo; least of all a sandal-clad, chummy, summer-vacationy photo. Yet I would like a picture too. 'There's got to be an opportunity that isn't terribly awkward, don't you think?' I say, hesitant. 'As long as we're not sitting by a candlelit table at a restaurant, smiling stiffly to the camera like we're on some messed-up date.' I recall that we're on our way to the beach so I add: '… and as long as I'm not in my bikini.'

'Don't flatter yourself,' he says teasingly, just as the bus appears.

My cheeks flush when I realize what he means. 'What?! No! That's not what I meant! Christ! I wasn't insinuating that you want a bikini picture of me!' I practically yell at him.

'No?' he asks, still in that teasing voice.

'No, it's got nothing to do with you! I ... for crying out loud, I've had a kid! This is a post-baby body!'

Despite having yelled at him about one of my most personal hang-ups in public in one of the most commonly spoken languages in the world, all I reap is a look of disbelief on his face. *Great. Here I am, letting it all hang out and he's not even convinced.* I turn away, frustrated with myself. I made it sound like I'd fallen victim to some ridiculous, sexist beauty standard. No wonder he doesn't buy it, he knows me better than that. But I'm sure as hell not going to clarify that my awkwardness has less to do with the changes motherhood brought on, and more to do with how my body has changed since Tom last saw it. Why the hell do I even care? Am I being self-conscious because he remarked that my looks haven't changed, as I know that isn't true for every inch of my body? *Oh vanity. What a fucking drag you are.*

The bus stops in front of us, and I stride onboard. The seat I choose on the upper deck is hot from the sun, matching my cheeks. Tom gets into the seat next to me and says in a comforting voice: 'Don't forget who you're talking to. I'm the guy who had laser treatment to be able to take his shirt off, remember.'

Looking at him from the corner of my eye, I sigh. 'So we both have our hang-ups.'

'The best thing to do is to say it out loud, laugh at it, and move on,' he says with a grin.

'You're a fast learner, Stranger.'

'I'm thinking about stealing that and making it my own, actually,' he says, and leans back into his seat.

Minutes later, we climb off the bus at Camps Bay. It's late afternoon, the sun is hot, and the beach is crawling with people. As we walk down to the shore, my thoughts are on the emotional remnants of the past I share with Tom. This time around, I'm determined to leave no loose ends, nothing that can be allowed to fester. Unsure of how to word my thoughts, I speak with hesitation. 'Shame is a feeling that bears no fruit. It's a breeding ground for destruction, does nothing but silence you and stunt your emotional growth. Anger is an active feeling and can even be constructive, as an outlet. But not shame. If you harbor shame, that's where you need to be working on yourself, to treat the cancer that it is.'

He nods, and I know he understands what I'm trying to say. The paralyzing effects of shame are all too familiar to him. We come to a halt amongst kids playing in the waves and families building sandcastles. A second after Tom's backpack hits the sand, so does mine. Our shoes land in a pile, his shirt next to my dress. Finally, we're standing opposite one another wearing nothing but swimwear.

'Fuck shame,' I whisper.

Without further ado, we run into the water. Tom takes a swim but I'm content with wading in the freezing water up to my knees, which in turn drives my shoulders up to my ears. Refreshing, nonetheless.

After getting our fill of salty splashes, we walk back onto the shore and towards the rocks we climbed a few days earlier.

'Of course,' I hear Tom say when he sees the tattoo on the small of my back. 'Now I remember.'

On our way, we pass a couple in their forties engrossed in their smartphones, side by side yet light years away from each other. Meanwhile, the man walking next to me leads a life that's far removed from mine in every way possible, and yet he's closer to me at this moment than most other people I've met.

He squints his eyes and gazes at the sky. 'We ought to be able to see the green flash when the sun sets.'

'The green flash?'

'Yes, when the sun slips down behind the horizon and the last rays shine through the surface of the ocean, there's a green flash. It's very brief — if you blink you can miss it.'

After throwing our clothes back on, we climb up on a nearby cliff. The rock is warm under our bare feet, and my heart beats heavily in my chest when we sit down and gaze out over the golden sea. Beneath us, a retriever plays happily on the shore, shaking water from his glittering fur with gusto.

Tom gestures with his head towards the ocean. 'I brought a wetsuit, to be able to bodysurf here.'

'Bodysurf?'

'If you know the right technique, you don't need a surfboard to be able to surf, you can use your own body,' he explains. 'The waves today aren't good for that, though. They're too ... straight.' He turns to me with a more serious expression. 'It's something that I've learnt, that I need daily physical exercise for at least half an hour. If I don't, I can feel myself getting tense and impatient. I'm hyper-sensitive about getting to this point, and there is an element of selfishness that I hate about being ... pent up, or feeling like I need to expel something. For me, movement is necessary for a balanced head.'

I look at him — a man who has developed a workout system to defend against himself. Yet I don't believe him to be destructive. I see no blood-thirst in him. At this very moment, I trust him wholeheartedly.

'When exactly did you send me that initial email?' he asks.

'May 2005.'

'Eight years.'

'Yeah.'

He shakes his head and sighs. 'You don't know how many times

I've written paragraphs and deleted them.'

'I have too.'

'We'd have three hundred emails by now ...'

'I know. The correspondence has been so ...'

'... impersonal at times. Never too familiar, too funny nor critical in any way.'

I nod. 'Careful.'

'Devoid of excitement or anger or anything that could be misconstrued ...'

'... emotionally ... stale.'

'Yes. You're right.'

His eyes rest on me. 'I ... feel I've learned so much this week. About the nature of rape, about myself and the effects of my actions on you. I definitely now know that there is nothing to be gained by being the judge, jury, and executioner of one's self-imposed sentence. I feel like I should share this ... this awareness of the damage you can cause, and maybe some of the ... "why". Not that I have some "catch-all" explanation, but still, I *know* I'm not unique or alone. I'm one of many. And yet there's an awkward silence. A fear of digging deeper, maybe. I just want say *something*. Like you did in your book. I want to speak up, and minimize the chance of our history being repeated, Thordis. Plus, if we'd kept on writing to each other, and not met face to face, I know I wouldn't be talking like this. I wouldn't be speaking about going public, and I sure as hell wouldn't be on the path I'm now on ... learning to love Tom again.' A smile flashes across his face. 'That was one of the easiest things I have ever said to you, so it must be how I feel. If I do speak out, there would be an acknowledgement of the patience and understanding you've shown me all these years.'

His elbow brushes mine when he adds: 'You have kept a momentous secret for me. Perhaps it's time it isn't a secret any more.'

'Perhaps you're right.'

We sit in silence, watching the last sunlight color the horizon from vivid amber to a shade of peach that gradually fades into blue as the stars light up above our heads, one after the other. Out on a nearby cape, people gathered to enjoy the sunset turn into tiny shadow puppets forming a razor-sharp contrast to the glowing background.

'You ready?' he asks. 'Here comes the green flash.'

We both hold our breath as the last strip of sun lets go of the horizon and slips down behind it. I don't dare blink, but no matter how hard I stare I can't see any flash of green. 'Did we miss it?'

'No, I don't think there was one, this time,' he says, perplexed. 'What a shame.'

I shrug but honestly, I'm not surprised that even the laws of nature are changed after this week in Cape Town. Nothing will ever be the same.

The sand is still warm as we climb down from the rock and slip into our shoes. He gives me an inquisitive look as I hand him my phone. 'Will you take my picture?'

My body celebrates the opportunity to sprint up on a three-meter-tall cliff that protrudes into the sea. Adrenaline rushes through my veins as I reach the top and gaze into the glowing, rippling eternity stretched out in front of me. When I leave tomorrow, I want to leave my past behind. Here, in the healing embrace of the Mother City herself.

'I think I got a couple of good ones,' he says once I've climbed down. Our eyes meet as I accept my phone from his hand, and, before I know it, the words are upon my tongue. 'I realize I've never said "I forgive you" to your face, but I do. I forgive you, Tom.'

His eyes open wide. 'Oh my God, did you just say that?' he gasps.

Before I know it, his arms wrap around me and sweep me tight up against him like a ragdoll. I hug him back, surprised by his strong reaction when the sobs tear through his throat. His crying shakes my body, and I hear myself whisper into his ear: 'It's over. I forgive you. It's over.'

We embrace for a long while before he lets go of me, wipes a tear from his cheek, and says: 'I accept your forgiveness.'

The Tom who walks off into the sand a moment later seems different, somehow. His step is lighter; his head held a bit higher than before. I'm moved by the sight. *I wonder if forgiveness can literally change the way people walk?*

I stop to quietly enjoy the effect: the peace of mind and the load that's been lifted off my chest. Strange, this all too common misconception that forgiveness is somehow sacrificial, which leads to it being wrongly associated with selflessness and nobility. As I'm standing and watching Tom walk away into the golden sand, every cell of my body confirms that my forgiveness was no less beneficial to me than to him, allowing me to stop drinking the poison of bitterness, stop torturing myself with unanswered questions, stop living life looking over my shoulder.

The colors grow even more vivid after the sun sets on this last night of ours in South Africa. The palm trees along the beach rise out of the blazingly golden horizon and their leafy heads stretch far up into the violet night sky. The splendor is one of the most romantic things I've ever laid my eyes on, and, before I know it, I've punched Vidir's number into my phone. When he answers, a goofy smile lights up my face. 'I bought your ring. It's one size too big, but hopefully we can have it resized.'

'Or I'll just wear it on my right hand instead,' Vidir answers lovingly. 'We'll figure it out.'

'Yeah, I'm told it's really about your lifelong love and devotion for me, in the end.'

I can hear him smile when he replies: 'Funny, that's exactly what I had planned.'

I bask in the blazing sunset before adding: 'The last night in South Africa before I come home to you ...'

'Soon, honey.'

'Very soon.'

Tom arrives at my side just as I slide my phone back into my bag. Shaking my head, I gesture at the dazzling sky. 'That's clearly Photoshopped.'

'I know. Just ... breathtaking.' He shakes his head, too.

'When you meet the love of your life, you need to bring her here. Never before have I seen a backdrop that screams as loudly for romance.'

He smiles faintly but remains silent.

'I think she'll come knocking soon,' I tell him. 'Sooner than you think.'

'Who?'

'The love of your life.'

He shrugs a bit awkwardly. 'I don't know about that.'

'I do. I'm certain of it.' *Because now you don't have an excuse to lock people out of your heart any more.* I can feel it, just like I can feel the cool sand between my toes.

It's odd to think that this is the last time Tom and I will walk together along the paved sidewalk in Sea Point. The darkness is thick with buzzing insects, and I try to memorise the sound. Two people may leave this place permanently changed, but life here will go on as usual.

Tom is also lost in thought when we sit down on the low wall in front of the Ritz. He rubs his hands together, opens his mouth but closes it again. Finally, he asks: 'Is there any part of you at all that feels like you've been unfaithful this week, Thordis?'

The question surprises me, and yet I understand where it comes from. The emotional processing of the last few days was the equivalent of many relationships, even though it was entirely platonic. I shake my head. 'No.'

He exhales in relief. 'Good. I would've hated that.'

'Besides, Vidir was with us in every step,' I add. 'Without him, I would never have been able to embark on this journey in the first place.'

'He was surely a welcome support,' he says quietly. 'What time is your flight tomorrow?'

'Three thirty,' I tell him. 'And yours?'

'At noon. Want to meet up in the morning and have a last coffee together before I go to the airport?'

'Yeah, let's do that. As a matter of fact, I was going to suggest that we go together to the airport.'

He looks at me, hopeful. 'You're up for that?'

'I think I'd just feel lonely and stranded in Cape Town on my own.'

'Agreed,' he says with a smile. 'See you in the morning then.'

When I lay my head on the pillow, I'm painstakingly aware that this will be the last time I'll sleep in a bed for the next two days. I wonder if it's also the last time I will see Tom? Forgiveness was our goal. Now that we've reached it, why don't I feel like screaming from rooftops and dancing a victory dance? Sure, I reaped relief and liberation this week, but never did I expect the grief that envelops me now, thick like the darkness of my hotel room. My thoughts seesaw over the steady hum of the air conditioning; agile and restless. For years, I was chained to the bed where Tom left me. My escape from there became a lifestyle that catapulted me through a jungle of people, challenges, and experiences. By saying goodbye to Tom, I'm parting with my defense mechanisms. Finally, I can stop pulling on the chains.

The startling discovery shocks me to an upright position. *My unease has less to do with the thought of parting with Tom than parting with everything he's represented in my life.*

I lie back down on the pillow, but I can't stop myself from staring wide-eyed into the darkness, scared of the uncertainty ahead. *Relax,* my heart coos. *You'll grow, love, challenge yourself, lose yourself, find yourself again, and take off to crazy destinations, like you always have. Nothing will change that.*

Nevertheless, I find myself tossing and turning until my mind seeks solace in a little boy who will be ecstatic to reclaim his mother from the airplane. The last dregs of consciousness wash away my chaotic thoughts, leaving only one word behind. *Home.*

From Tom's diary

Wednesday

I pushed through the gate and left the front yard of Rape Crisis, scanning the street for some shade. I stepped towards a large rusted fence that was casting the desired cool shadow. I leant my back on the corrugated iron, swallowed the potato-sized lump in my throat, and put my head on the ribbed metal.

The exhale was half sigh, half gurgling groan now that I'd found the shore. What had come before had been a three-hour episode of part swimming, part drowning, with all the anxious symptoms of trying to keep my head above water in large unruly seas. That internal voice was producing powerful roaring waves, each pushing into me the sense that I was being disrespectful just by being under that roof. The relief I felt leaning against that fence was a gasp of guilt-free air.

I'd predicted the stabbing guilt I would feel. I knew the labels of 'rapist', 'hypocrite' and 'perpetrator' would inevitably surface, and there was no illusion about what my head would produce. In entering the safe haven for women, I *knew* I'd be figuratively beside myself, firing a volley of berating and shame-laden terms. I'd readied myself for the noise.

I am one of the 'they'... the ones who have inflicted such hurt. The ones to be feared. A bad man. A man who has committed sexual violence.

I'd anticipated the attempts to unsettle myself, but also hoped that the immensity of being there would envelop me in its importance. I hoped that the opportunity to just be there would have more power than any campaign I could set up against myself.

I knew I wanted to be there.

I wanted to feel what it was like to be on the right side.

I've worked with many immensely resilient young people who have survived abuse and sexual violence. Going to the Rape Crisis service represented the coalface for me. The very front line of the issue I need to know more of. I hoped that walking with Thordis into that environment would help me better understand the experience of others.

Some of the remaining concerns faded out momentarily when I surrendered to today being part of this whole journey. Like every other turn and twist this week, I knew it would result in growth and healing.

I wasn't prepared for the shock that registered when learning of the details of the problem in South Africa. The sheer number of people affected, the legal minefield to navigate when the survivor's trauma is so raw. Young children being abused. So much hurt in the heart of this country.

I had many questions for Shiralee, but I stuck to the safe ones.

Amidst the intimidation I felt while listening to Thordis and Shiralee speak with such crystal clarity, I was so grateful to be there as a 'youth worker from a service in Sydney'. I tried to reassure myself that I've worked in community services for a while now, and comprehended the majority of issues that Shiralee and Thordis spoke about. I also genuinely knew anything I was to learn today would have professional use for me, and not just personal.

I'm glad I was able to quash the anxiety attack that threatened when we were speaking with Shiralee, even though parts of my shirt were saturated. *Why did I wear that red t-shirt?!* My composure was cracking at the end there, though. With that awkward quip about the 'Man' book, I was scrambling for the door.

After all, I went in there with Thordis for personal not professional reasons. And that is perhaps why I was leaning on a metal fence afterwards, full of relief that my 'performance' was over. Being inauthentic in such a space, at such a crucial service ... came at a risk.

If that was a test I set for myself, if I urged myself to go in there as some form of challenge, then I risked being disrespectful in order to confront that.

I'm so glad we spent some time by the ocean after that. Just being able to put my feet in that icy water settled me down.

She said the words today. *Those words you've been waiting to hear, Tom.* That three-word sentence that felt like it could possibly end another kind of sentence.

I didn't expect to react the way I did. I even feel a bit embarrassed about grabbing and hugging her ... but those tears were held onto for more than sixteen years. I guess they were always going to be hot and irrational. Thankfully, it felt like that hug was shared.

I also like to think that I didn't *need* her forgiveness to be spoken aloud. I haven't been counting the days, waiting for it. I didn't want for there to be any pressure on her, either. This week, just by being able to talk it all through and sit near each other, it's as if the air between us had a quality of being forgiven.

But in saying that, to hear her say it was sublime. I understand why I was a mess.

Who knows if these words can carry the weight we've put on them. All I know is that she gave me something today that sends me skyward with hope, and that giving it was something that she knows more about than I ever will.

Day Nine

4 April 2013

When the alarm goes off, my body refuses to get up. Not until I've said a proper goodbye to the luxury of having a bed and a pillow at my disposal. After all, sleep is best when it's practiced horizontally.

The journey I'm about to take calls for comfortable travel clothes and I pick out my coziest jeans along with a soft cotton shirt. The combination isn't likely to win any fashion prizes, but given that I have to sleep in these clothes for the next two days, they're not bad.

After I'm done packing, I reward myself with a long hot shower. The water gurgles in the drain along with a stream of fleeting ruminations about what life will be like AC: after Cape Town. *What will come out of this molt?* Will it leave me soft-skinned and at ease with myself or did I grow a tough hide while wrestling my fear? Until now, my contributions to the field of sexual violence were a result of a constant itch that was only soothed by rubbing up against the rough surfaces that enclose it: the flaws in the justice system, the social inequality, the silencing. How will I carry the lessons learned in Cape Town into my future? Or will it perhaps be the other way around; will they carry me to places that I can't even guess? Rubbing the water from my eyes, I'm reminded how geckos become visually impaired when shedding their ocular scale. Perhaps I should lay the questions to rest and accept the fact that I'll be temporarily blind until I've grown into my new skin.

A little while later, I'm enjoying my last meal on South African soil; my standard bowl of yoghurt and a boiled egg out in the hotel garden. The sun is shining brightly, and it looks like it'll be the prettiest day since I arrived in South Africa. *Ha! Just when I'm about to leave.*

I'm sitting on the floral sofa, reading a local newspaper, when Tom walks into the Ritz lobby with a giant rucksack on his shoulder. 'Hi,' he says, cheerfully. 'Please tell me there's good coffee here.'

'Coffee yes, but good? Not even close.'

'I'll take my chances.'

On our way to the breakfast room, we pass Nigel's little shop. He is just finishing a phone call when we step inside.

'How was the chocolate?' Tom wonders.

Nigel's face lights up and he places one hand on his chest while shaking his head humbly. 'Too beautiful. I couldn't eat them. And with the note ...' He sighs. 'Too beautiful. I almost got into trouble, though. They were lying here,' he says, and points eagerly to a drawer by the back wall, 'and my wife came here and said "What is this?" I told her to read the note and she says: "Who is this and what is going on?" He pauses and frowns theatrically. 'I told her to read the other side and then she nodded and said, "Oh. Something must've happened at the tree of life. Something that changed their lives."'

Tom and I exchange looks and nod.

'Maybe he proposed to her, my wife said.' Nigel's eyes are glittering with excitement; his sincerity is so genuine that the moment is neither awkward nor embarrassing.

Smiling, I tell him: 'Nothing like that, but it was just as life-altering and powerful,' and Tom agrees with a nod.

Nigel crosses his arms and sizes us up, content. 'Well, let me say that you two would make a beautiful couple.'

'We went down that road many years ago and it ...' My words dry up and I shrug.

'... didn't work out?' Nigel asks softly.

'No, it didn't. But I did receive a proposal recently. It just wasn't from him,' I gesture towards Tom.

'Well, I wish you happiness,' Nigel says, smiling with his entire face. Something about this man melts my heart. Suddenly, I feel like crying.

Tom leans on the desk. 'Regarding the mystery person who asked you about the baobab tree ... did she ever come back?'

Nigel looks at me, unsure of how to answer, before looking back at Tom. 'She just ... came in here, asking about this tree. She really needed to know where it was. She didn't tell me why.' He glances at me before adding: 'But it was very important to her.'

I shrug, in no need to question the matter further. 'I was obviously intended to find the tree of life.' *Life simply made it happen.*

'We're headed upstairs to have a quick last coffee in the sun,' Tom says to Nigel.

'Come by before you leave and say goodbye.'

The tanning chairs in the garden are hot to the touch. Tom sits down carefully to avoid spilling his horror-coffee.

'I have to warn you, that tastes like ear wax,' I tell him.

'How would you know? Do you know what ear wax tastes like?'

'Of course I know what ear wax tastes like! Don't you?'

'No!' he answers, aghast.

'Bullshit. You expect me to believe that you've never scratched your ear and accidentally bit your nail, afterwards?'

'God, no.' He shudders.

'Well, I have and it's gross. Almost as gross as that coffee.'

'Oh wow,' he says after tasting the brew. 'This is unbelievably bad.'

The sun warms my face as I stick my hand into my jean pocket. 'I've got something for you.'

'What's that?'

I pull out a purple button. 'I organized a fundraiser for the Women's Shelter in Iceland recently, selling buttons. The idea was to challenge people to do something creative with their button, take a picture of it, and put it online. For me, the message was how we need to think creatively when it comes to battling violence. I hereby challenge you to do something creative with this button, take a picture of it, and send it to me.'

'Challenge accepted,' he says, and plays with the button. He pulls a beaded key-ring that forms the letter 'A' out of his pocket and hands it to me. 'They gave me this at the villa when I checked out this morning. It could be a nice reminder of Cape Town. So much beading in this city,' he says in an admiring voice. 'I don't know what the 'A' should stand for, though.'

I take the key ring from his hand and run my index finger across the colorful beads. *Always,* maybe? The lessons we learned in Cape Town will always stay with us, that's for sure.

On the way back down to the lobby to say goodbye to Nigel, I realize that in spite of all his help, he hasn't taken any of our money. *That's it. I'm buying souvenirs.* Just as I get the idea, I walk past a glass cabinet in front of Nigel's shop. I must've passed it every single day and yet I've never noticed it. My jaw drops when I see five hand-carved turtles in the cabinet. *No way.* I've been treading Cape Town back and forth in search for turtles that stared me in the face every day.

I reel in my jaw, walk straight up to Nigel, and tell him: 'I want to buy one of your turtles.'

Shaking his head with a smile, he tells me: 'No, let me give it to you. It will be a gift.' He ignores my pleas to pay and opens the cabinet.

I pick up a turtle made of soapstone, like so many crafts around here. All of the turtles are sporting a carving of an animal on their backs. At a glance, I recognize a leopard, a rhino, a lion, an elephant, and what looks like a buffalo. 'Are these the big five?'

'Yes, the big five game animals are only found in Africa. Nowhere else in the world,' Nigel says with pride.

The turtle I'm holding has a rhino carved on its back, and he brushes it lightly with his fingertip. I hand it to him. He reacts with a generous gesture. 'You can have it.'

'The idea was to buy it from you, Nigel—'

He interrupts me: 'It's a gift.' Placing a hand on his chest, he adds: 'From the bottom of my heart.'

My eyes water as I nod in humble appreciation. Suddenly, I get a genius idea. 'Can we have our picture taken with you?'

Nigel smiles in surprise. 'Yes, of course.'

A moment later, we've found a helpful lady from the lobby who's willing to take our picture. Tom stands on Nigel's right side, I'm on his left, and he puts his arms around us. When the lens shuts, the smile on my lips is genuine. *Two birds with one stone.* A long-awaited picture of Tom and me, with Nigel the Fate Shaper as a bonus — a bonus who also makes the picture look relaxed and natural. *Bingo.*

After the photo, Nigel prepares to shake my hand goodbye. Looking at his outstretched hand, we both get the same idea and open our arms simultaneously. The hug is tight and warm.

'Come here, you,' Tom says, and they hug too. A handshake wouldn't have been enough and we all know it.

Outside the Ritz, a taxi awaits us. My heart grows heavier with each step, almost as heavy as the suitcase I hoist with difficulty into the trunk. The itch at the back of my throat has developed into a painful lump. To add insult to injury, the ballad 'Hero' by Mariah Carey is being blasted in the taxi. I look to the sky and scoff. *A bit on the sentimental side, are we?*

As the taxi takes off, I quietly say my goodbyes. First to the Ritz, to the lobby that hosted our awkward reunion, the palm trees, the street. When the taxi driver enters the highway and Cape Town stretches out before us in all its glory, Mariah Carey is belting out the most epic part of the song. The lump in my throat balloons. *Hell no, this is too much.* My eyes fall upon Tom's iPod, lying next to him in the car seat. 'Will you play me some of your music?' I plead.

'Sure. Now?'

'Yes. Now. This minute.'

'Wanna hear "Stranded on Earth"?'

'I'd love to!'

He looks up the song and hands me the earphones. 'Normally, it's an eyes-closed song, but we can make an exception. This would be a great backdrop.'

The song slides across my eardrums like a rattlesnake, full of mystique and grace as the landscape flies by at lightning speed. It forms an amazing soundscape as I say farewell to Robben Island, the busy street corners, and the tourist buses. It grows and incorporates more instruments as I say goodbye to Shiralee, Rape Crisis, and the church. Just as I say my farewell to the tree of life, a female vocalist starts to sing in a powerful voice. The effect is so captivating that when I hand Tom back his earphones, I admit: 'I see what you mean by a spiritual experience.'

The stylish airport overlooks the city, and the taxi drives us right up to the sliding doors. Words are unnecessary as we drink in Cape Town one last time. The sun is hot and the air doesn't stir. *Goodbye, Mother City. Thank you for letting us rest in your arms*, is the last thought I have before entering the terminal building.

The Mother City promptly responds. In the entrance, Tom stops dead in his tracks and points to a giant sign above our heads.

I look up and read out loud: 'Doesn't it feel good to move forward?'

Tom reaches for his camera, speechless.

I gesture towards the sign with a beaming smile. 'That's for you, Stranger.'

He nods and takes a picture.

After Tom checks in (my check-in hasn't even opened yet), we sit down at a restaurant overlooking this part of the airport, ordering one last drink on South African soil. 'Cheers to Nigel,' he says with a grin. 'I love the fact that you've been looking for a turtle all week and on the last day, you're given one!'

'Cheers indeed.'

We touch glasses. The smile on Tom's face fades. 'The South African friend I'm going to visit now is one of my closest. It feels weird to not share with him what I think about his amazing home town.'

'Then tell him.'

He cocks his head. 'Yeah. We've come too far for there to be any lies at this stage, haven't we?'

He pulls out a pretty card from his backpack. 'Better get started on this.' The front is decorated with various African animals made of clay and glued to the paper along with patterned pieces of cloth. He writes 'Vidir' on the envelope in delicate handwriting.

I leave the restaurant to complete my check-in. As I wait in line, I watch Tom through the glass as he writes to the man who did the most heroic deed of all this week by staying at home, trusting Tom and me unconditionally.

He arrives just as I accept my boarding pass from the clerk and hands me the envelope. It's sealed, and I don't ask. In fact, I'm glad that he felt up for it on his own — and even more glad that I feel the same way.

After an uneventful security screening, we enter a tidy Duty Free full of African souvenirs. I'm shaking my head over a wide selection of ostrich eggs (*won't they become extinct soon?*) when Tom holds a beige, hand-painted linen cloth up to my face. The smell is strong and musky. 'Earthy, you know?' he says, excited. 'I'm buying it.'

A little while later, we follow signs down a staircase and into a smoking lounge that turns out to be a stylish glass cage. Tom lights a cigarette before pulling a plastic bag out of his backpack heavy with change. 'Here, can you take this for me and give it to a local charity or something? It's almost thirty rand in there.'

'Sure.' I play with the throw he bought from the souvenir shop, admiring the hand-painted pattern.

'My mother will love that,' he says, eyeing the throw. 'I'm thinking about keeping it at my parents' house, so they can enjoy it too.'

'That's where you … told them, right?'

'Yes.' His eyes darken. 'I'd decided I couldn't keep them guessing any longer. I asked them to sit with me outside. It was a lovely clear night, and I tried to look up at the stars while talking between sobs. I explained the events of the night to the best of my recollection, the cab ride to your place, carrying you to the room. I stopped at the point when I said that I undressed you … I couldn't say that word. Instead

I said something along the lines of "there was no consent". There was silence. Then, my parents spoke of making their own "mistakes", and of forgiveness, and how long I'd kept this in and hurt myself. They moved closer and spoke of unconditional love. I told them we had been in contact for years, and they said I was very fortunate to be able to be speaking with you around this.'

'You're fortunate to have them as parents too.'

He smiles. 'I know. It's a night I'll never forget.'

'Can you give them my best regards?' I ask him. 'And ... no.' I bite my tongue. 'Never mind.'

'Hey. No stopping in the middle of a sentence.' He pokes me playfully in the shoulder.

'It's just ... do you think you can find a way to convey to your mother that I don't blame her in the least?'

He frowns. 'I don't think she blames herself.'

'I think she may, Tom. I've seen my own mother search herself tirelessly for explanations to the things my siblings and I have been through. Just like your mother did in the letter you read out loud to me, when she questioned whether her anxiety during the pregnancy could've had a negative effect on you. I'd appreciate it if you could find a way to tell them that I wish them nothing but well.'

'I will.'

I get a sharp stab of anxiety when he puts out his cigarette. I want to rewind, whirl the ash out of the ashtray again, blow it back onto the cigarette between his fingers, watch it grow longer and longer until the ember turns into a flame that's sucked backwards into the lighter, leaving us with five more precious minutes.

He shrugs awkwardly. 'I should probably get going.'

As we reach the top of the staircase, his gate awaits, where the last passengers to Australia are boarding the plane. Twenty more steps until we part. *Nineteen. Eighteen. Seventeen …*

After twelve steps, we stop simultaneously before throwing our backpacks on a nearby bench. My jacket goes the same way along with my sunglasses. My heart cracks when he locks his arms around me.

He shivers as he whispers to me: 'I thought about what I'd be leaving in Cape Town, and it is being left here. I am not distancing myself from it, but thanks to you it is now being held by the big, beautiful tree of life. I'm not scared any more, Thordis.'

We both sob. He hugs me tighter and lowers his voice. 'I'm so grateful for this week. Thank you. You saved me.'

For a few eternal moments, we're standing still. I bury my face in his neck and enjoy hugging him wholeheartedly, without hesitation or fear. At last, I muster the willpower to let go of him.

'I don't have much to add to that,' I tell him. 'Thank you too, Tom. Be yourself. Be safe. Be happy.'

He nods, suppressing a sob.

'Text me once you get there.'

'I will. You too.'

I wrap my arms around him one last time, whispering: 'We're going to be OK, Tom. More than OK.'

He picks up his backpack from the bench. I gather my things too. Finally, we're standing face to face, and I can see an impatient stewardess waiting for him at the end of the gate.

'Don't be a stranger,' are my last words to Tom Stranger.

'I won't. Goodbye, Thordis.'

'Goodbye.'

My ears are ringing as I watch him walk towards the gate. When I've realized that he isn't going to look back, I turn around and go back to the Duty Free. Inside me is a void. The jars that used to be full of unspoken words are now empty. There's nothing but marks in the dust where the bitterness and chaos used to be. The wrappings from my forgiveness are scattered around my heart.

I am here. Unmistakably here, in this body, within the shifting clockwork of this very moment. Alive. One. Whole.

The feeling is novel, and I sink down on a bench, examining my hands as if they've taken on a new shape. Minutes turn into hours of contemplative rearrangement of my self-image; a quiet inspection of the voids within, and the conclusion that they will soon be replaced with new images, sounds, sensations. When a couple with a bright-eyed toddler interrupt my solitude, loneliness comes crashing in full force. It'll be another two days until I see Vidir and Haflidi, on the other side of an inhumanly long trip. And who knows if I'll ever see Tom again? *How can this be, dear life? How come I feel like I just lost a precious friend?*

When I get on the plane to Istanbul, my inner stockroom worker pulls up his sleeves, yanks the numbness out of my heart, lines the tear tanks up in the front shelves, and uncaps them all. The first tears hit my lap as the words *you saved me* echo in my head. My lobster shawl comes in handy and I pull it over my head, where it forms a private tent around my overflowing emotions. My tears stream unhindered for the next few hours until the stewardess brings dinner in a lukewarm aluminum tray. The woman next to me turns out to be vegetarian. I disappear back into my tent to cry some more.

Eleven tear-stained hours later, an exhausted and emotionally drained woman walks into the Istanbul airport. *Coffee. Now. Can we make it intravenous, please?*

I shuffle into a café where a nerve-racked waiter takes my order. I can tell it's his first shift as he rushes towards the kitchen with large sweat stains under his arms. *Please let my coffee arrive soon, though.* I start up my laptop but find myself staring blankly at it for the next half hour, the cursor blinking in a word document as empty as I am. *Typical*. When I finally have nothing better to do than write, I'm blocked. If I weren't so empty, I might even find it ironic.

Suddenly, my phone beeps. My face lights up when I discover it's from Tom. It must mean he's landed safely in Australia.

> *Got to tell you, just sat by the ocean and told my friend our story. He listened. I cried. I said the word that I haven't been able to whisper. He thanked me, spoke of respect, mistakes, and a second chance at life. He sends his warm regards. Can I call that a small semi-graduation test?*

The joy that shoots through me hits the café like a shock wave, jolting the sweaty waiter who straightens his back, looks around in surprise and sees me. He gulps. 'I'm so sorry, Miss, here's your coffee,' he says, bringing me the cappuccino I ordered forty minutes earlier. I give him an understanding smile, preoccupied with my reply.

> *Wow, that's not small nor semi, Tom! Congratulations. My heart is swelling in my chest. Happy for you, glad you have such a good friendship and deeply moved that you're stepping out of the cage. To quote the sign in Cape Town: Doesn't it feel good to be moving forward?*

The text lifts my writer's block and I pound the keyboard for the next few hours, until the screens around me scream at me to go the hell to my gate. I'm still writing away in Stockholm airport, a bit perkier after a short nap on the plane, a strong cup of coffee, and a bowl of fruit, when I see a collection box from the International Red Cross at the end of the hall. It has a picture of a distraught man running with a child in his arms, under the headline: *Do you have humanity? We accept donations in every currency.* I dig up the bag with Tom's change and empty my own pockets too. No less than a pound of coins lands in the collection box, topped off with a bill sporting Nelson Mandela.

Humanity turns out to be the theme for my 36-hour-long, four-plane ordeal to Iceland. In Istanbul, a woman saves me from forgetting my passport at the café. During the flight, I give a little girl my unused earphones from the tourist bus, happy that they can be of use to someone. Both times that I manage to nap, my seatmate accepts a bottle of water for me, awaiting me like a salvation when I wake up. *We're all vulnerable during flights,* I note to myself. *We all have to put up with long lines, uncomfortable seats, rigid security measures, and an interruption of our daily routine. We're all equally doomed if the plane crashes.* And out of all this unpleasantness, compassion grows.

Sitting on the last plane from Stockholm to Iceland, I entertain the hope that the newfound lightness in my chest will root itself there, permanently. The past still happened, but the thought of it doesn't come with the claustrophobic feeling of being locked inside the memory any more. Not even the subsequent string of misery hurts as much, in recollection. *Funny how a chain reaction can go both ways,* I note, gazing at the foaming Atlantic miles below me. A ripple that once was destructive has been reversed, pulsating backwards through my life, leaving clean streaks in the mud. Leaning back into my seat, I enjoy the novel feeling of not having to dig around in the past. Beneath the celebration, my realism raises her gray head and scoffs at the self-congratulations. *Think it'll all just go away now?* she says in a rusty voice. *It'll always be a part of you. Not just the scars left by Tom, but by the others too.*

I know, I tell her. *But look on the bright side. If ghosts from the past come charging, I now have an empty room in my head that can be turned into an armory.*

Iceland is not a popular tourist destination in early April, and, as a result, the other seats in my row are empty. After sitting for more than thirty hours, my back feels like it's been pelted with bowling balls. I lift the armrests that separate the seats and attempt to lie down, only to have the seatbelts stick mercilessly into my thigh and ribs. *Oh for crying out loud*. Suddenly, I'm jealous of Tom and his luxuriously brief 14-hour flight to Australia. Blink of a goddamn eye.

At least he's used the spare time wisely. Admitting to a friend what he did all those years ago was no small step. I wonder if he was the first in a long line of friends and family that will now be let in on the truth, one by one? Tom's words from the rotating restaurant echo in my head: 'Because I couldn't speak to anybody about my past, it seemed futile to hold on to it and collect it as part of my self image.'

Will it be a part of him from now on?

I close my eyes and try to ignore the relentless humming of air pushing past me at eight hundred feet per second. Something was born that night in '96, a sickness that we suffered from for years before having the guts to accept the diagnosis. Both of us shouldered the blame and shame, manifesting itself in similar symptoms. Fragmented and sweating from self-medication, we stumbled through the worst of it, but the tumor kept growing until it filled our mouths and the words that managed to squeeze past it were malignant. Saturated with the lie that stemmed from not being able to share our single most influential experience with a living soul.

Breaking my silence took me a long time and yet I'm years ahead of Tom, having made his violence toward me publicly known. Ridding myself of shame was the hardest part, but I eventually got there by accepting the truth that evaded me for so long: the fact that I was not responsible for Tom's choices that night. He will not have that at his disposal. What lies ahead for him, I wonder? Is there a possibility that both of us had grown dependent on our roles and that Tom, too, will have to separate himself from everything I represented in his life until now? He told me that self-blame was a pattern he'd grown addicted to. I battled that same addiction myself. Blaming oneself and taking responsibility for one's actions are two separate things. The former leads to self-flagellation that feeds the self-pitying ego; the latter looks beyond the self and acknowledges one's role in relation to others. I wonder if taking responsibility will set Tom free? Will it loosen his grip on the whip and help him reason with himself, even when guilt beckons? The man I parted with at the airport was a changed person, relieved by my forgiveness. Will it become the foundation on which he can build his own absolution? Curling up on my plane seat, the ultimate question rings in my head: *Will he ever be able to fully forgive himself?* As much as that would make a grand finale to our story, I realize that there's nothing more I can do. From now on, Tom and I will be writing our separate narratives, independent of one another. When faced with the uncertainty of the future, I find comfort in the fact that although the past will always be a part of us, our former survival strategies will become unnecessary after the detox of Cape Town.

The floor in Keflavík airport billows beneath my feet as I text Vidir and Dad that I've landed safely in Iceland. As I'm fighting my jetlag in the Duty Free check-out line, with standard sweets for the family in a shopping basket, a rack of rune necklaces catches my eye. Reaching out, I grab the Thurisaz rune off the rack and read the back: 'The meaning of this rune is that you undergo suffering to learn from it, and with discipline and contemplation you will succeed in turning your life around. Something that appeared at first to be negative and hard will be a blessing and will renew your life.'

Indeed, it feels good to be moving forward.

My last fellow passenger yanks a dark-blue suitcase off the baggage belt and hurries away. Knowing that my suitcase isn't compliant enough to show up twice in a row, I still wait dutifully until the same cardboard box has rattled past me three times before filling out a lost baggage form.

I call Vidir as soon as I've settled into my seat on the fly-bus. Hearing his voice makes me melt like butter, only to break out in a cold sweat when he tells me that my stepdaughters Hafdis and Julia are on their way. I'm startled. Is today Friday? Is it our weekend with the girls? My fatigue hits me full force at the thought of a family-of-five action weekend. For the first time in hours, I feel like crying again.

My self-pity dissolves when I arrive at the bus station and hear a voice I'd recognize anywhere in the world. 'MOMMY!' A three-year-old boy comes running and throws himself in my arms. He looks at me with beaming excitement, flaps his blonde butterfly wings in my face, and asks in a hopeful voice: 'Can I come with you on the plane, Mommy?'

Before I'm able to answer, he looks at the fly-bus behind me. 'Or are we going on the bus, Mommy?'

Anywhere with me.

Standing behind my child is the man who loved me, trusted me, and respected me enough to support me on a crazy journey across the globe. My knees turn into spaghetti when he hugs me tightly. 'Welcome home, honey,' he whispers into my hair. Knowing that we only have a few precious moments to ourselves for the next few days, I drink them up like a desert flower. His scent. His arms around me. The warm smile on his lips.

The first thing that meets the eye as I walk through the door to our apartment is a banner that says 'Welcome home,' decorated with clumsy drawings. Hafdis, my 14-year-old stepdaughter, appears with brand-new freckles that she got in Florida, where she went with her mother to mark her confirmation and spend some (if not all) of the money she was given by relatives on the occasion. We hug and take turns in welcoming each other back home, and I note a pink iPad and iPhone sticking out of her pocket. I lock eyes with Vidir and mouth the words '*Thanks, Jesus*'. He grins and rolls his eyes.

A bouquet of roses and freshly baked banana bread await me on the kitchen table. 'You'll have to excuse that I can't give you any souvenirs yet,' I tell Vidir in an apologetic voice.

'Your suitcase?'

I sigh. '... took off to Tahiti or who knows where.'

Vidir sits down in a kitchen chair, and I sink into his lap. He gives me a long hug and exhales deeply. 'I'm so glad you're home. I've been so worried about you ... or maybe worried isn't the right word ... but you know.'

I respond by placing a kiss on his neck.

'Do you feel like you managed to ... get what you wanted out of this trip?' he asks.

I contemplate my answer. 'I believe so. The long-term effects have yet to be revealed, but for now, I feel ... whole. And ... lighter, if that makes sense.'

My words fall preposterously short of describing the immensity of what I just experienced. Summarizing it in words feels futile, like attempting to explain a concept of philosophy with a stack of Lego. Fortunately, I know Vidir understands. He pulls me closer, and I'm reminded of my intention to make his embrace a part of my daily routine until I run out of days.

'Want to see the rings?'

He lights up. 'You bet! You have them?'

'Hand luggage, of course,' I explain, pleased with myself.

Vidir opens the box I hand him and is stunned by the ring. 'It's amazing,' he whispers, studying the hypnotizing pattern.

Haflidi is sitting at the kitchen table, happily munching on banana bread. The girls are laughing in the living room, immersed in the iPad's wonders. The house is more peaceful than I dared to imagine, and relief at being back overpowers my jetlag.

I take the box from Vidir's hand. He looks questioningly at me when I bow down on one knee on the kitchen floor in front of him.

'Vidir Gudmundsson ...'

He smiles in the sharp spring sun that flows in through the window.

'... will you marry me?'

Our eyes meet when he answers: 'Yes.'

'Love me and honor me?'

'Yes.'

'In sickness and in health?'

'Yes.'

I slide the ring onto his finger and kiss him on the mouth. 'And don't you forget it.'

The weekend is unusual in many ways. Meals and sleep routines are upset due to Mommy's debilitating jet-lag. The children float around the house, their mouths stuffed with duty-free lollipops. The weirdest thing of all is postponing the travel story. Vidir asks me a thousand unspoken questions every time his eyes fall upon me, all of which are answered silently, in my mind. The result is what we like to call *present distance*. A distant soul in a present body.

On Sunday night, after the girls have gone back to their mother in a cloud of vanilla perfume from Florida, we finally have a moment to ourselves. When I'm done putting Haflidi to bed, Vidir is waiting for me in the candlelit living room. Despite his best efforts, his anxiety is palpable. Quavering, I get started on the story, equally nervous after having waited this long. Vidir's shoulders relax as the story progresses, and he squeezes my hand when I describe the talk I had with Tom in my hotel room, in the eye of the storm.

It takes me three nights to complete the story, once Haflidi is asleep after long workdays. I would've understood Vidir's need to judge Tom, but I find him doing the opposite when he identifies with him in numerous vulnerable places.

The silence that ensues once I'm done with the story is warm and saturated. We're lying in each other's arms in bed when I reach out to caress Vidir's cheek.

'It's an amazing story,' he says in a hoarse voice. 'Thank you for telling it to me.'

'Thank you too.'

We embrace the silence, and I feel how the tree of life wraps its branches around us, rocking us softly. A dim light from a lamp on the bedside table draws shadow puppets on the walls; rhinos, mountains, rocks, turkeys and — if I squint — a smiling Nigel in a well-ironed shirt.

Sitting up, I turn to Vidir. 'I have something for you.'

He looks at me in surprise as I disappear into the hall and return with the card from Tom.

'For me?' he asks, and studies the handwriting on the envelope.

I nod. 'Want me to step outside so you can read it in private?'

'It's up to you,' he replies, busy studying the clay animals on the card.

Tom didn't ask me to read the card; it was meant for Vidir only. Out of respect for both of them, I wander into the bathroom, where I turn on the faucet and gulp a few mouthfuls of cold water.

'Thordis?'

Springing up like a jack in the box, I yell 'Yes?' while rubbing a stream of water off my chin.

'I don't understand the handwriting. Can you help me?'

My heart is pounding in my chest as I enter the bedroom. Sitting down next to Vidir, I take the card from his hands.

To Vidir,

Simply
Thank you.
This week I have listened to Thordis talk of your loving, trusting and supportive union/relationship/self. I am so ... happy that she has you. I deeply wish you and your family a celebratory and soul-nourishing future. Thank you for helping make this time a success.

Sincerely,
Tom.

Dropping the envelope on the bed next to him, Vidir pulls me into a tight hug. Visibly moved, he whispers into my ear: '*Now* you're finally home.'

Something tells me he's right.

From Tom's diary

That blurry smile shared was the last gesture before I turned and started walking towards my departure gate ten meters away. Deep breathing to address the light-headedness felt more important than wiping away those tears, and besides, I felt no need.

My spine was more vertically aligned than it's ever been, and I felt ... so strong. So incredibly together and strong. Each step was a celebration of movement. Mindful but light movement, because that helium balloon had again been blown up in my ribcage and it was squeezed up against my throat.

The ten meters were whittled down to five, and I felt an urge to look over my shoulder. It would've been nice to celebrate the grand occasion with one more acknowledgement. I thought I could feel her looking at me, but I refrained from turning around. I wanted to honor how complete we have made it all, and nothing felt left to be done. It *did* feel good to be moving forward.

I handed the hostess my ticket, smiling and sniffing. *She must see lots of men cry*, I thought to myself.

Turning left to enter the glass-lined gangway down to my plane, and before I knew it, I stole a glance over my left shoulder. There she was, walking back towards the waiting area and about to take one last turn before she disappeared.

My ears opened and I registered the song that was playing over the airport speakers as I watched Thordis walking. Shit. It's Gloria Gaynor defiantly launching into the disco-laced 'I've got all my life to live, I've got all my love to give, and I'll survive, I will survive.' Just like a bad 70s Hollywood ending. Now I was teary *and* on the verge of bursting into laughter. I imagined the credits smoothly appearing at the bottom of the screen.

She disappeared and a flashing thought bolted across my mind space. *Was that the last time maybe?*

I turned to make my way down the glistening ramp and the sun was lighting up its flat surfaces. In the distance I made out a parched northern mountain range gracefully pushing its way upward into the hot sky.

Right. That's done it.

I stretched my hands up above my head, closed my eyes and leant my head back in surging celebration. I put as little distance as I could between my heart and the heavens, and let it out.

We did it!

The tears came, again, and they were so very welcome. Side effects of the knowledge that all fears were faced and conquered and everything was released. The light from that once-dark cave was so bright it may as well have been a sunrise.

I took a breath, wiping some tears away while handing my ticket stub to the smiling man greeting me at the airlock. Now I'm in my seat, I've draped the coarse but comforting throw I purchased for my folks across my legs. I'm soothed by having this small sliver of Cape Town to carry with me.

I want to record the ocean's worth of learnings sitting in my head and torso, the dizzying heights and freezing fears I've seen and felt this week, to never forget how they have changed and will change me. The blessings and events of these past days have felt like they were guided, and I want to dignify this ethereal force with at least a written memory of what I've learned.

I'm glad to have hours in the air to myself, to spill out onto the page these grand and dramatic notions. An individualized quasi-religious list of the simple lessons I've been shown. Life lessons learnt in a week. Lessons for *my* life at least:

There is something up there. Don't be concerned about what shape or form it holds, just be thankful and grateful that your soul is in communication with it. Look up and be humbly thankful. Often.
Exerting power over another is a display of fear, greed, or self-interest. It is born of fear of what you do not know, cannot control, and is based in an insecurity that is blinding. Greed is psychological, cannot be sated, and is an internal emptiness. Self-interest can be a smothering and selfish narrowing of your humanity, so that you see only yourself in this world.

With enough shame/guilt and self-judgment, you can block memories, and black out your involvement in past events.
But with love and patience you can go back there and uncover yourself.
Life goes on. Utilize it fully. There is not much that you own, but this one is certainly yours.

Such lofty attempts at spirituality feel a bit theatrical ... but then again, if forgiveness was a religion, I'd be a follower.

My soul feels free.

Epilogue

7 April 2016

There are so many stories to tell. I could start by telling you how upon his return to Australia, Tom fastened the Women's Shelter button to his surfboard so it would always accompany him on that soul-nourishing exercise. I could tell you how two weeks after I got back to Iceland, I gave a speech in the Westman Islands and used the opportunity to visit the spot where the awful truth was first spoken out loud. How I discovered a monument nearby that shows the tree of life in Norse mythology carved into a rock. I could tell you how I found out through internet research that the tree of life in the paradise of Kirstenbosch was planted there in the winter of 1996, when Tom and I first met. And how the playwright in the sky appreciates wordplay, because a male turkey is apparently called a 'tom'.

I could tell you how shortly after he got back home, Tom sat between his parents and told them about our week in Cape Town. How when he described the moment of forgiveness during the picturesque sunset, they each reached for his hand in tears. How his mother stated that finally, *finally* they'd recovered their son from the incomprehensible darkness he'd resided in all these years. How after Cape Town, it'd be a joy to watch him step out of the shadows and into the light.

I could tell you about grand victories, like when Tom came to Iceland a year later and I introduced him to Vidir. How two hours after nervously shuffling their feet, unable to look each other in the eye, they were sitting by our kitchen table and patting each other on the back in silent respect. How on midnight leading up to my thirty-fourth birthday, all three of us sat in my backyard by candlelight, feasting on champagne and cheese. How Tom and I marched together in the Slut Walk 2014 along with thousands of others, united under banners against rape. I could tell you how my best friend, who met up with Tom and me in a hostile, defensive mode, caught himself having a heart to heart about sexual violence with Tom later that same night. How he turned to me afterwards, bewildered, and said: 'This is why you guys need to tell your story to the world — it gets the most guarded of people to talk about these matters.'

But my favorite thing to tell you would be that my hunch proved to be right. A few weeks after Cape Town, Tom met a woman: Cat. Intelligent, beautiful, and equally concerned about the environment — she turned out to be the love of his life. Three months after they met, he decided to tell her the truth, resulting in the following email exchange between Tom and me:

> I suggested we go up into the park above the Opera House
> after I had a beer and she had a water. The park sits on the very
> edge of the harbor looking out over the bridge and Sydney
> waters. It was guaranteed to be a good sunset, so I somewhat

used that as an excuse. I knew there was also a big old fig tree just up in the park.

So we sat down, commented on how lucky we were and how colored the view was. Then I started with the ominous 'Cat, I need to open up to you about something' and of course she became uncomfortable and joked that 'this doesn't sound good'. I then spoke around trusting her, getting closer, the fact that on the first date we spoke about vulnerability, and that I have a history that I don't want to hide from any more, and want to communicate to her plainly.

I began by telling her that I had lied to her once. When watching a documentary from South Africa she asked if I have been there, and I somewhat automatically said no. That 'no' has been sitting uncomfortably with me ever since. At the very end of the conversation, she said being lied to was perhaps the most difficult part to hear.

I apologized for lying and went on to say I had been to Cape Town with a woman named Thordis Elva at the end of March/beginning of April this year. I then spoke about meeting you in 1996, and then chronologically went through the events of our past.

I used the word rape. I spoke about my blacking out the choices and my part in that night. I told her about the years since, and our miraculous communication. I then told her about Cape Town and the week of slowly moving through each other's life story. Robben Island. Kirstenbosch. Camps Bay. That touched and inspired week that we had. I told her that since then my days have been different.

I obviously trust her implicitly and chose her to be another to be let in to the secret. She listened and leant on me while

I spoke. Then as soon as I had finished she began saying that from where she sits it seems like I have taken responsibility for my actions and owned my choices. She spoke around 'to err is human, to forgive divine'. She said she wasn't belittling my deed or the hurt I had caused, but said she believed in the capacity of us all to forget our humanity and make horrendous errors. She said I had gone a long way in an attempt to make amends and pay the price for the pain that was in the past. We spoke about the stigma around the label 'rapist', after I said you have given me the strength to part with it. I don't remember her response word for word, Thordis, but it was beautiful. Respectful to us both. The sunset was blazing away at this point, too.

We walked back over the bridge and since then it's seemed very comfortable, and even closer. She said she was so glad we could share the 'good, bad and ugly' about ourselves.

Her reaction was of course staggeringly wonderful and exceeded my highest hopes. I've got a lightness about me today that means my shoes aren't even making a sound.

Thank you for your support, again Thordis. You inspired me to move through any fear and not just to hide or seek cover. We've come too far. Trusted too much to not be vulnerable, comfortably.

I hope this finds you well.

Hugs,
Tom.

Tom,

Reading your email left me feeling humble and moved. I had hoped that after Cape Town, you would shed the misconception that people couldn't possibly love you if they found out what you did. I say this because I had the same misconceptions. I thought if I told people about the rape, they would either be overwhelmed by it or render me down to it. I thought nobody could possibly have a normal relationship or friendship with me, if they knew.

I've never been as happy to be wrong.

When I told my mother nine years ago, it was much like your experience. I sobbed and choked on the words and couldn't look her in the eye. At the core of my shame was the fact that I had been drinking that night. After all the gut-wrenching worries and sleepless nights my mother had suffered due to my sister's alcoholism, I felt that my drinking would be the ultimate form of treason. In my mind, kicking her would be kinder. My fears were unfounded as my mother grabbed my hand and squeezed it after I told her the story of what happened that night in '96. To my great relief, the sorrow written across her face didn't carry the slightest bit of blame towards me.

I also told her, years later, that I was corresponding with you in hope of reaching forgiveness and closure. She never asks about these things. Her face has a way of closing up when I talk about them. It's unlike her and it pains me to think of her mind being occupied with resentment and bitterness on my behalf. I know from experience that such feelings usually end up hurting the person who harbors them far more than the person they're directed at.

Earlier today, she came over for coffee. She sat in my kitchen and held her coffee cup with both hands, carefully sipping on the cappuccino I made her, when I decided to brief her.

'Mom,' I said. 'Tom told his parents.'

She didn't answer.

'He has owned up to what he did.'

Still no answer.

'He is more sorry than we'll ever know, Mom.'

She took another sip of her coffee before meeting my eye, remaining silent.

'Mom?'

'Yes?'

'I want you to consider something.'

'What's that, dear?'

'To forgive Tom.'

She drew in a quick breath and put her coffee cup down. This time avoiding my stare.

'Mom?'

'Yes?'

'Do you think you can do that?'

My mother is one of the strongest people I've ever met, equipped with an elastic heart that can stretch to fit any circumstances. She believes in letting go. She believes in the power of beauty and the wisdom of humility. Because of these qualities, she is the family's mediator and confidante. She's the only person who can soften my father's sometimes unwavering stances. For this, she's had to suffer his criticism for being 'too lenient', when in fact it is her leniency that has kept us together all these years.

The tension in her face was replaced by a sudden calm. She looked me right in the eye, a faint smile on her lips.

'Oh honey,' she said. 'You know me. In the end, I'm such a softie.'

Mahatma Gandhi once said that the weak could never forgive. That forgiveness was an attribute of the strong. My mother is living proof that it takes strength to be soft.

When she left my house this afternoon, I could tell that she had taken the first steps towards forgiving you.

One step at a time.

There were moments when I had doubts about peeling the scab off the past with you, but something good really did come out of this in the end. Like you once said yourself: You have a purpose. Believe it.

Take care, now and always.
—Thordis

This book is the result of a co-operation between Thordis and Tom, with invaluable support from Vidir and Cat. It's written as a contribution to the public discourse on sexual violence: one of the most common and serious threats in human society, and is dedicated to those who want to see an end to it. Violence is never a solution — condemnation excludes understanding, and without understanding, we will not learn.

If you recognized yourself in this book and it brought up difficult emotions, know that help is available.

You are not alone.

Authors' Note

The abuse perpetrated by Tom against Thordis is widely considered to be rape and has been defined as such in Icelandic law since 2007. However, in 1996, having non-consensual sex with someone who was unable to fight back was defined as a lesser form of sexual misconduct in Icelandic law, which carried a lenient sentence and statute of limitations. Due to her misconceptions, Thordis was unable to identify what Tom had done to her as sexual violence. Similarly, Tom didn't see his actions for what they were and sustained a denial. Years later, when Thordis had confronted Tom and he had taken responsibility for the violence he perpetrated against her, the statute of limitations for his crime had passed. As a result, Thordis and Tom's case wasn't processed by the criminal justice system for situational reasons – not because they think that sexual violence should be met with legal impunity in any way.

In terms of working method, Thordis kept a daily diary throughout her week in Cape Town, which provided the essential foundation for the reconstruction of the week's interactions and events. She started writing them out in a detailed, narrative style on the journey home from South Africa, a task that kept her busy for a year and a half.

She then extracted all the dialogue from the manuscript, to have it moulded and approved by Tom in person when he visited Iceland mid-2014.

On a few occasions, they turned to their eight-year-long correspondence to seek clarity on how they phrased certain thoughts and feelings. However, Tom did not yet read Thordis's narration of the journey, which she completed a few months later. Tom's diary entries were written independently, drawn from his scribblings post-Cape Town and his recollection of the week's emotions. This way, both Tom and Thordis ensured that they wrote from a purely personal perspective, without being influenced by the other person's memories or feelings. The editing process that followed took another year and a half, with countless emails exchanged and frequent Skype calls with editors in the UK and Sweden.

Acknowledgements

We want to extend our thanks to: Guðrún Eva Mínervudóttir and Margrét Sjöfn Torp for editorial advice and moral support; Elísabet Grétarsdóttir for being our agent when we didn't have one; Jonas Axelsson, Siri Lindgren, and colleagues at our wonderful agency, Partners in Stories; Adam Dahlin and Matilda Lund at Forum publishing house for editorial advice and soul; Philip Gwyn Jones and Marika Webb-Pullman at Scribe Publications for shaping us up, guiding us forth, and killing our darlings; Pat Mitchell for tireless encouragement; Elizabeth Rapoport, Betsy Scolnik, and everyone else who read our book and gave us valuable feedback; and last but not least, Vidir, Cat, and our families for supporting and believing in us every step of the way. Thank you.

About the authors

Thordis Elva is known to Icelanders as a writer, journalist, public speaker, and Woman of the Year 2015. Nine of her plays have been professionally produced and her book about gender-based violence earned her a nomination for the Icelandic Literature Prize. In 2011, she founded an equality campaign that sparked a national debate, and in 2012 she was commissioned to reinvent the approach to violence prevention and sex education in Icelandic schools, resulting in award-winning short films. She has been the Chairman of the Board of the Icelandic Women's Shelter, has served on government committees, and is a sought-after speaker on subjects like gender equality and non-consensual pornography. She holds a BA in theatre, an MA in Editing and Publishing, and currently resides in Stockholm, Sweden with her partner, Vidir, and their son.

Thomas Stranger is based in Sydney, Australia. He holds a Bachelor of Social Science, a Certificate in Youth Work, and has recently completed a Masters of Cultural Studies at the University of Sydney. His career path has seen him work in various sectors (community services, youth, outdoor recreation, charity, construction, and hospitality). For now, he is working locally as a landscape gardener and residing by Sydney harbour with his wife Cat.